PRAISE FOR
THE SHOPPER MARKETING REVOLUTION

Paco Underhill
CEO, Envirosell Inc.
Author of *Why We Buy: The Science of Shopping*

"For the ambitious marketer, the path to the Fortune 100 C-suite runs through emerging markets. Success in Brazil, Latin America, and Asia will burnish a resume faster than years spent in middle management at corporate HQ.

"*The Shopper Marketing Revolution* is a treatment on modern marketing, with many of its examples pulled from the trenches of China, Southeast Asia, and Oceania. It is elegantly written and comprehensive, and for those on the fast track of modern business, it is a must-read."

Herb Sorensen, PhD
Scientific Advisor, TNS Global
BrainTrust Member, RetailWire
Author of *Inside the Mind of the Shopper*

"*The Shopper Marketing Revolution* provides a rare look into the inner workings of the relationship of retailers to their brand manufacturer customers! It also provides a detailed account of the essential components of shopper marketing, and usefully delineates the relationship of shoppers to consumers. But perhaps most importantly, it is a terrific blueprint for successfully managing the components within the retail environment. The economics driving the industry on the retail side are too little understood, even by very many who work in marketing for the major brands. Too many people
tangent to retail reality. This book is invaluable to the caree
the marketing professionals in the industry, who can save t
wheel spinning by studying the book to inform their own pr
I am very grateful to Mike Anthony and Toby Desforges fo
book. It transformed quite a lot of my observations and su
industry observer, into documented facts!"

Dr. Brian Harris
Chairman, The Partnering Group

"*The Shopper Marketing Revolution* represents the first comprehensive book on the important topic of shopper marketing. As the authors correctly point out, shopper marketing is the next "big wave" of consumer and retail marketing, and it will be the most significant change to occur in marketing in the last fifty years. The book does an excellent job of providing the rationale for the logical emergence of this new shopper-focused era. Importantly, it also provides a clear and practical framework to guide organizations in making the necessary changes to successfully navigate and prosper from this new and exciting business environment.

"While shopper marketing has been around for some time, confusion still abounds on many fronts, including how to define it, what its scope is, how to do it, and how to organize to sustain it in a productive and profit-building manner. The book tackles these issues head on and makes a major contribution to adding knowledge and clarity in each of these areas. Most importantly, the book addresses several of the most significant obstacles that have held shopper marketing back from delivering on its enormous promise. The foremost of these are organizational issues—how to change the culture that exists in many CPG [consumer packaged goods] companies as to the role of the marketing function (namely, that marketing owns the consumer while the shopper domain lies at the retailer level and therefore is a sales role, not a marketing role); and how to organize to do shopper marketing. Perhaps the most important contribution of the book is the assertion that shopper marketing is part of marketing and as such must be managed with an integrated Total Marketing (consumer and shopper) perspective. This requires a major shift in mindset for most traditional marketing departments and marketing managers. There must be no doubt, as the book propounds, that the new world of marketing, with a balanced focus on both the consumer and the shopper, has arrived. As with all major change points in our industry, those organizations that accept this change and visualize its opportunities and success requirements first will be the first to reap the competitive advantages and business growth opportunities that this new era brings.

"*The Shopper Marketing Revolution* is a must-read for all CPG manufacturers, retailers, and the agencies that provide support for this business function that is rapidly coming of age. Toby and Mike have provided a strong and clearly written case and roadmap for succeeding in the new world of shopper marketing."

Chip Hoyt
Managing Director, The Tetrarchy

"A comprehensive, practical, and principled guide to shopper marketing. What it is, why it evolved, why it's important, and how this knowledge will likely revolutionize the packaged goods industry is covered. This highly readable book is essential for anyone interested in shopper marketing, from the novice to the advanced practitioner, and for other members of the firm, especially executive leaders."

Choon Lan Kong
Regional Sales Capability Development Manager, Fonterra Brands (Singapore) Pte. Ltd.

"*Revolution*—personally I like the word very much. It shakes us up; it calls for drastic changes in the way we think and the way we manage this dynamic industry! Toby and Mike bring to us this very pragmatic five-step Total Marketing model, demonstrating clearly how it works. This is a must-read book, whether you want to learn more about shopper marketing or want to be part of the consumer goods companies' transformation."

Tan Diep
Managing Director, OgilvyAction China

"Mike Anthony and Toby Desforges know their business. And they have the perfect combination of shopper marketing mastery and astute business understanding. *The Shopper Marketing Revolution* is a superb handbook for FMCG professionals at all levels who are looking for that extra edge. Just when you think you are in the know . . . read again."

John Berenyi
Managing Director, Bergent Research

"Finally, a sensible, usable book about shopper marketing. *The Shopper Marketing Revolution* mixes sound theoretical insight with important case studies from the world's biggest brands to show how to break through in today's ever-more-challenging retail environment. Toby and Mike's sensible approach to what research can and cannot deliver gives you real power to unlock significant opportunities. Add to this their understanding of how retail really works around the world and you have a book that is entertaining and eminently practical and that will lead to significant sales value growth.

"Shopper marketing is more than bundling up a cute deal and sticking down some floor decals. This book shows you how shoppers really shop and how you can break the seemingly endless cycle of price promotions."

David Glaze
Associate Vice President, Kao Hanbai Co., Ltd.

"*The Shopper Marketing Revolution* is a must-read for all managers in our industry. Leading edge yet approachable, this is a very accessible and stimulating book that delivers a much-needed wake up call for all of us involved in the consumer goods business. Providing practical solutions and new ways of thinking for how to resolve key issues (many of which have been of our own making), it also provides clear direction, opinion, and ideas for how to achieve the opportunities that we are all striving to realize.

"Reflective and visionary in equal measure, the book is both refreshingly honest and inspiringly constructive. By explaining current trends and hot topics in a clear and motivating manner, it helps to make sense of an industry that has sometimes lost its way. By cutting through previously confused terminology and by providing a balanced evaluation of many of the latest industry practices, it is refreshingly honest. It's full of realistic suggestions as to how to evolve any company's thinking and process towards a much-needed revolution based on a systematic integration of all marketing efforts towards the ultimate achievement of common defined customer goals. I hope that others will be equally inspired to take a long hard look at how we can adapt existing patterns and behaviors and strive towards changing our industry model quickly for the benefit of all stakeholders."

THE SHOPPER MARKETING REVOLUTION

CONSUMER – SHOPPER – RETAILER:

HOW MARKETING MUST REINVENT ITSELF IN THE AGE OF THE SHOPPER

THE SHOPPER MARKETING
REVOLUTION

CONSUMER – SHOPPER – RETAILER:
HOW MARKETING MUST REINVENT ITSELF IN THE AGE OF THE SHOPPER

TOBY DESFORGES MIKE ANTHONY

Writers of the Round Table Press
PO Box 511, Highland Park, IL 60035

www.roundtablecompanies.com

Publisher: Corey Michael Blake
Executive/Lead Editor: Katie Gutierrez
Staff Editor: Aaron Hierholzer
Post Production: David Charles Cohen
Directoress of Happiness: Erin Cohen
Director of Author Services: Kristin Westberg
Facts Keeper: Mike Winicour
Front Cover Design: Nathan Brown, Sunny DiMartino
Interior Design and Layout, Back Cover: Sunny DiMartino
Proofreading: Rita Hess
Last Looks: Jess Place
Indexing: Linda Presto
Digital Book Conversion: Sunny DiMartino
Digital Publishing: Sunny DiMartino

Printed in the United States of America
First Edition: June 2013
10 9 8 7 6 5 4 3 2 1

Library of Congress Cataloging-in-Publication Data
Desforges, Toby
The shopper marketing revolution: consumer — shopper — retailer:
how marketing must reinvent itself in the age of the shopper /
Toby Desforges and Mike Anthony.—1st ed. p. cm.
ISBN Paperback 978-1-939418-27-2
ISBN Digital 978-1-939418-28-9
Library of Congress Control Number: 2013941445

RTC Publishing is an imprint of Writers of the Round Table, Inc.
Writers of the Round Table Press and the RTC Publishing logo
are trademarks of Writers of the Round Table, Inc.

CONTENTS

PART III: THE REVOLUTIONARY'S HANDBOOK

ACKNOWLEDGEMENTS

A large number of people have contributed not just to this book but also to bringing "Project **engage**" from inception to reality. I'd particularly like to thank my wife, Simonetta, and my three boys, Oliver, Matteo, and Iacopo, for their patience, love, and motivation throughout the project. I'd also like to thank Mike Anthony for his unswerving loyalty, friendship, and inspiration.

I'm grateful to the **engage** teams across Asia for cheering us on through the process and for their hard work and commitment, but particularly to K. Ple (Nuchreeya Mahuttanagovit), K. Chompoo (Saowanee Suwannasit), and K. Mod (Watcharewan Hundasiri), who joined us right at the outset and have stayed the course. I'd also like to thank John Griffiths and Howard Bryant for being great mentors since the early days; Lynne Klapecki and Geoffrey Blake for opening my mind to greater possibilities and Martin Jimmink for the advice he gave me when I needed it.

I'd like to make special mention of some individuals who have bought our services and given Mike and me the opportunity to work with their teams and develop our thinking: my thanks go to David Glaze, Nick Williams, Zainudden Bin Mohd Hussain, Gerard Gereats, Chris Stratton, Carlo Mendoza, John Knox, Mark Weir, and Laura Ashton.

Special thanks goes to K. Dia (Parujee Phadhana-Anake), Sue Publicover, and the RTC team for their efforts in helping us complete the book. I'd also like to thank the following for contributing their thoughts and insights in the process: Herb Sorensen, Darren Marshall, Anson Dichaves, Brian Harris, Chris Hoyt, Hans Olaf Hallan, Tia Newcomer, and Mark Weir.

Last of all, I'd like to thank my mum and dad and brother, Giles, for being the best—love you guys.

—*Toby Desforges*

. . .

"That took more effort than we thought" should be, if not inscribed on a tombstone, written on the walls of my office as a reminder at the onset of any new endeavor. This book has been no exception, and it is no exaggeration to say that it simply would not have happened without the effort, patience, contribution, nudging, cajoling, supporting, nagging, and bucket loads of encouragement from a very large number of people.

The journey to the publication of this book started many years ago, with an idea that has encompassed the creation of a vision, a transformation in our lives, the creation of a company, and the engagement of support from so many places. I am humbled to be able to even conceive of writing this, let alone actually doing it.

That journey would not have begun without the love and support of my amazing wife, Nicola, and my inspirational daughter, Ellis, or without the passion, energy, and friendship of Toby.

Team **engage** has grown enormously over the years, and I'd like to thank all who have shown and given passion and commitment to the cause. I'd especially like to thank K. Ple (Nuchreeya Mahuttanagovit), K. Chompoo (Saowanee Suwannasit), and K. Mod (Watcharewan Hundasiri), who joined us very early in the journey and stayed the course, for their faith and belief in two strange guys from another country who had a crazy idea about changing the world. I'd like to thank Howard Bryant for his straight-talking advice and support; Richard Cowley for his enthusiasm and all those difficult questions; Jon Rigg for always being there to lend a helping hand; Lynne Klapecki for afternoons of coffee and thought-provoking conversation; Martin Jimmink for encouraging me to think differently about so many things; and the many, many people who have sat and listened to me opining over a pint as these ideas took root.

The ideas that form the heart of this book required extensive testing, proving, polishing, and perfecting: thanks to David Glaze, Nick Williams, Zainudden Bin Mohd Hussain, Andrew Pooch, Chris Stratton, Carlo Mendoza, John Knox, Mark Weir, and Laura Ashton for engaging with us and allowing us to work with their teams so extensively.

I'd like to thank a number of individuals who have made massive efforts to make this book a reality: K. Dia (Parujee Phadhana-Anake) for thinking of all of the things we didn't think of and for making it all happen; Sue Publicover and the team at RTC; and all of the people we spoke to who willingly gave us the benefit of their wisdom and experiences—Herb Sorensen, Darren

Marshall, Anson Dichaves, Brian Harris, Chris Hoyt, Hans Olaf Hallan, Tia Newcomer, and Mark Weir.

And last but by no means least, thanks to my mum and dad; my sister, Cathy; and my brother-in-law, Chris, for putting up with a wayward and often absent son, brother, and brother-in-law who probably doesn't express his thanks and gratitude for everything you have done nearly often enough.

—*Mike Anthony*

INTRODUCTION

Life for a marketer used to be a lot simpler, or at least it felt that way. Brands were grown by pulling two simple levers: build a brand and drive distribution. If marketers got that right, all was well and good. And within each of these areas, the options were well documented: consumer goods brands were built with advertising (mainly TV and radio) with a sprinkling of public relations and events; distribution was about putting the product into as many of the stores across the country as possible.

But over the decades, things have gotten more complicated. The number of media channels that consumers feast on continues to increase, driving up the complexity and cost of pinning down a target market. Some retailers have grown to stupendous size, and getting that distribution is expensive and a long way away from a foregone conclusion.

And then there is shopping. Before the Internet, before cell phones, and before the explosion of brands, innovation, and new categories, shoppers had far fewer choices of what to buy. If they wanted to buy a television, shoppers typically went to a local appliance or department store, checked out the picture, asked the salesman a few questions, and made a purchase. Done.

Today, shoppers are faced with myriad choices about what to buy: which brand, what screen size, what level of audio quality, what resolution? Will it mount on the wall? What about the impact of aspect ratio? Wouldn't it be fantastic if one didn't need an engineering degree to make a purchase decision? Shoppers are also faced with many more choices of where to buy: mega retailers such as Best Buy, hypermarket chains such as Walmart, or one of countless online retailers who will ship the product to the home without the shopper needing to step out of their front door.

Because so much has changed in the consumer goods world over the last sixty years, it may come as a surprise that the vast majority of consumer goods companies are still using the same model to drive their business as they did in the 1950s.

The consequences of that inertia are terrifying. Marketing monies spent on persuading consumers to desire brands are becoming less effective. Driven in part by this, and by the increasing power of "Big Retail," more money is being spent on achieving distribution and discounting products in stores than ever before. And the problem with that is that up to 70 percent of this retail investment loses money.

The consumer goods industry is no longer fast growing. Its profits are under pressure. Yet the majority of companies in this industry continue to use a growth model built for yesteryear.

Recall the words of the American retail giant John Wanamaker: "Half the money I spend on advertising is wasted. The trouble is, I don't know which half." Although Wanamaker made this statement a century ago, the reality remains. Consumer goods companies are failing to gain the return on investment (ROI) they need from their marketing because they don't get "it." Most continue to be invested in twentieth-century thinking that fails to take into account the shifts in the industry—including e-commerce shopping choices, cluttered stores, limited shopping time, and other factors—that have changed the face of shopper influence. We're over a decade into a new century, yet far too many companies have failed to dip their toes into this bubbling whirlpool of opportunity.

We have both spent most of our working lives in this industry: we love it and are grateful for the experiences and opportunities it has given us. But we are saddened by the state of affairs we see today. The industry we joined two short decades ago was vibrant and exciting—it was "the place to be." Today it is no longer the industry of choice for people at the beginning of their career. There is no reason in our minds that this should be so. Something needs to change.

We have dedicated ourselves to creating and propagating a new marketing model that takes into account the reality of today and tomorrow rather than that of yesterday. For years, we have worked with savvy executives from global entities, helping them untangle their marketing strategies and their teams. With a step-by-step approach—five in all—we've discovered and tested a method that builds a stronger, more symbiotic relationship between the retailer and manufacturer. Every recommendation in this book has been extensively tested and proven. The approach works, and it delivers better results for these companies, their partners, their shareholders, and the people they employ.

At the heart of this model lies a concept and a practice called *shopper marketing.* Shopper marketing requires that marketers connect with the consumer and the shopper—often two separate people—to better understand these two fundamental elements in the "supply and demand" of the consumer goods industry. Shopper marketers then use this understanding to form more meaningful propositions for, and therefore relationships with, retail customers. This revolutionary shopper marketing method drives better brand engagement with consumers and more effective results with shoppers in stores (be they virtual or real). It drives the goal of all consumer goods companies: profitable growth.

This book attempts to reach out on many levels. The first part explains more about the industry's issues, the potential solution, and how that solution works in the real world. The second part explores the key concepts that drive a new marketing model. The third part is designed to be a "how to" guide—to help practitioners (be they consumer marketers, shopper marketers, salespeople; whether they work for a manufacturer, a retailer, an agency, or a market research company) take steps toward a better, more effective marketing model.

Shopper marketing is of interest to everyone. The whole world is a shopper, and we are all being marketed to by retailers and manufacturers alike. In this book, we attempt to deliver insight into how this world works (and how it doesn't!) and to show how it could be done so much better. But the book isn't just about shopper marketing. Shopper marketing is a revolution—a revolution in marketing driven by shoppers. The trends we outline here affect anyone working in the consumer goods or retail industry, which together represent potentially 20 percent of global GDP.[1] And as with any revolution, each of us has a choice: to rally and drive the change or to be dragged along in the tailwind of those blazing the trail. This book is an invitation, an outstretched hand, if you will, to come and join a revolution, and that is an opportunity that comes along perhaps once in a lifetime.

Welcome to the Shopper Marketing Revolution!

T. Desforges and M. Anthony

---

1   The World Bank estimated global GDP to be $69.98 trillion in 2011 (World Development Indicators database, accessed March 14, 2013, http://databank.worldbank.org/databank/download/GDP.pdf.); Herb Sorensen, author of *Inside the Mind of the Shopper*, in discussion with the authors in November 2010, estimated that the retailing industry is worth $14 trillion.

PART I

THE SHOPPER MARKETING REVOLUTION

CHAPTER 1

THE $200 BILLION CRIME AND HOW IT HAPPENED

For nearly 60 years, the consumer goods industry has been a powerhouse of economic growth. In that time, the term *brand* has become common parlance, and we are now surrounded by instantly recognizable brands. No part of contemporary culture has been unaffected; no continent on earth has been left untouched. Consumers in every corner of the world buy and enjoy products like Pepsi, Coke, Mars bars, Colgate toothpaste, and Persil detergent.

Consumer goods marketing hasn't just given us iconic products; it's also produced some of the greatest creative and commercial talent of the last century. Many of today's composers, artists, film directors, entrepreneurs, politicians, and leaders in almost every field began their careers in companies like Unilever and Procter & Gamble, or worked on those brands in the offices of advertising agencies like Ogilvy & Mather and Leo Burnett. As just one example, brothers Ridley and Tony Scott worked in advertising before becoming two of the world's most successful film directors.

Today, the consumer goods industry represents nearly a fifth of the world's GDP, but it is also an industry on the brink of decline. According to Deloitte, its growth has slowed to an all-time low—in the last four years, the top 250 companies have grown by less than 4 percent per annum on average.[2]

---

2   Average of growth rates from Deloitte's *Global Powers of the Consumer Products Industry* reports for 2010 (http://www.deloitte.com/assets/Dcom-Global/Local Assets/Documents/ Consumer Business/dtt_globalpowersconsumerproducts_150210.pdf), 2011 (http://www.

The profitability of leaders and followers alike is becoming increasingly thin.

The consumer goods industry is no longer the place to be for bright young things. Promising individuals today prefer sexier alternatives in tech or communications, or they seek to get rich quick in the halls of investment banks, and manufacturers are finding it harder to locate new talent. This is an industry that is hemorrhaging money, an industry that is leaving as much as half of its profits on the table. In this chapter, we will show that a crime is being committed—one that's potentially robbing the industry of nearly $200 billion a year, and we'll show how it happened. In the following 15 chapters, we'll explain what needs to be done.

WHEN MANUFACTURERS RULED THE WORLD

After World War II, European and American manufacturing shifted from supporting the war machine to fulfilling the needs and desires of consumers. In the United States, the economy was emerging from the gray cloud of those dismal years, and its citizens were entering a new era of affluence. The United States didn't have to rebuild its infrastructure, but in the European countries on whose soil the war had been waged, that wasn't the case. In Europe, economies had been destroyed and companies bankrupted by the war's outcome. Americans were embracing vibrant living standards that hadn't yet stretched across the Atlantic.

The rebirth of American consumerism provided the opportunity for companies to dive into massive production. Big businesses forged in the late nineteenth century, during the Industrial Revolution, could now focus on consumer goods with renewed zeal. Manufacturers were producing and selling consumer products in vast quantities, and this mass manufacturing brought prices down to levels of affordability unheard of in the prewar years. Demand soared. If you made it, people would buy it.

Back then, the market was not flooded with brands like it is today. There were fewer choices, making the shopping experience far simpler. With fewer brands available, competition was thinner and shoppers easier to influence.

Along with fewer brand choices, consumers and shoppers also had far

---

deloitte.com/assets/Dcom-Kenya/Local Assets/Documents/Deloitte Reports - Global Powers of Consumer Products 2011.pdf), and 2012 (http://www.deloitte.com/assets/Dcom-Guam/Local Assets/Documents/Global Powers of CP 2012_Deloitte_Web.pdf), all accessed March 14, 2013.

fewer ways to spend their money. A teenager with a dollar or two could choose to buy a movie ticket, a record, a comic book, or a milkshake. He didn't have options like mobile phone top-ups, video and music downloads, apps, video games, and the clothing brand du jour.

During this early phase of consumer goods' evolution, marketing and advertising gained momentum. The "4 Ps" (Product, Promotion, Price, Place) defined a new strategic framework for coping with the emerging marketplace. A simple but effective business model developed: marketers built brands for consumers, and a network of salespeople secured distribution for the company's products in retail outlets across the marketplace.

Then, in the late 1950s and early 1960s, television gave marketers a new, exciting, and effective tool for reaching an audience that was captivated by this video marvel. Viewers weren't flooded with commercials; advertisements in those days were an integral part of the program—not an excuse to leave the room for a few minutes. Nor did television viewers have hundreds of cable channels or the option to record a show and watch it later while fast-forwarding through the commercials that funded the broadcast. So, when a consumer goods marketer planned a television ad campaign, he could advise the retailer that if he didn't stock the item, shoppers would look elsewhere, and the retailer would miss out on the almost-guaranteed demand.

Salesmen in the 1950s and 1960s could walk into their retail customers' businesses and (almost!) just write their own orders. In fact, demand was so strong that sales reps sometimes had to tell retailers they couldn't get everything they wanted. The retailer simply had to accept that reality.

At that time, the mass retailing model barely existed. Walmart, today the world's largest retailer by revenue and the world's largest company by the same measure,[3] was not incorporated until October 31, 1969, seven years after Sam Walton opened his first store in Arkansas.[4] Across the Atlantic, Europe's largest retailers of today, Tesco and Carrefour, were in their infancy. Carrefour, now the world's second-biggest global grocery retailer,[5] started as one store at a crossroads in Annecy, France, in 1960,

---

3   Deloitte, *Switching Channels: Global Powers of Retailing 2012*, accessed February 26, 2013, http://www.deloitte.com/assets/Dcom-Global/Local Assets/Documents/Consumer Business/ dtt_CBT_GPRetailing2012.pdf.

4   "History Timeline," Walmart, accessed February 26, 2013, http://corporate.walmart.com/ our-story/heritage/history-timeline.

5   "Global Retail Rankings 2012," Planet Retail, accessed February 26, 2013, http://www. planetretail.net/Presentations/grocery-2012-web.pdf.

and Tesco, the UK's leading retailer and one of the fastest-growing global players, opened its first self-service store in 1956.[6] In the 1950s and 1960s, it was manufacturers, not retailers, that dominated the marketplace, and their customers were small, relatively powerless store owners.

THE RISE OF THE RETAIL MACHINE

But then things started to change. The small retailer became bigger and bigger. Walmart had 24 stores in 1967 but had grown to 125 stores just eight years later. In 1977, Walmart acquired the Mohr-Value chain of stores. By 1980, the company's 276 stores amassed $1.2 billion in sales.[7]

In the UK, Tesco was experiencing similar growth. Not long after acquiring numerous grocery store chains in the 1950s, it expanded from supermarkets to department stores. The company opened its first 40,000-square-foot superstore in Sussex in 1961. By 1976, Tesco had 900 supermarkets and superstores.[8]

As retailers began to acquire smaller chains, they gained more clout with the manufacturers. The sheer expanse of their real estate and their growing appeal to shoppers gave companies like Sainsbury's, Tesco, Walmart, Kroger, and Carrefour more negotiating power with manufacturers. They proved they could consistently deliver great volumes of both shoppers and sales. The world in which retailers had to stock a product if the manufacturer advertised it was changing. The tables were turning. By the early 1980s, if a manufacturer had a consumer product on TV, it absolutely had to get the product on the shelves of the big retailers; otherwise, it wouldn't get a return on its media dollars. To achieve that goal, manufacturers began to make concessions to the big retailers that would have been unheard of in the industry a decade before.

Retailers also extended their strength and influence by launching their own brands. These "no names" were shelved side by side with nationally recognized brands but cost a fraction of the price. Most of the products were privately labeled, sometimes manufactured in the same plants as the

---

6   "Business Profiles: Tesco Plc," InternationalTrade.co.uk, accessed February 26, 2013, http://www.internationaltrade.co.uk/articles_print.php?CID=44&SCID=&AID=687.

7   "Wal-Mart Stores, Inc.," Hoover's, accessed February 26, 2013, http://www.hoovers.com/company/Wal-Mart_Stores_Inc/rrjiff-1-1njhxk.html.

8   Jay P. Pederson, *International Directory of Company Histories*, vol. 24 (Farmington Hills, MI: Gale, 1998).

name brands. Capitalizing on the low price of the no-name item and the store's high traffic, retailers gained share of basket (the proportion of products bought by a shopper), feeding their own bottom line at the expense of the consumer goods companies. Retailers began realizing it wasn't their job to make money for manufacturers. Their new goal was to increase the number of customers and the sales per customer in any way that delivered a profitable result.

The 1980s saw massive growth in retail. At the end of the 1970s, Walmart operated 276 stores; it was running 1,928 stores in 1992.[9] Its revenues had leapt to $26 billion by 1989.[10] In the same period, Carrefour opened stores in Argentina and Taiwan and began the globalization of retail.[11] Across the world, supermarket retailing had become the norm rather than the exception.

Net sales ($)

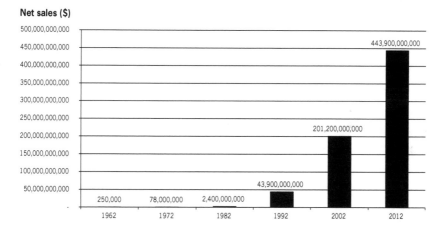

Source: Walmart, *2012 Annual Report*, accessed February 26, 2013, http://www.walmartstores.com/sites/annual-report/2012/WalMart_AR.pdf.

After a long stretch of holding the retailers' reins, manufacturers had discovered that brand power was not enough to convince stores to carry their products, at least not without additional financial incentives. The promise of running television ads to drive demand was assumed, not a bonus, so that investment no longer enticed the retailer. To retain their presence in the retailer's kingdom, manufacturers had to serve up more rewards—such

---

9   "History Timeline," Walmart, accessed February 26, 2013, http://corporate.walmart.com/our-story/heritage/history-timeline.

10 "Store Wars: When Wal-Mart Comes to Town," PBS.org, accessed February 26, 2013, http://www.pbs.org/itvs/storewars/stores1.html.

11 Ashok Som, "Carrefour in South America," in *Marketing Management: International Perspectives*, eds. M. S. Raju and Dominique Xardel (New Delhi: Tata McGraw-Hill, 2009).

as slotting fees (payments made to the retailer in exchange for shelf space) and funds to support promotions.

Manufacturers had lost the upper hand in the relationship; they no longer owned the shopper. A consumer goods company could work hard at marketing to someone outside of the store, but it couldn't exert the same influence the retailer had once the shopper was in a store. If a shopper's local store didn't stock a particular product, the shopper often just bought whatever substitute was available. The companies that produced consumer goods had to adjust their thinking and shift their focus to finding new ways to persuade the empowered retailer to support their brands.

THE BIRTH OF CATEGORY MANAGEMENT AND TRADE MARKETING

With the power of their brands diminishing, manufacturers were hit by a further shock in the 1980s. The strength of network television, which had for decades been the dynamo of demand creation, began to decay. The advent of cable (and later, satellite) brought with it a massive explosion in channels, fragmenting traditional audiences around the world and challenging the core of the traditional brand-building model. No longer could a manufacturer rely on reaching a huge chunk of its target market by advertising on popular network TV shows. Communication with consumers was about to get a lot harder and a lot more expensive.

The pace of fragmentation was staggering; cable TV's early growth in the United States had been stymied in the late 1960s by a regulatory freeze put in place to protect local networks, but subscriptions exploded with deregulation in the early 1970s. Satellite-to-cable distribution systems allowed HBO and Ted Turner's WTBS to reach new audiences. By 1979, 16 million U.S. households subscribed to cable, up from just 850,000 in 1962. In 1989, nearly 53 million households subscribed to cable, receiving access to 79 networks—up more than double the number available in 1980.[12]

Across the world, similar upheavals were taking place with the introduction of satellite networks in the UK in 1989—an event that broke the traditional hold of ITV—and the introduction of the global Astra satellite network in 1991, which opened up the global market. In one short decade, a new media model had been born.

---

12 "History of Cable Television," National Cable & Telecommunications Association, accessed February 26, 2013, http://www.ncta.com/About/About/AboutNCTA.aspx.

And with all of this complexity came a steep change in the volume of advertising. Consumers were now bombarded with ads from every direction, and they started tuning it out. Advertising recall started to drop. The old method was becoming less effective.

The time had come for the manufacturers to retune their approach. For all the issues that consolidating retail presented, there was at least one benefit; big-box retailers provided homogenous environments in which to communicate directly to shoppers on the verge of making a purchase. But with retailers demanding deeper and deeper discounts, leading manufacturers recognized that they needed something to rebalance the equation.

Then leading consumer goods manufacturers hit on a golden opportunity for collaboration. They discovered something they could bring to the table that would spark interest in the retailer. While Walmart knew a lot about retailing, it couldn't be an expert in everything—surely Procter & Gamble would always know more than Walmart about shampoo. Could that knowledge be valuable? If Proctor and Gamble (P&G) could help Walmart sell more shampoo or make more money from shampoo, wouldn't that rebalance the equation?

This revelation gave rise to the Category Management movement in the late 1980s. Dr. Brian Harris coined the term and created a blueprint for this emerging approach. He observed that brands were often focused on stealing share from their competitors, even though the shopper's choice of which brand to buy had little or no effect on the retailer. If a shopper chose Pepsi over Coca-Cola, the decision would not necessarily increase the retailer's overall sales in the soft drinks category; the benefit would be the manufacturer's side alone. Category Management provided an approach focused on developing the total category, thereby giving both the retailer and the manufacturer the opportunity to improve their results.

Dr. Harris proposed a system whereby the manufacturer and retailer collaborated more fully, based on their common ground. Since both entities were striving to get more shoppers to buy more products, they clearly had a shared interest in growing total sales in the category—not more Coke and less Pepsi, but more Coke and more Pepsi.

Category Management, as defined by Dr. Harris, leveraged the brand marketing savvy of the manufacturer and the real estate advantage of the store. Manufacturers recognized that by increasing sales in the overall category of their product, their sales would grow even if their share didn't. But by being the co-architect of the strategy with the retailer, they had a good chance of taking the lion's share of the growth and therefore growing their share, too.

Harris's Category Management strategy included placing certain brands in multiple locations within a retail location. Merchandisers saw that large packs and large bottles of beverages, for example, could belong in the soft drink aisle, while individual-sized bottles and cans of the same beverages could occupy coolers at the front of the store. The strategy met the needs of two different soft-drink shoppers: one who wanted a cold drink now and the other who wished to stock up for later consumption. Placing the refrigerator case near the checkout further promoted impulse buys.

To support closer collaboration with retailers, a new function was created within manufacturing companies and bolted on to their sales teams: "trade marketing" teams were given the task of managing the mechanics of trade promotions and driving the strategic agenda for groups of brands within discrete categories or for specific channels.

THE AGE OF THE SHOPPER

By the end of the 1990s, consolidating retail and fragmenting media had put the traditional business model of consumer goods marketing under enormous strain. If the model wasn't already at a breaking point by then, a number of profound changes in the last decade have brought it the rest of the way. Simply put, we are in the midst of a revolution in the way consumers and shoppers interact with the products they buy. Three dramatic changes have placed shoppers at the center of the equation in a way that leads us to believe that a corresponding revolution must take place in the way we market consumer goods.

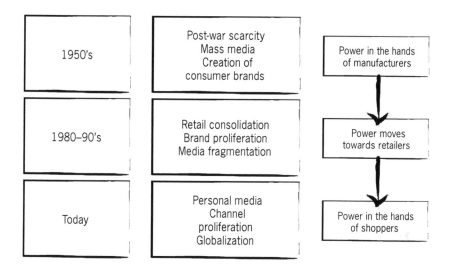

CHANGE #1: MEDIA HAS BECOME PERSONAL

Products like TiVo, Sky Go, Netflix, and Apple TV, which enable us to consume film and TV at any time and almost ad-free, massively reduce the impact of the traditional TV commercial. Paradoxically, while we see more ads than ever before—one estimate suggests the average 65-year-old American will have seen over two million ads in his or her lifetime—advertising recall was at an all-time low even back in 1990, at just 8 percent as compared to 34 percent in 1965. In 2007, people could hardly name two commercials they'd seen in a given day.[13] Yet as we move away from the forms of media that have traditionally supported advertising, expenditure on media (traditional and online) continues to rise. Globally, compound annual growth in advertising expenditure runs at 5.6 percent over the last decade.[14] Media expenditure has grown 11 times since 1965, and yet it has become eight and a half times more expensive, in today's terms, to create one advertising impression.[15]

Of course, it's not even guaranteed that the ad will reach the target market. The option to illegally download and stream content online means

---

13 EmpireResearchGroup.com front page, Empire Research Group, accessed March 1, 2013, http://www.empireresearchgroup.com/.

14 Saul J. Berman, Bill Battino, Louisa Shipnuck, and Andreas Neus, IBM Institute for Business Value, *The End of Advertising as We Know It*, http://www-05.ibm.com/de/media/downloads/end-of-advertising.pdf.

15 Author calculation based on information available on EmpireResearchGroup.com front page, Empire Research Group, accessed March 1, 2013, http://www.empireresearchgroup.com/.

that viewers might easily watch a version of the content that has the expensive American ads stripped out of it.

We're also watching a lot more than just network TV, with hundreds of cable channels to choose from. And when we watch any kind of TV, we are increasingly engaged in other media simultaneously: we surf the Internet, play a game, or talk on the phone. Facebook and YouTube are the upcoming generation's entertainment of choice. As of March 2013, the top-viewed video on YouTube has been seen nearly 1.4 billion times,[16] while the lead show on the U.S. network TV the week of this writing was seen by only 20.6 million Americans.[17] Facebook stats today show over 1.06 billion monthly active users[18] spent an average of 6.4 hours per month on the site in September 2012.[19] Smartphone apps make content immediately available anywhere and anytime to a global community.

In short, media has become personal, and as a result, the central pillar of consumer communication since the 1950s—the TV ad—is, if not dying, clearly not the force it once was. As a consequence, the importance of intercepting shoppers at the point-of-purchase in an attempt to influence their decisions is more important to consumer goods companies than ever before. The rush to produce new ideas and leverage new technology that makes in-store communication more impactful has driven the power into the hands of the shopper.

Deloitte, Bain, and Nielsen all report that over the last three years, manufacturers have increased annual expenditure on in-store promotions by 65 percent. Today, a Midwestern housewife can use a smartphone to compare prices at the aisle and redeem any number of coupons immediately. The shopper is now an important component of value creation for retailer and manufacturer alike.

---

16 "Charts: All Categories," YouTube, accessed March 7, 2013, http://www.youtube.com/charts/videos_views?t=a.

17 "Top 10: TV Shows," Nielsen, accessed March 7, 2013, http://www.nielsen.com/us/en/insights/top10s/television.html.

18 Emil Protalinski, "Facebook Passes 1.06 Billion Monthly Active Users, 680 Million Mobile Users, and 618 Million Daily Users," TNW, January 30, 2013, http://thenextweb.com/facebook/2013/01/30/facebook-passes-1-06-billion-monthly-active-users-680-million-mobile-users-and-618-million-daily-users/.

19 "September 2012: Top U.S. Web Brands and Food & Cooking Websites," Nielsen, accessed March 7, 2013, http://blog.nielsen.com/nielsenwire/online_mobile/september-2012-top-us-web-brands/.

CHANGE #2: THE SHOPPER'S CHOICES HAVE PROLIFERATED

At the same time, shoppers have more places to shop than ever. While retail sales continue to consolidate around key players, these retailers have also gone through enormous structural change. Since the late 1990s, players like Tesco, Carrefour, Metro, and others have chased market share not by doing more of the same, but by creating multi-format approaches. Tesco's offerings now extend way beyond traditional supermarket goods; the store's stable now includes convenience stores, gas stations, community supermarkets, discount stores, shopping malls, and hypermarkets. The convenience store format is growing the fastest globally, bringing ready-to-consume foods and staple grocery products even closer to the shopper's home.

An Anecdote from Toby

In almost every key market in the world today, shoppers can choose from not one local supermarket but many different outlets tuned to meet their specific needs at a given point in time. In my hometown in rural Lincolnshire in the heart of the United Kingdom, my mother now chooses daily between at least 40 outlets that can service her daily household and grocery needs: Lidl, Aldi, Morrison's, Tesco, Sainsbury's, Marks & Spencer, Waitrose, Boots, Superdrug, Holland & Barrett, three branded wines and spirits retailers, five brands of gas station, a traditional weekly market, and at least twenty small newsagents, butchers, and greengrocers—all within a four-mile radius. That doesn't account for numerous other specialist retailers that might be competing for her monthly disposable income—sellers of fashion products, books and stationery, home improvement supplies, home electronics, mobile phones, and many others.

Leading retailers today compete for shoppers in a cutthroat environment, and many brands once thought to be unassailable—think Woolworths in the UK, Borders in the United States, and Blockbuster around the world—have become casualties in this battle. The average profit margin of the world's leading retailers is less than 3 percent.[20]

The modern retailer invests in its brand like never before, employing complex and well-crafted strategies to lock in shoppers' loyalty. In the postmodern retail environment, full of options for the shopper, price alone

---

20 Deloitte, *Global Powers of Retailing 2013: Retail Beyond*, accessed March 7, 2013, http://www.deloitte.com/assets/Dcom-Australia/Local Assets/Documents/Industries/Consumer business/Deloitte_Global_Powers_of_Retail_2013.pdf.

will not win the war. Complex and innovative loyalty programs like Tesco's Clubcard and AS Watsons' member card cost up to 1 percent of total sales to operate (and that is a huge percentage of profit for the thin-margined retail businesses). New retail formats drive growth, as do new services like insurance, healthcare, banking, bill payment, utilities, and Internet provision. Own-label sales now account for 14.9 percent of average retail sales in the markets where they are present,[21] and retailers leverage their brand strength to drive the cost of the regular grocery-store trip down while driving loyalty and margins up.

In this choice-filled environment, the shopper is both king and queen.

CHANGE #3: THE INTERNET HAS ARRIVED

The advent of the Internet has rewritten the rules of shopping. In 2011, U.S. shoppers spent $256 billion online, with over 60 percent coming from retail sales.[22] Geography is no longer an obstacle to finding and purchasing a product. Shoppers are not limited to the inventory on the shelves of their local stores. They recognize the value of shopping online and will pay a bit more for shipping to get exactly what they want and have it delivered.

Online retail is growing rapidly and exuberantly, and neither the traditional players nor traditional products are driving the change. iTunes's mastery of online sales has thrust a spear deep into the heart of traditional CD sales, and Amazon.com's 2010 entry into grocery and gourmet foods introduces a new, potentially global player to challenge the retail brands around the world.

With their relatively limited, localized online offerings, it appears that traditional retail players have been caught off guard by these newcomers. Global e-commerce in anything beyond travel and tourism is yet to become a reality. But how long can shoppers in Singapore be expected to browse products on a U.S. website without being able to buy them online? There is little, beyond archaic trade regulations, to stop a smart, innovative player like Amazon or Zappos from applying their skills in online marketing and supply-chain aggregation to realize their global potential.

Thus, with the personalization of media, massive channel proliferation, and the shift from shopping in person to online, the control of the retailer has

---

21 Nielsen, *The Rise of the Value-Conscious Shopper: A Nielsen Global Private Label Report*, accessed February 28, 2013, http://hk.nielsen.com/documents/PrivateLabelGlobalReport.pdf.

22 comScore, *2012 U.S. Digital Future in Focus*, accessed February 28, 2013, http://www.comscore.com/Insights/Presentations_and_Whitepapers/2012/2012_US_Digital_Future_in_Focus.

been transferred to shoppers, who now have many more options for where to spend their money and what to spend it on. The age of the shopper is here.

CONSUMER GOODS MARKETING IS BROKEN

So where are the consumer goods companies in all of this? Their absence is conspicuous. Yet they are essential in the mix—it is, after all, their products that we shoppers buy, their products that we consume every day, and their brands that we profess to love in survey after survey. But it's not their strategies driving the change in our behavior. In truth, the strategies manufacturers developed in the 1990s—Category Management and trade marketing—have not worked.

Category Management was the first step toward realizing that the needs and behaviors of the shopper played a key role in sales growth. The problem is that Category Management presumes that the manufacturer's goals could align with the retailer's. But real alignment is often elusive: retailers just want to sell more products and don't really care which brand. Manufacturers have a diametrically opposed goal: they want to sell more of their brand and don't care where it is sold. Category Management was founded on the belief that these fundamental differences could be overcome by focusing on growth of the overall category, but most in-store promotion is designed to serve the retailer's needs rather than those of the manufacturer (see Chapter 6, "The True Cost of Discounting"). Rather than solving the problem, Category Management has provided only a partial solution. And implementing Category Management has proven to be difficult for a number of reasons. Even Dr. Brian Harris recognizes that the way the process of Category Management has been used has made it "too complex." Streamlining the process has become essential. Globally, trade marketing and sales teams have been challenged by the amount of time and effort required to collect and analyze the necessary information. Retailers have had similar challenges and, as a result, many have delegated too much of the effort required to develop category business plans to manufacturers.

Manufacturers' other strategy, trade marketing, remains poorly understood, and we suspect many CEOs view it as something of a fad. When we surveyed trade marketers in 2006, we found at least four different ways of managing trade marketing. Further, across 40 interviews, we found not one consistent definition of trade marketing.

Yet it is the escalation of trade expenditure that marks the advent of the age of the shopper. Clearly, it's not surprising that traditional communication vehicles have become less effective, nor will it surprise anyone in the industry that retail is consolidating. What may surprise some, though, is the exponential rate at which trade expenditure has grown. Accenture CAS estimates that in 1980, trade promotions, the largest element of trade expenditure, accounted for less than 8 percent of leading consumer goods companies' sales in the United Kingdom. By 2005, they estimate that this figure had reached 25 percent.[23] A threefold increase—the fastest-growing cost within a consumer goods company's balance sheet in that time and now the largest cost after cost of goods for many manufacturers.

Around the world and across all types of consumer goods manufacturers, we estimate that promotion probably accounts for 10 percent of an average company's sales. Herb Sorensen, PhD, a shopper research expert and author of *Inside the Mind of the Shopper*, estimates the industry is huge. "Retailing is a $14 trillion industry globally—$8 trillion goes to the brands and $6 trillion goes to the retailers."[24] If this is the case, then consumer goods manufacturing and retailing is fully 20 percent of the world's GDP. Assuming all manufacturers spend 10 percent on promotions, as we estimate, the value of promotions is $800 billion dollars.

What we do know, from consolidated reporting by Deloitte, is that the top 250 consumer goods manufacturers worldwide had a turnover of $2.8 trillion in 2010.[25] Based on our 10 percent estimation, their expenditure on promotion is likely around $280 billion per annum. According to Deloitte, this is $40 billion more than the total earnings of these companies (estimated to be $240 billion in 2010). Every year, however, this expenditure increases as manufacturers struggle to respond to the declining efficiency of advertising. This has created an enormous market for retail real estate. Retailers now support their businesses by leveraging their suppliers' promotional funds, using that income to drive store expansion and soften hard operating margins. In a world where key retailers consistently deliver a huge number of shoppers, retailers are in a position to make significant and increasing demands on manufacturers.

---

23 Representatives of Accenture CAS, in discussion with the author, 2007.

24 Herb Sorensen (author, *Inside the Mind of the Shopper*), in discussion with the author, November 2010.

25 Deloitte, *Global Powers of Consumer Products 2012: Connecting the Dots*, accessed February 28, 2013, http://www.deloitte.com/assets/Dcom-Guam/Local Assets/Documents/Global Powers of CP 2012_Deloitte_Web.pdf.

At a management conference in Asia, the global CFO of a major consumer goods company observed, "If we do nothing to control the increase in our trade spend, the organic growth of multinational retailers alone may force us out of business in three Asian markets. But if we continue to meet their demands for increased expenditure at the same time, we will be broke in half the time."

Often these retailer demands are for increased promotional funding of one form or another. Promotions are an easy way for retailers to secure higher profit margins and to demonstrate to bargain-hungry shoppers the benefits of coming to their store. Many manufacturers accede to these demands for fear of losing sales to competitors or—even worse—losing a key product listing. This iron fist is typically wrapped in kid-glove assurances that promotions are part of a strategy to build shopper loyalty, but Dr. Sorensen remains to be convinced: "The fact of the matter is, many brands are laboring under the illusion that retailers have a clue in terms of what they're doing in managing the shopping process, and they don't, and it's a serious problem."

In this climate, it is expected that spend on promotions will continue to increase. Is this good news or bad?

Many argue that it's great news for shoppers, but this is only partly true. While millions of shoppers hunt bargains and seek lower prices every day, our research into shopper behavior throughout the last decade revealed ample evidence that a price point does not change behavior in the way once thought. In many cases (though not all), promotions provoke "forward buying." When a shopper "forward buys," she stocks up on a deal, but then, with extra stock in the home and no increase in consumption, the next purchase is deferred. The manufacturer responds to the resultant sales dip with another promotion, and the cycle is repeated. In some cases, over 80 percent of volume is sold this way, pulling the true price of a product down. This impacts manufacturer profitability and ultimately leads to reduced product choice, reduced innovation, and reduced spending on product formulation.

Logic suggests that this would be bad for the retailer as well as the manufacturer. But in fact, the retailers are insured by the manufacturer's funding of the offer. At the same time, those retailers build shopper perception of their brand as offering great value. This perpetuates the cycle as more bargain hunters flow into the stores. But price is easily replicated, and when a competitor offers price cuts plus an additional benefit (think Amazon's low prices and the benefit of convenience), the retailer who relied on price to drive traffic will suddenly have much quieter stores.

But the biggest losers in this scenario are the manufacturers. A recent study of 700 retail promotions delivered startling results: 70 percent of the promotions lost money for the manufacturer. When costs were accounted for, the incremental profit made from these offers did not cover the manufacturer's costs. We found an average return on investment of just 30 cents for every dollar spent. Yet, in 75 percent of these promotions, the retailer made money.

These figures are startling, but they are corroborated by Chris Hoyt, a veteran shopper marketer and founder of Hoyt & Company. He believes that in the United States, the average promotions ROI for manufacturers ranges between a relatively abysmal $0.55 and $0.65.

The combined effects of the failure of Category Management and trade marketing and the consistent application of a business model created in the 1940s and 1950s is bankrupting manufacturers. Looking at how this model affects consumer goods companies' ROI on promotions reveals the $200 billion crime:

The $200 Billion Crime

2010 total annual revenue of the top 250 consumer goods companies worldwide = $2.8 trillion

Assume 10 percent is spent on in-store promotions = $280 billion

70 percent of promotions investment loses money = $196 billion

This means that every year, these consumer goods manufacturers waste $196 billion. That's almost the annual GDP of Portugal, which in 2012 was $210 billion.[26] If you look at the combined net profit of these leading manufacturers, you'll see that the current arrangement is costing the industry almost half of its potential profits. As this behavior continues every year without a change, it gets progressively worse, and each year the consumer goods industry edges closer to bankruptcy.

---

26 Central Intelligence Agency, "The World Factbook," accessed February 28, 2013, https://www.cia.gov/library/publications/the-world-factbook/fields/2195.html.

IT'S TIME FOR A CHANGE

A popular quote often attributed to Albert Einstein defines insanity as doing the same thing over and over again and expecting different results. Is the consumer goods industry insane? We hope not. We do know that the perpetuation of this issue is not done purposely; of course, all manufacturers have every desire and intention of being profitable. Yet they continue to apply strategies that have been employed to increasingly poor results for 50 years or more.

What has been absent to date is a new, holistic set of strategies that will fundamentally change the way manufacturers do business. And the potential results are nothing less than a step change. With leading companies leaving nearly half of their money on the table, just breaking even on promotions could double their profits.

It's time to rewrite the rules of consumer goods marketing. A new business model is necessary—one that addresses the reality of today's retail landscape and acknowledges the rise of the shopper. Manufacturers must understand the types of shoppers who buy their products from retailers; they must understand how to influence those shoppers' behavior; and they must understand how to invest wisely in trade marketing and promotions. These "shopper marketing" strategies need to be integrated with existing "consumer marketing" approaches to create a "Total Marketing" approach. In the following chapters, we'll explore how this works, how it can benefit consumer goods companies all over the planet, and how it truly is a revolution.

CHAPTER 2

THE SHOPPER MARKETING REVOLUTION

W hat do infant and child nutrition, skin care, coffee, cooktops, televisions, and milk have in common? They are all big established product categories, stuffed with leading brands engaged in fierce competition. They all suffer from the pressures of consolidating retail, the elusive search for true innovation, and the difficulties of reaching out to an increasingly streetwise consumer.

But perhaps most importantly, they all face the challenge of achieving growth and doing so profitably. And while that challenge has become harder in recent years, we predict that the consumer goods industry is now heading into a "perfect storm"—a scenario so extreme that those companies that do not act now may not survive. Despite enormous efforts and massive expenditure (about a trillion dollars of marketing), most of these categories grow at rates that can be measured in single digits, or worse, don't grow at all! As we pointed out earlier, during 2008–2010, the top 250 consumer goods companies have grown by only 4 percent per annum on average.[27] And when one considers that this broad church of consumer goods companies includes such stellar growth performers as Apple and Samsung, it is clear that many (if not most) are struggling to drive growth.

---

27 Average of growth rates from Deloitte's *Global Powers of Consumer Products* reports for 2010 (http://www.deloitte.com/assets/Dcom-Belgium/Local Assets/Documents/EN/be_press_ global-powers-consumer-products-2010_020310.pdf), 2011 (http://www.deloitte.com/ assets/Dcom-Kenya/Local Assets/Documents/Deloitte Reports - Global Powers of Consumer Products 2011.pdf), and 2012 (http://www.deloitte.com/assets/Dcom-Guam/Local Assets/ Documents/Global Powers of CP 2012_Deloitte_Web.pdf), all accessed March 14, 2013.

Plus, the top 250 companies in this industry only make an average profit of 8.5 percent.[28] For all of that effort and all of that money, that's not much growth and not much of a return!

And those trends we discussed in Chapter 1—media fragmentation and retail consolidation—show no signs of slowing. Media fragmentation is certainly nothing new to the marketing world, but in recent years, that fragmentation has increased with renewed vigor—driven by completely new channels such as gaming, mobile devices, and social networks. And though the top 10 retailers in the world have doubled in size in the last decade, they are still barely scratching the surface of their potential to consolidate and globalize. A typical multinational consumer goods company may have offices in 80 countries; Walmart, in 2012, was in 27.[29] That's a decent increase from the nine countries where they were in 2001, but it still leaves plenty of room for growth. Tesco, the third-biggest retailer on the planet, was only in 14 countries. Target, the eleventh biggest, is yet to stray outside the United States.

As if increased media fragmentation and increasingly powerful retailers weren't bad enough, there are two new pressures on manufacturers' profitability that were virtually unheard of 5 or 10 years ago: global competition and rising raw material costs. These two developments make up the remainder of the perfect storm that threatens the existence of some consumer goods companies.

As manufacturers in countries such as China and India develop their own brands, moving from being merely low-cost production houses for big companies in the West and Japan, the global market for consumer goods is growing more competitive. As one example, Haier, the Chinese white goods manufacturer, was only founded in 1984 (and the brand wasn't launched until 1991), but it is already the global leader in white goods, according to Euromonitor.

And, as most people know, raw material costs are rising faster than at any time in memory. Oil prices are at record highs and show no sign of falling. After declining for decades, food raw material prices have increased by about 50 percent between 2005 and 2010.[30]

---

28 Deloitte, *Global Powers of Consumer Products 2012: Connecting the Dots*, accessed February 28, 2013, http://www.deloitte.com/assets/Dcom-Guam/Local Assets/Documents/Global Powers of CP 2012_Deloitte_Web.pdf.

29 "Our Story," Walmart, accessed February 28, 2013, http://corporate.walmart.com/our-story.

30 "Malthusian Mouthfuls," *The Economist* online, November 17, 2010, http://www.economist.com/blogs/dailychart/2010/11/economist_food_price_index.

Now that growth is harder to come by, competition is global, and costs are increasing—both in terms of retail, media, and raw material—that industry-wide 8.5 percent profit margin is looking rather thin. And if we consider the estimate made by our friends at Accenture CAS that UK manufacturers' trade spend has tripled (from 8 percent of sales in 1980 to close to 25 percent in 2005), it becomes clear that unless there is a radical change in the way these companies perform, many of them will simply not exist in 10 years.

Yet some consumer goods companies are growing twice as fast as the categories in which they operate. Some manufacturers today have succeeded in growing their business rapidly, even in markets once believed to be stagnant or declining. We can tell you about a consumer electronics company that managed to double its sales while returning a loss-making business unit to profit. We can tell you about a baby nutrition company that found opportunities to grow its brand fourfold. We can tell you about a company whose ROI on promotions moved from negative to 200 percent in a year.

What is the common thread that connects these companies? They have taken themselves away from the traditional way of marketing their products—a methodology that was not only outdated but that threatened their very existence. Instead, they adopted a revolutionary approach. They reinvented their business model and changed the way they engage with their consumers, shoppers, and retail customers.

These companies were faced with the simple choice that all consumer goods companies now face: continue using a business model that is no longer appropriate or seek a new business model that is better suited to the environment in which they now find themselves. We see this as a stark choice: a decision between extinction and survival. Since it is impossible to imagine anyone choosing the first option, change is clearly required. The real question is whether the consumer goods industry requires evolution or revolution. Do we make the change progressively or all at once?

An evolutionary response calls for a gradual change—making incremental improvements to the business model as time passes. Retail consolidation and media fragmentation have slowly grown more significant over a period of four decades—a relatively gradual change. The age of the shopper has, in practical terms, only just begun. Surely then, the industry can take its time to evolve to this new situation, right?

We say, "No!" The consumer goods industry has already tried the evolutionary approach. The introduction of Category Management and trade marketing were evolutionary; they attempted to augment the existing way of doing business rather than addressing the fundamental issues within the environment. Neither of these approaches has been truly successful.

We believe that companies that stick with this approach are like the proverbial frog in a pot of slowly heated water. It is time for these organizations to radically change their approach and jump out of the pot before they find themselves boiled to death.

In the age of the shopper, the environment is becoming harsher at an exponential rate—in some ways, the water is already boiling! As Darren Marshall, Coca-Cola's vice president of Venturing & Emerging Brands, puts it, "These are not new trends necessarily, but it's now, at this time in our environment, where we have got to start doing something about it."[31]

The pace of change is such that an evolutionary response risks leading a company to extinction. With global competition and rising raw goods costs, things may get worse—quickly. Increasingly, the only practical response is not evolutionary but revolutionary. A revolutionary response requires a radical rethinking of the way we market consumer goods and leads to a rapid change in the common order. To turn things around for consumer goods companies, we need a clear articulation of what the companies must achieve and a common understanding of how marketing needs to change to address this requirement.

DRIVING CONSUMPTION

Fundamentally, a consumer goods organization has a single purpose: it must grow its brands profitably. That sounds pretty obvious, but let's just stop for a moment and consider what we mean by "grow." Ultimately, consumer goods organizations need to expand consumption of their brands in a profitable manner. More of the company's products must be used, drunk, eaten, watched, or listened to at a low enough cost to the company.

Note that we use the term *consumption* and not *sales*. Readers with a more fiscal background may find this strange. After all, it is sales—revenue—that companies track. But though better revenues are what the organization must deliver to its shareholders, it appears obvious to us that the only way that those sales are sustainable is if they are achieved in association with

---

31 Darren Marshall (Vice President of Venturing & Emerging Brands, Coca-Cola), in discussion with the author, December 2010.

an equal and parallel increase in consumption. A sale is a single transaction, a unit of economic intercourse. It is not a measure of consumption. If you buy a product and don't use it, what is the likelihood that you will buy it again? How much more strawberry-flavored yogurt drink will you buy when your kids don't drink it? When the bottles of spirits you bought for last year's Christmas party still fill your liquor cabinet, how much more whiskey will you buy?

In all of these cases, consumer goods companies have registered sales, but they have not driven consumption. Let's think for a moment about the beer industry. Around the world, take-home sales of beer peak prior to major holidays: the winter holiday season, Chinese New Year, the Fourth of July, and so on. For one UK-based brewer, sales peak in November and December. Naturally, sales fall in the months of January through March. But oddly, sales in these months fall massively below the indices of alcohol consumption during the same period.

In researching why this pattern occurs, the brewer found that while families stocked up in anticipation of a Christmas binge, they drank little of what they bought. This left partially consumed cases of beer gathering dust in storage rooms and garages well into the following year. With shoppers wishing to avoid piling on further stocks, sales shrunk. Perhaps more interesting was the question of why Britain's beer drinkers didn't finish what they'd started in December. The answer was that the beer was not in the fridge; it was in the garage—making it either inaccessible or not cold. Because of that inconvenience, it remained untouched.

As you see, a sale is not a measure of consumption. Without an increase in consumption, any increase in sales is likely to be short-lived, and the associated costs of achieving that increase are likely to dramatically reduce the profitability of the brand or company.

In the same way a strong wind creates a vacuum that pulls a sailboat along, it is the desire to consume more that powers sales growth. Without wind, the sail is impotent; without consumption, the sale is worthless. Clearly, the more efficiently a company can drive consumption, the greater the return on effort and investment will be. If the manufacturer hopes to achieve the goal of profitable growth, it must primarily focus on driving consumption, but its secondary focus must be on doing so efficiently.

Author and marketing guru Jay Abraham teaches that there are only three ways to grow a business: increase the number of customers the business has, increase the frequency at which they purchase, and/or increase the value that they spend. These dimensions all apply to our primary goal of growing consumption: a company's total consumption is a result of the number of people who use a product, the frequency at which they use the product, and the quantity that they consume each time. Therefore, to increase consumption, a company must achieve one or more of the following:

1. Find and motivate new consumers to use the brand
2. Motivate existing consumers to use the brand more frequently
3. Motivate existing consumers to use larger quantities of the brand every time they use it

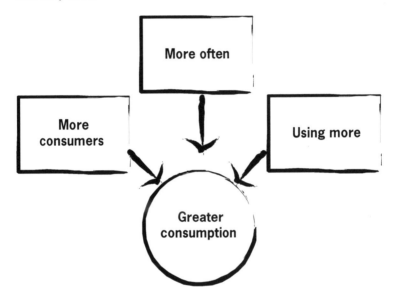

Expanding any one of these dimensions will lead to a corresponding rise in consumption; a 10 percent increase in the number of consumers will boost total consumption by 10 percent. But by growing these measures in combination, consumption increases geometrically. If 1,000 consumers each eat 20 cookies a week, the annual consumption is 1,040 cookies per person. By adding 10 percent to each of these dimensions (100 more consumers, 5.2 more consumption occasions and an extra two cookies on each occasion), consumption grows by 33 percent.

The business model of the 1940s and 1950s was, in the context of its environment, effective at driving consumption. Building brands via television was very efficient: a small number of television networks served a large number of households with relatively few competing brands vying for advertising. And a hub-and-spoke system of distribution points and distributors, paired with massive postwar investment in infrastructure (think American freeways, for example), enabled logisticians to optimize supply chains, making it feasible to get brands like Coca-Cola to even the farthest-flung store at a reasonable price.

Yet today, the profitability and growth rates of many leading brands are declining. Many organizations blame the economic environment for this drop, and it is true that consumers make different choices about what and how much they consume during a slowdown. But the claim that we are consuming less as a global society doesn't bear much analysis. With huge growth rates in electronic gadgets, Internet use, telecommunications, and Asia's enormous markets, blaming the difficulties of the consumer goods industry on the global economy seems vacuous.

We think that a more useful conclusion is that the industry's business model no longer does an effective or efficient job of driving consumption. Thus, that business model needs to be redefined.

REDEFINING THE CONSUMER GOODS BUSINESS MODEL

Decades ago, management consultant, author, and "social ecologist" Peter Drucker espoused the idea that companies needed to look at their entire business from the perspective of the only person who matters: the customer. He once said that the purpose of a business is "to create and keep a customer" and that the aim of marketing is "to know and understand the customer so well the product or service fits him and sells itself."

What Drucker's perspective does not do, however, is define who the customer is for the consumer goods industry. For decades, this industry has relied on a business model that identified two specific customers: the consumer (the person who uses the product) and the retailer (the entity that purchases the product for resale). Manufacturers have always understood the peril of not satisfying consumers' needs and, in recent years, they've ignored their retail customers' needs at their own peril.

In every consumer goods business, specific functions within the organization are focused on these two distinct customers. Marketing focuses its attention on understanding consumers' needs and desires, and on building brands that satisfy these needs on every occasion. Sales, on the other hand, concentrates on motivating retail customers to purchase and support the company's products so that consumers can buy them in stores. Long term, this business model dictates that equity is built in the brand, which is monetized through sales to retailers.

The big problem with the model, though, is that it ignores one major "customer"—the person who actually buys the product: the shopper. It is the shopper that connects the product sold in to a retailer to the end consumer. Without shopping, consumption is impossible. Without shopping, inventory piles up at retailers, and orders from manufacturers dry up. The shopper decides how the buying will be done: what, when, where, how much, and at what price. It is, therefore, the shopper who creates value for the brand and the retail customer. The only time economic value is created for either party is when somebody actually buys the product.

Having worked in the industry for over 20 years, we can assure you that selling cases of product to retailers is easy—you can secure an order almost anywhere by giving an extra discount, committing to a promotion, or having a clever selling story, or just by asking for a favor. But when the retailer doesn't sell that product, it costs you. Simply adding to a retailer's inventory of your brand is an artificial way of growing sales. With many retailers holding between four and six weeks' worth of stock, adding an extra week is most likely to lead to a deferred order or, worse, to that stock being promptly returned. Getting a retailer to buy is no guarantee that your sales will grow.

But, if you can get more shoppers to buy a product, to buy it more frequently, or to spend more on that product, sales will grow for everyone and, as a manufacturer, you get the payback from the investment you made in building brand equity.

This may all appear to be Marketing 101, but many organizations virtually ignore the shopper, assuming that the person buying in stores is the same person who consumes the product.

Is this true?

Let's think about cat food and diapers. Clearly, we don't see too many infants pulling Pampers off the shelf or cats prowling the aisles for a good deal on Whiskas. Let's think about aftershave—used by men, but overwhelmingly bought as a gift, often by women. Hans Hallan, Sales Development Director for the Asia and Africa Region at Carlsberg, a Danish brewing company, says, "Traditionally, we've looked at the consumer and the [retail] customer, but now we've started to realize that there is that third interface. It may be the shopper; it may be someone else. We therefore need to adapt our thinking, particularly in Asia. The shopper can often be a maid in some markets, a driver in another market. Quite often, the household decision for stocking is made by the matriarch of the family and not necessarily by the consumer, which, in 95 percent of occasions, turns out to be a man."[32] (We'll explore this theme in much more detail in Chapter 4, "Cats Don't Buy Litter, But Men Buy Perfume.")

What is now known, however, is that even when the shopper and the consumer are the same person, the factors that influence consumption are massively different from those that drive a purchase. A person in the shopper mindset is not the same as a person in consumer mode. And the same shopper can exhibit different behaviors from one aisle to the next. He might be brand loyal in razors but far less particular about tissues. A parent might spend more time choosing a juice drink for her family than shampoo. And a consumer who was motivated by advertising to check out a particular cell phone might look quite differently at the options when faced with various models and options in the store.

Often, these differences are ignored in the traditional business model. Darren Marshall observes, "We've got so many data points on the brand love component of things but virtually nothing around how people buy."[33]

Chris Hoyt, founder of Hoyt & Company and a pioneer of shopper marketing, says, "Brand people need to understand that no matter what they've spent to build brand awareness, when that consumer gets into a shopper mindset, it changes."[34]

The industry is only just beginning to recognize that there exists a diverse array of shoppers with an equally broad range of behaviors. Motivators to purchase vary from product to product and from shopper to shopper. One buyer in search of a television will do extensive research and know exactly the make and model he wants to purchase, along with the price he wants to pay. The in-store experience for this shopper comes down to availability. If the store has the model he wants at the right price, the shopper will buy it. He doesn't need a salesperson; he needs an order taker. The decision was made before he walked into the store.

Conversely, another shopper in search of a television may not be sure

32 Hans Olaf Hallan (sales development director for the Asia and Africa region, Carlsberg), in discussion with the author, December 2010.
33 Marshall, discussion.
34 Chris Hoyt (founder, Hoyt & Company), in discussion Sue Publicover, assistant to the authors, December 2010.

about the advantages of one model over another. He goes to the store and expects a savvy salesperson to fully explain the features and benefits of various models and then steer him in the direction of the best one to meet his needs. Now let's say he walks into a store and encounters an order taker instead of a sales pro. This salesperson doesn't grasp the features and benefits of the models on display. Maybe he usually works in the camera department and is just filling in, but he can't enlighten and educate the shopper on televisions. All he can do is tell him which one is on sale, read the features on the label, and tell him which models are in stock. Not prepared to make a decision with such flimsy information, the shopper leaves, and that particular sale will happen in a store where he is better served—or worse, the sale will not happen at all.

The crucial nature of the shopper, as distinct from consumer and retail customer, leaves us with the simple conclusion that if we are to redefine the consumer goods business model, we need to redefine it from the perspective of three different customers:

1. The consumer who ultimately uses the product
2. The shopper who purchases the product
3. The retail customer who buys the product for resale

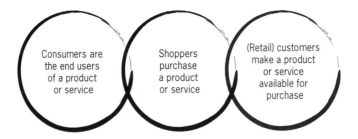

For the new business model to be efficient, it must identify a marketing strategy that reaches each of these three customers.

THE PURPOSE OF MARKETING

There are a huge number of terms and definitions in the world of marketing; even the word *marketing* has several competing definitions. As practitioners of this mystical art of marketing, we like to think of it in the way that the

UK's Chartered Institute of Marketing does, that is, as a process of, "identifying, anticipating, and satisfying customer requirements profitably."[35]

But what is the purpose of that process? Why do it? Many business processes increase profits, but we believe marketing is the only one that drives sales *and* profits. This is because the outcome of great marketing is a change in a customer's behavior, whether consumer, shopper, or retailer. Getting someone to try a new candy bar for the first time requires a change in consumption behavior. Getting a mother to stock up on cheese requires a change in her shopping behavior. Persuading retailers to stop discounting a product requires a change in their commercial behavior.

The consumer goods company's marketing efforts must change behavior of all three types of customer. The new business model must focus on the following:

1. Creating consumer desire to use more of a brand
2. Maximizing every opportunity to persuade shoppers to buy more of the brand
3. Motivating the retailer to support the brand in achieving these goals

This subtle yet revolutionary change in the way we market consumer goods is making a difference for the successfully growing manufacturers we talked about at the beginning of this chapter. It is the distinction between these three customer types—the behavior of retailers, consumers, and above all, shoppers—that is driving the growth of leaders in this revolution.

WHY CHANGING SHOPPER BEHAVIOR IS CRITICAL

It's almost inconceivable that a manufacturer would develop a new product without also considering how to motivate retailers to stock and distribute it. But how much effort is put into considering how to influence someone to buy the product once it's on store shelves?

We've worked with over 50 of the world's leading consumer goods companies across three continents and in all sorts of categories. We get particularly excited when we are asked to help with new product launches. We've read detailed marketing plans that discuss at length the target consumer,

---

35 The Chartered Institute of Marketing website front page, accessed February 28, 2013, http://www.cimhk.org.hk/.

the results of product and advertising testing, the forecasted profit-and-loss accounts, the media plans, and the launch timing. We've immersed ourselves in sales plans discussing target channels, pipe-fill procedures, and investment requirements from key customers and merchandising objectives.

Yet, in all of the plans that we've read to date, not one has discussed how the company intends to persuade shoppers to buy the product. These companies seem to believe that the weight of advertising and the depth of distribution will be enough to get shoppers to buy a product and then keep using it. Often this belief is based on product testing; using a number of sophisticated and credible approaches, the company has asked potential consumers, "Would you buy this product?" But let's illustrate the dangers of this approach using an imaginary, oversimplified, and a slightly exaggerated example.

Suppose for a second that we ran a product test targeting one hundred beer consumers. Let's say that acceptance exceeds 65 percent. For most companies this would meet the minimum hurdle rate and lead testers to conclude that a launch will likely be successful. On the basis of this information, the launch may go ahead. But in a category like beer, we already know from our discussions with Carlsberg's Hans Hallan that, in some countries, up to 95 percent of products, including beer, are bought by people who aren't the ones using or consuming the product.[36]

So in this test, our consumers might actually buy only 5 percent of the total category sales—meaning that because we neglected the shoppers, only 3.25 percent of the shoppers (65 percent of our 5 percent) have made a positive statement that they would buy the beer. The vast majority of shoppers—and therefore the majority of the opportunity—remains untested. In focusing on the end consumers and targeting their efforts toward them, and not the shoppers, the company has aimed at the wrong mark.

Will advertising messages tailored to the (male) drinker influence or even reach the (female) shopper? Will giveaways, loyalty-building promotions, and attractive displays—all configured to appeal to the lifestyles of the target (male) consumer—appeal in any way to the (female) shopper? Will posters that feature young women in short skirts impress this shopper? The answer to all three questions is almost certainly "no." We can expect our marketing effort to have little or no impact on shopper behavior. Even if we have created a desire for the beer in the consumer base, it won't be available for them to drink because the shoppers are not purchasing it.

---

36 Hallan, discussion.

In an average year, there are just over 10,000 new product introductions in the United States, and a 2005 McKinsey survey suggested that the vast majority of these brands take only tiny slivers of the market.[37] Their report tracked 134 new product launches and found that the average category share secured by a new product was 2.5 percent. Yet nearly two-thirds of these products secured shares of less than 1 percent. Product innovation is a risky, cost-intensive, and lengthy process. If the majority of product launches are destined to disappoint, surely it is worth investing in changing shoppers' behavior as well as that of consumers and retailers.

We believe that the need to invest in shopper behavior extends beyond launches, to every one of the manufacturer's activities. The relationship between shopping and consumption is equal and symbiotic: if a product is bought but not consumed, it is unlikely that product will be bought again; if a product is desired by a consumer but not purchased by a shopper, then it won't (or can't!) be consumed. No matter how good the proposition to the consumer, any marketing effort is destined to fail if shoppers don't buy. And even if retailers are persuaded to support a great product, when shoppers don't respond in their stores, retailers will revoke their support in short order. This is even institutionalized by some retailers. Within Japan's innovation-rich consumer packaged goods market, Seven & I (the company that owns the 7-Eleven brand) gives products from its suppliers as little as two weeks to prove their worth before they are out.

So if manufacturers owe it to themselves to consider the shopper (as well as the consumer and retailer) in their marketing plans, what of the retailers themselves? The increase in retail brands and outlet choices has diminished loyalty among shoppers. While shoppers state in research that prices and discounts are their primary reason for visiting a certain store, the arrival of new forms of retail in the shape of companies like Amazon and Zappos has put brick-and-mortar stores at a disadvantage (see Chapter 6, "The True Cost of Discounting"). Shoppers now have access to more data, in more convenient ways, than ever before; while standing in the aisles of a Walmart store, they can now use their smartphone to quickly check the price of nearly any product on Amazon or a host of other sites and choose a cheaper or better alternative.

Encouraging more shoppers into their stores, persuading them to visit

---

37 Erik A. Roth and Kevin D. Sneader, "Reinventing Innovation at Consumer Goods Companies," *McKinsey Quarterly*, November 2006, http://www.mckinseyquarterly.com/Reinventing_innovation_at_consumer_goods_companies_1870.

more frequently, and convincing them to spend more per visit is the lifeblood of retail. Indeed, retailers' marketing strategies have long been configured towards achieving these goals. As Anson Dichaves, the former head of Global Shopper Marketing at Philips (currently Managing Director Shopper APMEA at Nielsen) says, "Retailers have to market to their customers, who are shoppers."[38] By introducing the shopper into their business model as well, manufacturers can find a point of commonality with retailers, a central focus that allows them to share common objectives and strategies.

In today's world of inflating costs, deflating prices, and rancorous competition, neither manufacturers nor retailers can ignore the importance of changing shopper behavior. Both parties need to create a new way to engage shoppers, and they need to recognize that shoppers have the power.

THE NEED FOR SHOPPER MARKETING

In the world of marketing, there are early adopters abuzz around any new idea or product. Very often, this buzz creates a loud clamor among those eager to hop on the bandwagon. In this frenzy, the actual purpose of and context of the idea can get lost and, as a result, misconceptions arise and pace is lost. Since the term *shopper marketing* was first coined early in the 2000s, this is what has happened to this crucial concept.

The pioneers of shopper marketing are a mismatched bunch: idealists like us looking for a better way of doing things; consultancies watching the environment and seeking new solutions; advertising agencies hoping to develop more coherent through-the-line propositions; and manufacturers who have understood the potential ahead of the curve. And there are a smattering of snake oil salesmen, dressing up old ideas in new clothes. With such a diverse group of people thinking through the issues (or not!), observers may be easily confused by conflicting ideas, propositions, and definitions. So before we go much further, let's clear this up!

You can read about the explosive growth of shopper marketing in many places. There are ample resources from the American Grocery Manufacturers Association, and in-store marketing associations around the world, as well as consultancies and advertising agencies, all attempt to quantify

---

38 Anson Dichaves (former head of Global Shopper Marketing, Philips), in discussion with Sue Publicover, assistant to the authors, December 2010.

the growth of the shopper marketing concept. Often a startling array of statistics is presented, all telling you that this is "huge" and that you need to get involved. Many a conference hall around the world has been packed with people giving breathless presentations on shopper marketing. Yet we've observed that, in most cases, the point is almost completely missed. And it's missed for three reasons: first, many people remain confused about who the target of all this activity is; second, the industry appears to define *shopper marketing* as being just those activities that companies execute inside a shop; and finally, there appears to be a fundamental misunderstanding about what marketing even is.

Let's first have a look at how shopper marketing is currently defined by Wikipedia: "Understanding how one's target consumers behave as shoppers, in different channels and formats, and leveraging this intelligence to the benefit of all stakeholders, defined as brands, consumers, retailers, and shoppers."[39] We find this odd. Is the target of the process a consumer or a shopper? In the Wikipedia definition, we are only interested in our consumers when they are shoppers. What about the shoppers who are not consumers? The definition ignores this category of customer. This might seem like pedantry, but the failure to account for this significant distinction weakens the whole definition. The very point of marketing is to change behavior; the point of shopper marketing must be to change shoppers' behavior. The link to consumers is important in that what the shopper buys must be consumed, but the focus of the marketing effort in shopper marketing is the shopper, not the consumer. Therefore, a correct definition must focus on shoppers.

Within the consumer goods industry, there is an ongoing debate as to the boundaries of shopper marketing. Some marketers believe that the methodology strictly controls in-store activities. They cite the various studies that show the large number of decisions made in the store. "I take the hard line," says Herb Sorensen. "No one is a shopper if they're not inside the four walls of a store. Certainly, for bricks and mortar, this is true. If someone is driving to a store and gets run over by a bus and they're asked what they were doing when they were hit, they don't say, 'Well, I was shopping.'"[40]

But we believe any decision that affects purchase behavior is a shopping decision, and any effort to influence a shopping decision is shopper marketing. Think of it this way. When an individual decides where to go shopping, is

---

39 "Shopper marketing," *Wikipedia*, last modified February 26, 2013, http://en.wikipedia.org/wiki/Shopper_marketing.

40 Sorensen, discussion.

that a consumer decision or a shopper decision? We'd argue it's a shopper decision—and clearly it's one that happens outside the store. The reality is that the line between consumer and shopper marketing has blurred—and that is why we argue for a new, integrated approach that reflects the way people truly behave. Shopping decisions are made outside a store; consumer influences invade the in-store decision-making process. Clearly it's time for a new definition that addresses that overlap.

A UNIVERSAL DEFINITION

Let's think about defining shopper marketing as, well, a form of marketing. Much of the current excitement focuses on new ways to communicate to people while they shop, better methods of promoting products, or new merchandising propositions. This is all very interesting and certainly represents a dynamic stream of innovation. But these are activities: none of these are marketing. Think about it this way: is advertising marketing? Advertising is certainly a marketing activity; it is a subset of Promotions, one of the 4 Ps that make up the "marketing mix." However, a product can be very effectively marketed without advertising. To define marketing based on a component of the 4 Ps is nonsensical and exclusive. Isn't research part of the marketing process? Should we ignore the teams engaged in creating marketing strategies and plans? What of the evaluation process?

In short, the industry needs a clearer definition of shopper marketing that focuses on the shopper, changing her behavior in order to create consumption growth. As Anson Dichaves puts it, "It is marketing: Analyze data, understand the insight, and propose a solution to activate that insight. What's happening right now is it's either a promotion or a merchandising solution."[41] So we need a more effective definition.

We define shopper marketing this way: *"Shopper marketing is the systematic creation and application of elements of a marketing mix to affect positive change in shopper behavior and drive consumption of a brand."*

In this definition, shopper marketing focuses on building an in-depth understanding of the shopper's behavior and then applying that knowledge to drive sales *and* consumption—by developing offers, messaging, and merchandising that influence the purchase process.

---

41 Dichaves, discussion.

THE SHOPPER REVOLUTION

Is this a revolution? The *Oxford English Dictionary* defines the word *revolution* as "a dramatic and wide-reaching change in conditions, attitudes, or operation."[42] We believe including marketing to the shopper in the way brand marketing is conducted is an opportunity to change performance in people and businesses. Yet for this performance to change, the entire business model that the consumer goods industry currently uses needs to change. The new business model needs to recognize, understand, and influence the behavior not only of consumers and retailers, but also of shoppers.

This calls for a fundamental change in marketing attitudes. Marketers must now recognize that consumers are not necessarily shoppers, and vice versa. Marketers must embrace the fact that if they want to grow a brand, they need to influence shoppers' behavior. To do that, they must understand how, where, why, and for whom the shopper shops. And they must understand that while purchasing happens in a store, the factors that influence purchase decisions do not necessarily occur there. If they wish to return to profitable growth, marketers need to know that not all shoppers are equal, and they need to be able to identify those who are most valuable.

Including shoppers in the way marketing is done demands new tools and new thinking, particularly in the area of in-store investment. The industry as a whole must become savvier in the way it spends money. Collectively, manufacturers and retailers can no longer continue spending money on activities that do not change buying behavior; it must be widely understood that this course of action is ineffective and wasteful. To survive, business leaders need to insist that making any marketing investment without evaluation of its ROI is hazardous, and that to avoid waste, new systems and oversights will be needed.

Introducing a new business model means that new working processes will be required. The traditional line between the roles of marketing and sales will have to shift. Trade marketing teams will need to think, act, and organize differently, and some will question the viability of the function overall.

Perhaps most fundamentally, relationships between manufacturers and retailers need to change. In many cases, this new marketing approach will lead to greater collaboration on common goals, and better working relationships should be the result. In other cases, it may open up new routes

---

42 *Oxford English Dictionary*, 2nd ed., s.v. "revolution."

to market, an outcome that will present interesting challenges and opportunities for both parties.

In all, shopper marketing could provoke major change if it's fully embraced and integrated into consumer goods businesses. Will it be worth it? The answer is a resounding yes, not the least because the environments demand a significant change. The results shopper marketing can deliver are spectacular: Deloitte found that U.S. companies that invested in shopper marketing efforts experienced growth that was 50 percent faster than their overall category growth rate; in some cases, the rise was double that pace. Chris Hoyt quotes data suggesting that shopper marketing initiatives, when properly planned and executed, can consistently deliver returns that are 300 percent more effective than Category Management (for manufacturers). Other studies have delivered more conservative numbers (25 percent or more), but all studies point to one truth: when you invest in marketing to shoppers, you get a strong ROI.

With these 25 to 50 percent increases in growth, this approach clearly shows great potential for overcoming the industry's middling 4 percent annual growth rate. To win, manufacturers need to take a step forward. They need to understand which shoppers are most valuable to their brands; they need to find out in which stores and specifically where in those stores shoppers can be influenced; and they need to learn what activities will have the best chance of

DEBUNKING SOME SHOPPER MARKETING MYTHS

1. **Consumers and shoppers are the same.** False. In all categories, a proportion of products are bought by people who never use the product. This can be very high or very low, depending on the category. In every case, though, the factors that influence consumption behavior and the factors that influence shopping behavior differ enormously.

2. **Shopper marketing only happens in a store.** False. Shopping begins when people start to think about filling a consumption gap. Shoppers decide where they will shop long before they go to a store, and influencing this decision is as much a part of the shopper marketing process as influencing what they do in a store.

3. **Shopper marketing is only relevant in large stores like Walmart.** False. People shop in a huge array of different outlets, small and large. Shopper marketing can influence people's behavior wherever they shop.

4. **Shopper marketing is part of an evolutionary change.** False. Shopper marketing demands fundamental changes in the business model, its tools and processes, its organization structures, and relationships. In return for these changes, it delivers a platform for sustainable, profitable growth.

positively changing the behavior of those target shoppers. In the rest of this book, we'll show how significant practical changes to the consumer goods business model can have a revolutionary impact. The time to shift your focus to the shopper and kick your marketing into high gear is here and now.

CHAPTER 3

THE FIVE-STEP TOTAL MARKETING MODEL

We've shown that the body of evidence supporting the need for change in consumer goods is compelling. We believe the adoption of a new marketing model is a financial imperative, and the managers we work with agree. Yet there is a huge gulf between this consensus on the need for change and the actual implementation of that change. Most of us grasp why change is essential; the struggle lies in how it should be made. The traditional marketing model is deeply ingrained in the DNA of the consumer goods industry, and to effectively reengineer that DNA is far more than an intellectual challenge—it is a mission that requires a whole new approach to marketing.

CHANGE THE BUSINESS, NOT YOUR TITLE

For decades, the most common response to a challenge of this sort has been to develop a specialist function to address the issue. The initial evolutionary response to media fragmentation and retail consolidation—the founding of trade marketing and Category Management functions—was exactly this type of reaction. Today, the industry is responding to change in precisely the same way. In the most recent report on the state of shopper marketing, "Shopper Marketing 5.0: Creating Value with Shopper Solutions," Booz and the GMA state that "many major CPG manufacturers now have shopper marketing organizations staffed with more than twenty dedicated employees (some have fifty or more)."[43]

In a large proportion of cases we work on, we find that these "new" teams are in fact the product of a wholesale rebranding of what was originally a trade marketing function. The teams have been augmented in some cases; often members of specialist consumer insights teams have been co-opted to play the role of shopper experts, but the teams themselves are doing the same work as before. A 2011 Australian study on shopper marketing conducted by the Point of Purchase Advertising Institute (Australia and New Zealand) and ShopAbility found that "companies are using a wide array of more 'traditional' promotional activities."[44] The 2011 Grocery Manufacturers Association's "Shopper Marketing 5.0" report suggests that shopper marketing is evolving towards "shopper solutions": a combination of cross-promotions and merchandising that bring products together to address a specific occasion.[45] But this is far from new: over the last three decades, hundreds of products have been bundled together in seasonal promotions, themed events, or simple pairings to encourage shoppers to, for instance, buy everything they need for the perfect summer barbecue or a night of watching football with friends.

Managers who live in the hope that this long-established tactic will address the new problems they face are to be sorely disappointed. Rebranding trade marketing teams and reworking well-used strategies is not a recipe for long-term growth. At best, this approach will lead to more efficient execution of these strategies; at worst, it will perpetuate the status quo.

Trade marketing has always struggled to define itself, and many organizations never fully understood where it added true value. But giving trade marketing a new title without giving it a fundamentally different function does nothing to fix the underlying issue the industry faces. Many trade marketers are highly competent in the field of managing promotional spend, but relatively few operate at a strategic level. They often lack the necessary guiding processes and skills of a shopper marketer. An article in ShopAbility's

43 Grocery Manufacturers Associaton and Booz & Company, *Shopper Marketing 5.0: Creating Value with Shopper Solutions*, accessed February 28, 2013, http://www.booz.com/media/uploads/BoozCo-Shopper-Marketing-5.0.pdf.

44 Inside Retail, "Shopper Marketing Gains Momentum," September 9, 2011, http://www.insideretailing.com.au/IR/IRNews/Shopper-marketing-gains-momentum-2324.aspx.

45 Grocery Manufacturers Associaton and Booz & Company, *Shopper Marketing 5.0: Creating Value with Shopper Solutions*, accessed February 28, 2013, http://www.booz.com/media/uploads/BoozCo-Shopper-Marketing-5.0.pdf.

Australian report claims "nearly three quarters (72 percent) [of shopper marketing teams] don't currently have a set or documented process for conducting shopper marketing activities."[46] Tia Newcomer, Hewlett-Packard's vice president of worldwide marketing, sums the issue up clearly: "You just can't take a trade marketer and slap [her] into a shopper marketing position. A good shopper marketer has some sales background, Category Management, and/or analytics—because that's highly important whether you're looking at insights or ROI—and some marketing background."[47]

All this suggests that the industry is again trying to evolve, seeing shopper marketing as the "new trade marketing," or as Dr. Brian Harris puts it, "the logical evolution of category management."[48] But as we showed in the previous chapter, we need not evolution but revolution. That requires an entirely new marketing model, and no team will be able to realize the potential of this model without fully comprehending how the new process works.

THE QUESTION-LED BUSINESS PROCESS

The traditional marketing process has at its heart a series of key questions: Who is our target market? What are their needs and desires? How can we configure a product that profitably meets these needs and desires? How can we persuade our consumers to use this product? How can we persuade retailers to support this product in their stores? The questions present a series of gateways the marketer must pass through to achieve profitable growth. But the new marketing model introduces a new customer—the shopper—and raises new questions that must be integrated into the traditional model.

When you market to shoppers, your goal is to influence a specific shopper's purchase behavior in order to drive the consumption of a brand. Thus, the new marketing process must first define which shoppers should be targeted. Since the goal is to drive consumption, the groups of shoppers you define should be those who are most likely to deliver products to the target consumer, whether themselves or someone else.

---

46 Inside Retail, "Shopper Marketing Gains Momentum," September 9, 2011, http://www. insideretailing.com.au/IR/IRNews/Shopper-marketing-gains-momentum-2324.aspx.
47 Tia Newcomer (vice president of worldwide marketing, Hewlett-Packard), in discussion with Sue Publicover, assistant to the authors, December 2010.
48 Brian Harris (chairman, The Partnering Group), in discussion with the author, January 2011.

Once the target shopper is identified, the marketer must pinpoint exactly how these shoppers' behavior should be changed to deliver the required result. Since shoppers buy products in a broad range of outlets, the marketer must seek out those outlets in which it is most likely that a target shopper's behavior can be influenced. In these outlets, the marketer must then apply the most appropriate marketing mix in order to positively affect behavior. So this new marketing approach creates a whole series of new questions: Which shoppers should we target? Where can we influence their purchase behavior? How can we influence purchase behavior?

THE FIVE-STEP TOTAL MARKETING PROCESS

These additional questions are crucial, but integrating them into today's marketing model risks overloading the managers who have to answer them. We've found that effectively chunking business processes into manageable steps helps individuals and teams work progressively towards an outcome. To that end, we've categorized the questions into logical groups and given them a logical sequence. What emerges is a five-step process:

1. Define *consumption* priorities
2. Define target *shoppers*
3. Prioritize *channels*
4. Develop the *marketing mix*
5. Invest

Let's take a closer look at these steps, one by one.

1. DEFINE CONSUMPTION PRIORITIES

If you want to grow your brand, additional consumption is required. Understanding which consumers represent an opportunity to drive that future consumption is key to your success. To grow consumption, we target consumers who either could consume our brands but don't or those who could consume more but don't. These are our priorities as we seek to increase consumption.

By answering three key questions—Who is our target consumer group? What opportunities exist to increase the consumption of this target group? Which of these opportunities should we prioritize?—we are able to clearly pinpoint the scale of the opportunity to be chased and, probably just as important, which opportunities to ignore. With these questions answered, we know where the product needs to be to make that growth happen: Whose shower do we need to put the shampoo into? Which fridges need to be filled with our products? Whose lunchbox do we want to get our snacks into?

2. DEFINE TARGET SHOPPERS

Understanding consumers helps us find our target shopper. If Jennifer should wash her hair with our product, we need to get Jennifer's mom to buy it; if Bill's fridge should be full of our beverages, we need to get Bill's wife to by them. On this foundation, we can hone in on the shoppers who should buy our brand but don't, as well as those who do buy our brand but could buy more frequently or spend more.

Answering three questions—Who are target shoppers? What opportunities exist to positively influence their purchase behavior? Which of these opportunities should we prioritize?—will help you determine whom to focus on and will help you define the scale of the sales opportunity of various groups. The answers will also help you deprioritize groups whose behavior might be difficult to change or who offer relatively low growth potential.

3. PRIORITIZE CHANNELS

We can only realize our sales opportunities when we get targeted shoppers to change their purchase behavior. In most cases, this happens in a retail outlet—either a shop or online. In both cases, we need to identify the groups of outlets, which we call "channels," where we are most likely to affect the change we want.

Let's focus on an actual case to make this clear. In the United Kingdom, chain grocery stores comprise a key channel for most fast-moving consumer goods manufacturers. For grocery products, the top four retailers—Tesco, Asda, Sainsbury's, and Morrisons—account for almost 77 percent of sales in the market.[49] A key business driver for leading chocolate manufacturer Mars is encouraging mothers shopping in these stores to buy products for the whole family during their regular weekly shop. But in these stores, research showed that less than a third of shoppers enter the confectionery aisle. Why? Simple: by not exposing themselves to such a sinful category, mothers avoid the temptation to buy for their family *and themselves*. If

---

49 BBC News, "Tesco Market Share Dips Below 30%," January 31, 2012, http://www.bbc.co.uk/news/business-16817254.

these target shoppers actively avoid the category, the potential to influence their behavior is low.

By answering two questions—Which channels do target shoppers use? How easy is it to influence their behavior in these channels?—the marketer can calculate the actual potential value of each channel, saving the team a lot of wasted investment and effort.

4. DEVELOP THE MARKETING MIX

Marketers are adept at creating marketing mixes to affect the attitude and behavior of consumers. In this new model, this must be extended to encompass a marketing mix for shoppers and retailers, as well as consumers.

Intriguingly, the same research on confectionery products in the UK showed that of those who did enter the confectionary aisle, close to 70 percent purchased a product. Clearly, confectioners want to encourage shoppers who currently don't buy their products to start buying them in the future, and finding a way to make their category unavoidable is a surefire way to tempt shoppers to do just that.

To make sure every shopper is exposed to candies, a confectioner might seek an alternate location for its product, perhaps next to a category with almost universal appeal, like say, milk. (That's precisely what Mars persuaded some retailers to do!). Alternatively, it might buy display space on the end of each aisle (known as "end caps" or "gondola ends"). Or it might place the product at checkout counters or entice shoppers to the confectionery aisle by making it more exiting or engaging. Today, Mars might choose to market directly by couponing loyalty-card holders, or it could purchase prime space on the landing page of the retailer's website. In truth, the world of retail offers a massive array of marketing opportunities, and as mobile devices and interactive technologies become ubiquitous, these options continue to expand.

The key questions to ask during this step are: Which marketing activities are most likely to influence target shoppers' behavior? And what is the optimum mix of marketing activities in each priority channel? The answers enable the marketing team to structure campaigns that offer the greatest sales potential at the lowest possible cost.

5. INVEST

Good brand managers plan and budget their activities very well. They build brand profit and loss (P&L) statements to understand how well their brand performs financially. But often their analysis is limited to their consumer-centric activities, and they frequently ignore the investment and spend against the other two customers: the shopper and the retailer.

With the relatively small exception of manufacturers who sell their products directly to shoppers, the vast majority of products are sold in environments that are owned by a retailer. In order to implement the marketing mix in these environments, manufacturers must collaborate with the store owners. Collaboration can take many forms. It could be as simple as a regular sales call made to the millions of independent store holders all over the world, or it could be in the form of extended close working with global behemoths like Walmart or Carrefour. Whatever mode of collaboration is chosen, it will require investment.

In part, the question of which customers to invest in is answered in defining priority channels; there is no value in investing in retailers that your target shoppers don't use or in environments where you can't influence their purchase decisions. At this stage in the process, however, there are still significant decisions to make. It may be important to evaluate whether Auchan, Leclerc, or Carrefour is the best hypermarket operator to prioritize, or to make a call between Lidl and Aldi if discounters are key. In countries with a vibrant and diverse independent retail trade like Indonesia or India, knowing which grades of outlets to target will be essential.

For marketers facing these challenges, it's important answer three key questions: Which retail customers can implement the marketing mix? What levels of investment are required? Where is the greatest potential for ROI?

∗ ∗ ∗

The power of this five-step process lies in the progressive prioritization it creates; it only focuses on the greatest consumer opportunities, the key shoppers, the prioritized channels, the optimum marketing mix, and the customers that offer the highest return. In doing so, investment that might be wasted is redeployed to fuel profitable growth, while taking unnecessary cost out of the system. Its greatest virtue, however, is its simplicity. At the most operational level, it enables managers in existing teams to introduce Total Marketing without the need to create new organizational solutions per se. Managers in existing marketing, trade marketing, and sales teams can easily collaborate on specific initiatives, as each team is often already equipped to answer the questions that the process poses.

We've seen the power of the process in action both at extremely strategic levels and at simpler operational ones, and we've learned that managers are happy to quickly embrace this new way of working because they see immediate and significant results.

THE FIVE-STEP TOTAL MARKETING PROCESS IN ACTION

A while back, Sony hired us to advance the sales of its Bravia brand in China. For those in the know, Bravia was the epitome of state-of-the-art flat-screen TVs, and the brand commands a significant premium over its competition. China's explosive consumer market is a top priority for manufacturers in the consumer electronics space, and as global companies jostle with rambunctious Chinese manufacturers for a share of the consumer's wallet, the competition can get rough. Needless to say, margins are slim—and thinned further by a surprisingly consolidated retail market in which two big players operate three retail brands. Gome, Yongle and Suning stores accounted for nearly 80 percent of Sony's sales.

TARGETING HIGH-VALUE CONSUMERS

Our engagement began with an orientation to the brand and its consumers. Breaking with other markets, most of which had chosen to play on Bravia's explosive multi-color performance, the Chinese team sought to position the brand as epicurean. They created sophisticated advertising imagery targeting the top end of Chinese consumers—a particularly wise decision in a market where less that 1 percent of China's 400 million households could feasibly afford the product. Still, with nearly 13 million potential consumers living in that top 1 percent of households, Sony has a significant target market.

We started by segmenting the market using preexisting consumer insights. It immediately became clear that two consumer groups, just 39 percent of the potential population, accounted for 79 percent of the potential sales of Bravia products. Both groups consisted of affluent successful males but differed in their age and motivation. The larger of the two contained family men who had achieved success at the cost of time with their families—these we dubbed "life enjoys"—and who sought high-end products as a vehicle for rewarding themselves and their families. The second group was younger, single or just married, and saw their choice of electronics as a validation of their lifestyle—we called them "individual show-offs." Our consumer data showed us that preference for Sony's product was high, with 63 percent and 57 percent of both groups expressing a strong partiality to the brand. However, only 22 percent of both groups bought a Bravia TV. Our key question, therefore, was how can we convert preference into purchase?

UNDERSTANDING SHOPPERS AND SHOPPING BEHAVIOR

Our next task was one that most traditional marketers would skip: we took a deep look at how our target consumer behaved when shopping. We found that the process of shopping for a TV was incredibly involved and long—it took up to six months for some people to buy a TV! The process invariably began with some exploratory browsing. Shoppers looked at TVs incidentally, perhaps taking a little time out to look at what was on offer. As they became more committed to the idea of buying a new TV, shoppers spoke to friends and browsed the Internet for reviews. Armed with a bit more information, they began to explore offers in earnest, visiting stores and talking to the promoters (salespeople and brand advocates who work in stores for the brands they represent) that haunt China's department store-style electronics retailers. They would visit each brand's displays, gathering detailed information about what the TV could do and why it might be appropriate for them. Again, they sought further information in Internet forums, in chat rooms, and by chatting with aficionados in their own network.

As they entered the third stage of shopping, people began to actively engage with brands—by this time they had weeded out the brands that were not for them and compiled a shortlist of two or three worthy candidates. Shoppers returned to stores, sometimes repeatedly, gathering detailed brochures and talking at length with promoters. But still they didn't buy. Now they spent time on the Internet not looking for information about what to buy but about *when* to buy—they were seeking a deal!

China enjoys three key holiday seasons, and retailers capitalize on these breaks to herd shoppers into their stores with discounts and deals. We found shoppers waited for these seasons, knowing prices would come down. They tracked newspaper ads and even asked store staff when the deals would start and what might be available. When the time came, they pounced and sales rocketed.

What was most interesting, though, was how shoppers, even if they fell into the same consumer groups, differed in this convoluted path to purchase. Those shoppers who had an absolute preference for Sony at the outset behaved completely differently than those who merely considered

Sony and those that did not consider the brand at all. We found that each group responded differently to what they experienced as they made their decisions, and—for all groups—preference for brands waxed and waned through the path to purchase. While our two target consumer groups made up the majority of the first two groups of shoppers (those who clearly preferred Sony and those who considered Sony an option), it was clear that segmenting shoppers in the same way as consumers was not going to work.

For Sony, the key finding was how its in-store presentation affected different shoppers. For those who had no particular preference or rejected Sony, repeated visits to outlets did nothing to sway their opinion; indeed, these shoppers became increasingly disaffected with the Bravia proposition. Those who considered Sony as one option among others tended to veer towards the others as they learned more. And even those who preferred Sony were enticed away by competitors, notably Samsung and Sharp. It became clear that, for Sony, rapidly converting shoppers who preferred or considered Sony before they were swayed way was key. Using behavioral benchmarks, we found that sales grew by a whopping 275 percent by focusing only on these two shopper groups.

PRIORITIZING CHANNELS: WHERE TO WIN?

Sony's next challenge was to define where it could capture this potential. Bearing in mind that most of the company's sales were concentrated in three major retailers, this was a challenge. Of the three, Suning was the largest sales maker, so it might appear that this chain offered the greatest potential. Indeed, the bulk of Sony's in-store investments were in Suning stores.

Suning, China's third largest retailer[50], with well-located stores and a broad range of products, attracts hoards of shoppers during the weekend. These shoppers find browsing the extensive offer an entertaining way to while away a few hours. Suning attracts people of all incomes, but it particularly appeals to shoppers with a budget. Retailer Gome, by contrast, offers a hard discount feel, and the more pressurized environment appeals to shoppers who know what they want and are just looking for a deal. Yongle, the smallest of the three chains (it's owned by Gome), offers a cleaner environment with more expansive space, allowing browsers to spend more time interacting with brands.

---

50 Deloitte, *Global Powers of Retailing 2013: Retail Beyond*, accessed March 7, 2013, http://www.deloitte.com/assets/Dcom-Global/Local Assets/Documents/Consumer Business/dttl_cb_GlobalPowersofRetailing2013.pdf.

When we analyzed the role that each chain played for the target shoppers, we found quickly that our two target groups spent significantly more time in Yongle. They found the crowds in Suning distracting and the feel of Gome too down-market. Suning and Gome were full of shoppers, but increasing marketing efforts in them would be a waste; most shoppers in these stores had little or no potential to buy a Bravia TV. By contrast, focused investment in Yongle would directly target the shoppers with the greatest buying potential. We were able to calculate that a dollar invested in Yongle would recoup almost twice as much return than the same dollar invested in Suning.

DEVELOPING THE MARKETING MIX TO CONVERT BROWSERS TO BUYERS

We zeroed in on Yongle to discover what would convert our target shopper's preferences into a buying decision more rapidly. For our colleagues in China, there were three specific challenges: driving traffic to the branded booths within the store, converting shoppers to buyers in the booth (or at least ensuring that shoppers became more committed to the brand as a result of their interactions), and increasing the value of the sale. In Yongle's stores, the range of potential marketing activities is both extensive and expensive. With every competitor chasing the prime positions in-store, both as an opportunity to capture as much traffic as possible and to build their brands, retail chains are able to augment their profits by auctioning off the top spots. As a result, prime real estate in the store required massive payments. Equally, with Yongle wishing to market itself with attractive price points, manufacturers' margins were further thinned by price discounting. The booths themselves represented a significant capital cost; each needed to showcase the brands as effectively as possible. Added to this, manufacturers provide the sales staff in the booth to promote their brands; they provide hardware to demonstrate what the products can do; and they provide promotional materials to ensure that shoppers can easily review what they've seen in the store. Marketing in these stores requires significant funding; to optimize this investment, we needed to know whether traffic, conversion, or value had the most impact on behavior.

Remember, the target shoppers either preferred Sony or consider Sony an option. We found that 92 percent of these shoppers would visit the Sony booth, regardless of its location, so we immediately concluded that prime location was not essential. We also found that the prime locations were the busiest, so salespeople were often busy talking about their products to shoppers, many of whom had no intention to purchase. Our conclusion was that not only could we save money by taking a less busy location in the store, but doing so also ensured more of our target shoppers would be able to engage with the brand.

Next, we turned our attention to what actually happened in the booth. As discussed earlier, we tracked what happened when people interacted with Bravia and Sony's sales team. The first thing we found was that people rarely bought—only 32 percent of shoppers who preferred Sony left the store with a Bravia TV, and worse, less than 2 percent of those who only considered Sony bought. Second, we found that brand preference was reduced. We looked at the disposition of shoppers after they spent time in the store. Nine percent of visitors who had preferred Sony (but did not buy on the day) left the store actually liking other brands more, and no one who had considered Sony initially left with a preference for Bravia. A full 10 percent rejected the Bravia brand altogether. Something was going drastically wrong when shoppers were in the Bravia booth!

Clearly, this had to be the priority; there was no way we could increase the value of purchase in an environment where people actually liked the product less after they saw it. Sony's engagement with shoppers obviously wasn't compelling enough, so we listened to what shoppers said about their interaction: *I don't understand what Bravia does that other products can't do. I don't watch much terrestrial TV, but I couldn't try my favorite DVD to see how it looked. The guy at Samsung told me they made Sony's screens, so I don't see why I should pay more for Bravia. [The booth] is very dark—it doesn't seem very colorful. The Sony sales guy couldn't explain why Bravia is so expensive compared to other brands.*

From these comments, it was clear that shoppers weren't being effectively told about the product's unique selling points. The booth and the salespeople weren't doing a good job of explaining why the Bravia was worth the higher price point. The solution presented itself clearly: sell Bravia on its specific benefits more effectively. With identical levels of capital investment, the in-store environment was rebranded to reflect Bravia's superior color engine, and the booths were repainted a vibrant red to emphasize the point. Sony invested in bringing in the latest home-cinema hardware to showcase a screen's performance when playing DVDs. Sales teams were retrained to explain what Bravia did that others couldn't, and brochures were rewritten to explain the brand's benefits in accessible terms.

INVESTMENT

As is apparent, this new approach required a different way of investing. Money formerly spent on massive TV campaigns that reached millions of people who would never buy Bravia was directed into more effective solutions. Money previously spent on inflationary location fees was spent on booth decoration, staff training, and new materials. Funds were diverted from Suning towards Yongle, where returns would be better. Investment decisions that historically had been based on assumptions and received wisdom were now being made based on facts and insight.

The Sony executive team was delighted with the results. Not only did sales return to strong growth, but they were able to redeploy hundreds of thousands of dollars in marketing money to activities with proven returns— and they could save money on costly locations in-store to boot!

THE POWER OF THE FIVE-STEP PROCESS IN DAY-TO-DAY LIFE

Our experience with Sony shows the power of the Total Marketing process to drive commercial strategy. By applying the process in developing annual plans and even in addressing short-term operational issues, managers all over the world have gained massive value.

For instance, we work with one of the world's largest processors of dairy foods. Managers across the Asia Pacific region have been using the process to develop focused activity plans, and they apply it daily. In the Philippines, this business was seeking relatively short-term gains in a tough trading period. The commercial team collaborated on a brand initiative to rapidly increase penetration. The marketing team contributed key consumer data showing relatively low comparative household penetration on a specialized premium milk product. The trade marketing team was able to find data showing that milk was a highly planned purchase and that key shoppers shopped weekly in hypermarkets in urban centers. Together with the sales team, they determined that relocating their premium brand next to the largest generic milk product would increase traffic flow past the brand. The sales team was able to identify one key retailer who had the ability to implement the concept quickly and demonstrated the value of getting current non-buyers to buy. The retailer enthusiastically embraced the proposition. And the best bit? Sales grew by 27 percent—adding a full

5 percent to the company's sales at no cost! That's right, the retail proposition was so strong that no additional investment was needed.

Part of the accessibility of the process is that it enables managers to effectively collaborate and drive growth every day. When it's broken down into five simple questions, every manager can apply it. Our friends in the Philippines were asking these questions:

1. Which consumer opportunity should we focus on?
2. Which shoppers should we target?
3. Which retail outlets can be used to influence our target shoppers?
4. What activity is most likely to deliver the results we want?
5. How should we invest across consumers, shoppers, and retailers to deliver profitable growth?

We work with managers who find that these simple questions help them make smarter calls on their brands. Recently we chatted with one of the sales directors we coach. He's observed the process and its impact close up, and he said, "You know it's amazing—I never thought we could persuade Carrefour to give us more support for less money, but we've applied the process and it works. We can show their senior team why our colleagues in marketing are focusing on a specific opportunity; we can explain what it means for people shopping in Carrefour. We've found they are really interested when we show why their hypermarkets are so important, and when they learn what they stand to gain, they've fully supported our in-store marketing proposals."

THE IMPLICATIONS OF THE FIVE-STEP PROCESS

It's been six years since we first introduced our thoughts to a few long-standing clients, and we are hugely grateful for their commitment to try our ideas and track their progress. Having applied the process across a wide variety of markets and businesses, we now know the impact it can have for consumer goods companies globally. We see five major implications: alignment, better investment decisions, competitive advantage, great execution, and better sales and better profits.

1. **Alignment.** For years, senior managers have lamented the development of silos within the companies they run. Carlsberg's Hans Hallan describes the situation and the need for change perfectly: "We need to tear down the walls. There's a lot of silo thinking. Sales sells and marketing markets, not realizing that everything you do markets and sells your product."[51] We find that with the implementation of Total Marketing, goals and objectives become clearer. It becomes obvious to marketers that consumer objectives are delivered by shoppers in retail environments; it becomes clear to trade marketers and sales teams that without driving consumption, their sales efforts are unsustainable. The process promotes alignment within the organization and enables clear decision-making paths through the organization.

2. **Better investment decisions.** In the world of traditional consumer goods marketing, budgets are often split based on organization structure. Marketing owns the "above-the-line" budget, trade marketing owns the "below-the-line" budget and sales own "trade terms." Each function has to fight the other for budget, and all behave in a way that suggests a key part of their role is to protect their own budgets. Adopting an integrated approach to changing the behavior of consumers, shoppers, and retailers enables the entire commercial team to see where value lies. As result, decisions about where to invest and what to invest in become clearer, and investments are focused on delivering returns.

3. **Competitive advantage.** In the war for the store, the smartest guys in the room win. The five-step process is driven on insight and prioritization. Competitive players who are armed with a clear understanding of their target consumers, their target shoppers, and their priority retailers are able to lead the strategic debate. Mark Horstman, cofounder and manager of Manager Tools LLC, said, "Great strategy is also about deciding what not to do."[52] We've found the companies who are able to focus their time, effort, and resources on the biggest bets invariably grow faster than their competitors, and the retailers they work with know this. Leading shopper marketers get great results because they get great support from the retailers they prioritize, and that's a major competitive advantage.

---

51 Hallan, discussion.
52 Horstman, discussion, March 2013.

4. **Great execution.** Great support from retailers means that execution in the retail environment becomes so much easier. It's easier to get buy-in on proposals, easier to negotiate the deals, and easier make change happen in the store. The five-step process supports this, but it also ensures that the organization is lined up to get the job done well. With clear goals and directions, all available resources can be deployed to get the job done rather than wasting time effort and money on distractions.

5. **Better sales and better profits.** Shoppers react to what they see. When shoppers see an incoherent offer, poor communication, or gaps in product availability, they respond erratically. But when faced with smooth, consistent propositions that resonate with what they believe, their behaviors change. The five-step process promotes consistency in all elements of the marketing mix, and it enables profound behavioral change. As Tia Newcomer says, "When we focus on the most valuable shopper, we get higher loyalty."[53] As new shoppers come to the brand or existing shoppers buy more often, the business grows. With the support of appropriate, targeted investment, stronger profits follow.

MAKING TOTAL MARKETING A REALITY

The five-step process really is for everyone. It drives growth in developed and developing markets alike. It works across a spectrum of consumer products—from shampoo to tablets—and it helps managers get better results at all levels of the organization. We have seen Total Marketing's potential to revolutionize the world of consumer goods, and our mission in writing this book is to make this new approach accessible to all. But it requires some significant changes, and it requires commercial teams to think and act differently. The rest of this book is designed to guide you through the key changes and processes needed to make this revolution a reality in your organization.

In the four chapters of part II, we'll delve into four concepts we have touched on that warrant a closer look:

---

53 Newcomer, discussion.

1. The consumer and the shopper are not the same.
2. The shopper's path to purchase is a sequence of subtle decisions that start long before a trip to the store and end with a purchase.
3. A shopper's behavior can be influenced throughout the path to purchase using effective communication, availability, and offer strategies.
4. Brands need to work for consumers, shoppers, and retail customers alike for them to grow in the long term.

With these concepts in hand, the last section of the book—part III—is a field guide that explains how to work through each step of the five-step process, how to organize your teams, and what the future might hold.

PART II

THE MANIFESTO

. . . .

CHAPTER 4

CATS DON'T BUY LITTER, BUT MEN BUY PERFUME

. . . .

As we've seen, the consumer and the shopper are two distinct entities. And shopper marketing isn't just about shoppers; it's also about consumers. However, many esteemed authorities appear to endorse a view that the shopper and the consumer are the same person, and most consumer goods companies and marketing agencies use the words *consumer* and *shopper* interchangeably. With so many people aligned with this view, surely the consumer and the shopper are the same—correct?

No. The assertion doesn't stand up to much scrutiny. Look back at some of the examples we mentioned in Chapter 2: cats don't buy cat food, and kids don't buy diapers. Men might buy perfume, but it will be for their wife or girlfriend, and many men don't buy their own shampoo, conditioner, shaving foam, or soap. In Malaysia, women buy almost half of all male grooming products purchased in supermarkets (and only a fraction of these were for their own use). And who buys most products for kids? Parents.

Tia Newcomer, vice president of worldwide marketing for Hewlett-Packard, knows that summer netbooks are used by teens heading back to school—but the shopper? Mom. Likewise, Hans Hallan, sales development director for the Asia and Africa region at Carlsberg, knows that while up to 90 percent of beer bought in supermarkets is consumed by men, up to 95 percent of that beer is actually purchased by wives and maids in some countries. Both of these experts are aware, therefore, that to create a purchase in a store, the marketer needs to do more than leverage the brand equity with the consumer—because that particular consumer isn't present at the moment of truth, when the purchase is made. These companies know they need to understand the *shopper*—what drives his behavior and what they can do to enable the purchase.

To be sure, in many categories, the consumer often buys for his own consumption. In some categories, that scenario applies to nearly all purchases. But in every category we've studied, it's not always the case. Even sanitary napkins are sometimes bought by men or by moms. Yet many marketers settle for "most"—one of the most dangerous words in the marketing lexicon (up there with "assume"). In a recent study in China, a client told us that most of the consumers were indeed the shoppers so we could assume they were the same. When we checked the data, "most" was measured as 78 percent, meaning that 22 percent of shoppers were not consumers. For that 22 percent of purchases, the assumptions made about the shopper were wrong. At best, 22 percent of the money spent on influencing the consumer wasn't used optimally—the consumer wasn't in the store making the purchase.

A TEEN EXAMPLE

Imagine you're launching a new strawberry scented hair mousse aimed at a consumer group of teenage girls, and the primary goal is to steal market share from a competitor's hair care product. Consumer research has demonstrated that this product has massive appeal among teenage girls, and the consumer marketing team has worked hard on a campaign that is going to whip these girls into a frenzy. The goal is to make your strawberry mousse *the* next thing that every girl between the ages of 12 and 15 must have. You even recruited the latest stars for the commercial. Everyone is confident that these teens will love it and want it.

With all this work done to appeal to the target consumer, is your job over? Maybe—or maybe not. In this case, the job wasn't done because the marketers didn't understand who would actually be buying the mousse.

The answer, most of the time, is Mom. But Mom will never put strawberry mousse on her scalp (unless there is a major hair emergency). Granted, some teen girls will whine, complain, and cajole their mothers into buying the product, but it is imperative for the marketer to acknowledge that the consumer and shopper in this case are two distinctly different people, with two distinctly different mindsets and motivations. Further, the marketer must acknowledge that unless we have considered Mom in our marketing mix—weighing her needs, motivations, and behaviors—then it is highly unlikely that the launch will be as successful as possible or that the big budget spent on the product will deliver the highest possible return.

Mom, you see, isn't impressed by pink labels or moved by giddy girls pleading for some chemical-laden mousse. But, if the product is readily available—meaning she doesn't have to hunt for it—reasonably priced, and not a threat to her daughter's head and hair, Mom will probably relent and make the purchase. So, while the consumer marketer's job is to excite the screaming hordes of fickle teen girls, the shopper marketer must focus on influencing the shopper to buy the mousse for her daughter. And if the shopper marketers in question know nothing about moms and their shopping behavior because the entire marketing effort has focused on the daughter, what are the chances of their efforts paying off?

One company that understands the difference between consumers and shoppers is Procter & Gamble. Its launch of Sunny Delight was a brilliant example.

Sunny Delight was a simple brand—a juice drink for kids. P&G knew that moms didn't like giving carbonated beverages to their kids because they perceived the drinks as unhealthy. But those kids loved Coke and 7-Up, so Mom reluctantly relented when she had to. Moms would rather the kids drank juice, but real juice was pricey and was rejected by their children—it was far too virtuous and not at all fun. Despite this truth, P&G launched Sunny Delight with massive TV spend and a media buy targeted at kids. The ads were fun, energetic, and trendy.

But P&G didn't assume that the brand would thrive on pester power alone. The marketers took time out to understand the shopper, Mom, and determined that she looked in the chiller—not on the ambient shelf—for healthy product. So what did P&G do? It paid the bill and put the product in the cooler, next to 100 percent juice. Sunny Delight contained around 5 percent juice and didn't need to be refrigerated, but if it was going to appeal to moms, this placement was critical.

The result? Within three months of launch, Sunny D was the best-selling grocery product in the UK, topping everything, including Coke. Sadly, the Sunny D story didn't end well—the brand got some negative PR for supposedly turning kids' skin orange—but it stands as an example of understanding the distinction between consumer and shopper.

Of course, many times the consumer *is* the shopper. But, even then, we must question whether, from a marketing perspective, we can treat a person in shopper mode the same as we do when she's in consumer mode. As Chris Hoyt puts it, "The mindset changes . . . Once they get into the car [on the way to a store, the shopper mindset] . . . overrides the mindset that was created by advertising."[54] In these two modes, people are in different states of mind. They behave differently as a result, and they desire different outcomes. If marketers want shoppers to make certain decisions, they need to consider them as different from the consumer, even if they are, corporeally, the same person.

As a consumer, I have different objectives than a shopper, and I rarely, if ever, consume in same environment where I shop. When I get into shopping mode, I'm in the store environment. My stimuli change, and my goals do, too. My needs and desires as a consumer are blended with, and often overpowered by, my needs as a shopper. I know which coffee I want as a consumer, but as a shopper, I know I need to buy many other items, and I've only got an hour, and I don't have the car, and I need to pick up the kids soon, and we're a bit tight on cash this month . . . As you can see, the consumer's image of a perfect cup of coffee can get easily lost in the flood of the shopper's needs. The brand's pull may be strong enough to survive all that, but time and time again, consumer needs and desires are compromised by shopper needs.

So, given that the consumer and the shopper clearly aren't the same—even when they are the same person—why is the conflation of the two so pervasive? Well, for the last 60 years, consumer marketing teams have led the strategic development of the business; in their minds, it was all about the consumer. These marketers recognized that if they wanted to overcome their competitors and achieve the Holy Grail—brand loyalty—they needed to get inside the heads of consumers and build strong emotional bonds with them. They developed strategies based on a belief that if enough of a bond were created with the consumer, the rest would fall into place.

Thus brand managers fixated on the consumer—and quite rightly so! Over the years, most brand teams have developed a healthy focus on consumers; without truly understanding the behaviors and attitudes of these people, their brands would simply die. Yet as an unfortunate and unintended consequence of this consumer focus, they often ignore of the importance of understanding shoppers. Marketers focused on consumers and, it appears,

---

54 Hoyt, discussion.

decided that shoppers were "a sales thing." In client meetings, in research presentations, and in many of the interviews we conducted during the writing of this book, experts often talked about "the consumer in the store"—and we have to say, we get confused. Apart from restaurants, we don't see too much consumption in a store. What we see is shopping.

The consumer-focused approach harks back to a time when the consumer and the shopper could easily be visualized as the same thing. Consumer goods were more often than not bought by housewives in their local store. Marketers knew that all they had to do to hook the housewife was put their products—the ones they'd been advertising on the only three TV channels available at the time—in front of the housewife-shopper in the store. But if you wind the clock forward to 2011, you'll find a very different situation. For one thing, according to data from Mariana Sanchez, chief strategy officer at Saatchi & Saatchi, up to 35 percent of grocery and mass-merchandise shoppers in the United States are now men.[55]

If marketers create and market brands to entice and delight the consumer but then overlook how their products land in the hands of these users, they will encounter problems. At best, the effectiveness of their efforts will be reduced. At worst, well, it isn't possible to consume a brand that hasn't been bought! The gap between the emotional power of a brand and the returns that power brings the brand owners is nicely summed up by Darren Marshall, vice president of Venturing & Emerging Brands at Coca-Cola: "We are passionate about understanding how much the consumer loves us, but not so good at understanding why our market shares don't match our heartshares."[56]

We've been involved in shopper work for over a decade, but we certainly weren't the first. The concept of a shopper in this industry is hardly new. Yet it appears that for most organizations, shoppers are seen as something that should be left to salespeople and retailers. Salespeople are great at being, well, salespeople, but they are not are trained marketers. Little research has been done on understanding shoppers, and the small amount of data we have was often analyzed by trade marketers who lacked sufficient insight development skills or by research agencies that struggled to understand that shoppers and shopping are fundamentally different concepts from

---

55 Store Brands Decisions, "Advertising Could Shift More Towards Men," January 18, 2011, http://www.storebrandsdecisions.com/news/2011/01/18/advertising-could-shift-more-towards-men.

56 Marshall, discussion.

consumers and consumption. In the consumer goods world, the consumer is still king.

But what is the goal of consumer marketing? Clearly, it's not to drive purchase. Consumer marketers attempt to understand and anticipate consumers' needs and then work to develop a marketing mix that changes their attitudes and behavior toward a brand or a category. A coffee marketer may identify a need for a smooth blend of relaxing coffee to be consumed just before bedtime. The consumer marketer helps create the product, communicates to consumers that this product is simply perfect for them, and then attempts to influence their behavior so they actually drink that cup of coffee. But while a consumer marketer can happily create an image and an attitude, she won't be able to create behavioral change with this focus alone. For a change in consumption to take place (e.g., an extra cup of coffee a day), the shopper has to shop differently. Therefore, our shopper marketer needs to create a behavioral change in the shopper. That behavioral change enables the change in consumption, which is the goal of the consumer marketer. As you can see, shopper marketing is different from consumer marketing. Each has distinctly different goals.

As you might guess, the marketing tools available to shopper marketers are different from those used by consumer marketers. As a consumer marketer, I may use a wild blend of different types of media and messaging to get across to the consumer. As a shopper marketer, I may use some or all of those same tools to communicate to the shopper outside of the store, but the tools available to me inside the store are often more limited.

Shopper marketing, in comparison to consumer marketing, has a different target, different objectives, and different tools. It's an entirely different kind of marketing.

THE CONSUMER STILL COMES FIRST

Shopper marketing is one arm of the marketing mix, not a sole provider of your marketing needs—just as consumer marketing should be one component of the brand plan. Shopper marketing is about being able to connect two pieces: (1) what your consumer marketers are doing to entice consumers, and (2) what the retailer is implementing to influence the behaviors of shoppers. As we've seen, the target of those two efforts, the shopper and the consumer, are separate entities.

If the consumer and shopper are so different, then it may stand to reason that there is a need for shopper marketing to sit alongside consumer marketing. However, this doesn't explain why a Total Marketing approach is required—why these need to be integrated. Shopping only occurs to meet some future perceived consumption need. To understand shopping, we must first understand the "consumption behind the shop." Let's take a closer look at why consumption is still vital to our understanding of shoppers.

To target shoppers, we need to recognize that they are a heterogeneous group that we must divide into segments. Through segmentation, marketers build the foundation of their efforts—they recognize shoppers aren't all the same, so they need to treat some groups differently than others. Without segmentation, there is no targeting.

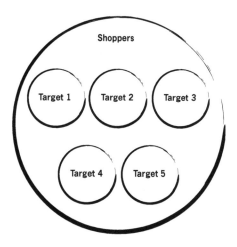

So which shoppers are the most valuable? Remember, an early premise of this book was that the growth of consumer goods companies comes from driving additional consumption. If that's true, then surely the most valuable shoppers to a consumer goods organization are those who are gatekeepers to the largest future potential consumption. To capitalize on this, we need to first identify the consumers who represent the biggest opportunity for potential future consumption. From there, an understanding of who does— or could—shop for that consumption opportunity helps guide the marketer to the shoppers who are most important to the brand.

Imagine two consumers, both men. One drinks two cups of coffee a day of Brand X and the other drinks one a day of Brand Y. Both their wives buy the coffee in a supermarket. Their wives are the same age, and their other demographic characteristics are similar. Which wife would you want to target? The one who buys for the two-cups-a-day guy, right? But as shoppers, these two wives appear to be the same. Suddenly, when the marketer understands the consumer behind the shopper, a small amount of consumption data helps create a brand new way of looking at shopping.

As you see, it is impossible to truly understand shoppers without first understanding consumers. A shopper's "journey" begins with his interpretation of what the consumer wants or needs. That interpretation may be very specific or quite loose—"six chilled twelve-ounce bottles of Heineken" or just "beer."

When the shopper *is* the consumer, he has a much clearer interpretation of his own needs. The influence of his consumer side is there at the point of purchase, interacting with his shopper side. Of course, it's impossible to separate the two entities completely. There is no magic point beyond which the consumer becomes a shopper or vice versa. As mentioned in an earlier chapter, Herb Sorensen takes a hard line on this and argues that "no one is a shopper if they're not inside the four walls of a store." On his blog at www.retailwire.com, he recognizes that this is not always strictly true, but he believes that any other model is too complicated.

However, as marketers, we would argue that the blurring of lines exists and needs to be recognized. Today, people shop from home—a lot. As Tia Newcomer states, "96 percent of consumer electronics shoppers go online before 79 percent go in-store to buy. In consumer electronics, the first moment of truth is nearly always online."[57] Shopping happens, and elements of the path to purchase happen, before the person pulls open the door of a store. One of the biggest shopping decisions—which store the shopper will go to—clearly happens outside the store. And when a person is thinking about where to go shopping, he is thinking like a shopper, not a consumer.

As a shopper, when I enter the store, I bring with me all of the accumulated messages and concepts I have already gathered about brands. When we ask shoppers in surveys why they don't buy a certain brand in-store, often their response is related to taste or performance—consumption characteristics, not shopping ones. You can't take the consumer out of the store any more than you can keep the shopper in there. And as mobile technology advances, the physical walls of the store are broken down such that the retailer no longer controls and limits the environment (see Chapter 10, "From Bricks

---

57 Newcomer, discussion.

to Clicks"). A shopper can stand in a store and visit your corporate website, check forums, ask their friends, and watch your commercial. In reality, it is impossible to separate the worlds of shopping and consumption completely, so they *must* work together.

THE CONSUMER OPPORTUNITY

The consumer goods industry has been fumbling around with shoppers and consumers for a long time. Marketers in this field can articulate who is going to use the product, how much they will pay, and where they will buy. They cultivate complex decision trees, attempting to map how the consumer or shopper will subconsciously decide which product she will ultimately buy. They create detailed paths-to-purchase maps. Many models study awareness, consideration, purchase, usage, and so on. These are long-standing brand-marketing actions. Yet, these marketers recently realized that the consumer may not be the person buying the products, which forces them to broaden their marketing perspective to address the needs of two customers: the consumer and the shopper. And with that knowledge, we have a greater opportunity to influence shoppers to buy more.

To create maximum value, the shopper marketing story must begin with understanding the consumer: the person who uses your product or service. How many times are items bought with no idea at all about who will use them or when? Without an individual desiring your brand, there is no spark to the purchasing engine—no one to influence the purchaser. Even an impulse purchase, sparked by a shopper in the store, is connected to a consumption occasion before the final purchase decision is made. ("That looks good; we could have that after dinner tonight," or "I'm sure Johnny would love that in his packed lunch.") And, of course, if a shopper buys a product that is not consumed (or does not delight the consumer), it is unlikely she will buy it again. In the latter scenario, there may even be significant detriment to the brand image.

Understanding the consumer gives us the biggest opportunity to identify which shoppers are most important to us. Consider three consumers:

- Consumer 1 uses your brand all the time, and there is no opportunity to increase her usage.

- Consumer 2 uses your brand once a week but needs to use it more frequently.
- Consumer 3 doesn't use your brand despite knowing that your brand performs better.

Now let's consider the three shoppers, one for each of these consumers (whether the same person or someone else). What shopping behavior do we desire in each? Do we want to change shopping behavior in the same way in each case? Of course not! The first one you *don't* want to change. As a manufacturer, we plainly want this shopper to keep right on buying, paying full price for a brand in which the consumer is clearly delighted. In the second case, perhaps we'd like the shopper to buy more (but only if we are simultaneously persuading the consumer to use more). In the third case, perhaps our goal is merely to get the shopper to take home a new brand for the consumer to try.

So far, so good. These shoppers are each different and potentially require different types of marketing. But how do we prioritize them? The answer to that question lies in understanding how valuable that behavioral change might be. And the answer to that lies in understanding which one unlocks the biggest future consumption opportunity.

If we are to increase sales and profitability, we need to drive incremental consumption of our brand and increase purchase. You can stimulate consumption through consumer marketing, but if you don't simultaneously change shoppers' buying behaviors to fuel that extra consumption, the returns from that investment will fall far short of their potential. In the same way, when you try to drive extra purchase but don't change consumption, you're increasing your promotional costs in return for, at best, short-term growth.

Is a price reduction or a buy-get promotion an effective way to boost consumption? It depends on the category. In categories where consumption is highly elastic (confectionery is a good example), then more buying often leads to more consumption. But a promotion that gets me to buy more soap, for example, is unlikely to persuade me to wash more. As you can see, it is imperative to understand the impact that shopper marketing activities have on consumption. Without that understanding, your assessment of the activity is limited to an understanding of short-term sales, which are, unfortunately, a poor lens through which to view longer-term brand health.

ONE PRICE FITS ALL

So without an understanding of the consumer, it's almost impossible to understand the true value of the shopping behavior you want to create. Depending on the impact your in-store marketing activities have on future consumption, they might be a raging success or an abject failure. That's a pretty dangerous gamble in a consumer goods industry that is spending around $280 billion a year on this stuff.

But it gets worse. A particular quirk of in-store activity magnifies the danger of loss: everyone gets the same offer. The sampling, the discount, and the buy-two-get-one deal are all made available to everyone.

Consider the example of three shoppers with three different consumers: the loyalist, the infrequent user, and the competitor's consumer. If I conduct a trial program indiscriminately, two-thirds of my promotional spend—the portion attributed to the infrequent user and the competitor's consumer—is likely to be wasted. Worse, my loyal and infrequent user may be using the trial pack in place of his usual product. That equals lost sales. If I use a buy-two-get-one promotion to load up my infrequent user, then my loyalist just gets lots of product at a lower price. Again, lost sales. And they're lost sales that a quick glance at my off-take would not reveal. An analysis based on off-take alone may show the promotion as a raging success, with a huge uplift. But the long-term value of my brand may have diminished. (For more on this see Chapter 6, "The True Cost of Discounting.")

And it gets even worse.

In most categories, there are what we call "deal shoppers." These shoppers are not loyal to a brand and will just buy the cheapest from a portfolio. Deal shoppers are tricky to pin down. They may be a deal shopper in one category and highly brand loyal in another. But collectively, they cost the industry billions. Anyone who has watched *Extreme Couponing* knows what we mean! In some categories, deal shoppers—who will never be loyal, buying your brand this week and another one the next—soak up over 80 percent of a promotion budget. Much of the remaining 20 percent goes to people who would have bought the brand anyway, discount or no discount.

Now, we're not saying that price shoppers aren't worth your marketing efforts, but an understanding of who buys your product and the impact those sales will have on consumption is extremely valuable. Even when you win a new customer, you might sell more product initially; but if the consumer doesn't love the brand and keep buying long term, the return on investment from the in-store campaign is negligible. It's impossible to properly evaluate an activity without knowing both your target consumer and shopper.

THE DRIVERS OF CONSUMPTION

For shopper marketing to be effective, it must be aligned with and support the efforts of the consumer marketing team. This requires a certain level of understanding of the consumer and the consumption opportunities. So let's take a simplified look at the four key elements that describe a consumption opportunity:

1. The needs and desires of the consumer
2. The occasions upon which those needs and desires occur
3. The consumer's experience with the brand
4. The availability to consume

Let's start with the *needs and desires of the consumer*. If a brand were attempting to grow its consumption, the marketing team would target a consumer need or want that was not being met. When coupled with the *occasions* upon which those needs and desires occur, it is possible to calculate the opportunity for a brand or category. Simply put, if a brand meets a certain need, and that need occurs every day among the target segment, then it's simple to derive the total possible number of consumption occasions. Expanding brand consumption requires persuading a consumer to use the brand to meet a different need or persuading them to use the brand on a different occasion (or both). Many brands have done this successfully—for example, Arm & Hammer found new ways to use baking soda (refresh your drain, contain odors in the fridge), and beer manufacturers in the UK have often heavily advertised in-home consumption to persuade consumers to drink at home as well as out of the home.

These first two consumption drivers—the consumer's needs and desires, and the occasions on which they occur—describe the large-scale opportunity to drive consumption among a consumer segment. Meanwhile, the other two—*the consumer's experience* with the brand, and the *brand's availability*—describe the enablers and barriers to that consumption. In simple terms, if a consumer has a need at a certain occasion but does not use your brand, it typically can be traced back to a poor experience or a lack of availability.

The consumer's experience of your brand is a major contributor (and barrier) to consumption. But that experience isn't always a firsthand encounter with your product ("I tried it and my hair wasn't shiny"). Instead, the consumer's experience is the accumulation of any direct use of your product plus every brand touch point: advertising, word-of-mouth, in-store displays, taste, packaging, etc. If she chooses not to consume your product, all of these things have added up to convince her that this brand is not the best way to meet this particular need on this occasion.

The other enabler or barrier to consumption is availability. If your product isn't there when the consumer needs it, the quality of the consumer's prior experience with the brand becomes irrelevant. If I don't have the particular brand of chips in my cupboard when that's exactly the snack I want, the opportunity to consume has been missed. Maybe I'll go for the pretzels instead and discover a new passion for them.

To drive additional consumption, the marketer must understand what is preventing that consumption from happening. If there is something wrong with the consumer's experience of the brand, that's a barrier the consumer marketing team can address. But if the product isn't available to consume, it's because someone didn't buy it or didn't buy enough. And that's when the shopper marketer jumps in!

Shopper marketers do not need to understand consumers to the same intricate level that we would expect from their consumer marketing colleagues. But they must be able to clearly articulate the opportunities that exist to drive consumption. Shopper marketers need to understand which consumers are being targeted, what changes to their consumption are desired, and how much that change might be worth.

This can be a challenge for some consumer marketing teams, as we found in many projects. If you are a marketing director, use "The Coherent Consumer Marketer Test" presented here to assess your team's clarity of thinking (page 74). It might seem simple, but we are continually amazed (and a little disappointed) to meet marketers whose goals are as broad as "to grow share" or who cannot tell exactly how much a particular growth driver is worth.

Shopper marketers need to know who the target consumer is—beyond the demographics and beyond the broad generic target beloved by brand managers: "We are targeting fun-loving teens who like to hang out with their friends and listen to music." As shopper marketers, we need to understand—like any self-respecting brand manager would—the actual behavior of the people we are targeting. Shopper marketing has behavioral change in its DNA; it thrives on payback. So, a shopper marketer needs to understand the target in terms of its behavior: "We are targeting fun-loving teens, ages 12 to 17, living in major urban areas who currently consume Brand X once a week during the weekend." Further, the shopper marketer needs to understand the *desired* consumer behavior: "Our goal is to persuade these teens to consume twice a week, at home, during the weekend."

Now, with a bit more data, the shopper marketer can begin to assess how much a consumption opportunity might be worth. Population, multiplied by an extra occasion a day, gives us that answer.

CONSUMER MARKETING AND SHOPPER MARKETING PARTNERSHIPS

As veterans of the consumer goods industry, we've seen that there isn't a clear division between consumer marketing activities and shopper marketing activities in the vast majority of companies. This line becomes increasingly blurred when a consumer and shopper are the same person—which is why an integrated marketing mix is the best solution. The consumer marketing team should develop the consumer profiles and use their skills

THE COHERENT CONSUMER MARKETER TEST

Can each member of your marketing team, for each brand they manage, clearly articulate the following?

- What are the key drivers of growth for the brand in the next 12 months?

- Which consumers are being targeted to achieve that growth?

- What is the current behavior of this target consumer group?

- What behavioral change needs to take place to realize that growth?

- How much (in dollars) is that growth worth?

to get the consumer excited about the brand, thereby influencing consumption. The shopper marketer, for his part, must understand the consumer but also profile the shopper—regardless of whether the consumer and shopper are the same person. Then, the shopper marketer takes on the job of creating a mix that will encourage the shopper to meet the consumption needs for the brand.

The consumer marketer, for example, knows that he wants to get a 12-ounce bottle of Heineken into the beer lover's refrigerator. He knows the touch points that will appeal to the consumer. The shopper marketer takes this to the next step: "We want shoppers to buy this beer for these consumers so that they have it in their fridge, ice cold, on the occasion when the consumer wants it." He then jumps in to determine who the shoppers are for the product.

As a shopper marketer, here is your mantra: "Know thy shopper!" You need to know your shopper so well that you can identify the precise stores that he shops in—and the outlets that know how to help you achieve the outcome you want. Having statistics to prove that contention, you can make the right investment in the right customers. (But that, too, is for another chapter: Chapter 8, "Understanding Shoppers.")

When we developed the five-step Total Marketing model, no matter what the scenario—in-store or out-of-store, brand loyalist or newcomer—we always came back to the importance of the consumer and the shopper as the first links in the chain. We realized that shopper marketing could only achieve optimum results if the program was totally integrated with consumer marketing activities. They are separate mindsets—if not separate people—but have equal importance in the path to purchase.

CHAPTER 5

THE PATH TO PURCHASE (OR, DEBUNKING THE BIGGEST SHOPPER MARKETING MYTH)

Marketers have been concerned about purchase for a very long time, but interest in the topic has really heated up over the last few decades. As media fragmented and retailers consolidated, smart marketers looked to the one place left where they knew they could still reach their targets by the million—the stores where they shopped.

Around 2005, Alan Lafley, then president and CEO at P&G, coined the phrase "the first moment of truth," referring to the moment in a store when shoppers decide whether they will buy your brand. (Interestingly, Lafley called them consumers!) While the concept of moments of truth was borrowed from Jan Carlzon of Scandinavian Airlines System, this was new to the consumer goods industry. The notion excited the industry, and marketers were eager to take advantage of the opportunity to reach shoppers at that crucial moment. They realized that if the shopper passed up their brand in the store, there at the shelf, then they'd lost. It didn't matter what had happened before, and it didn't matter how wonderful the consumption experience (the second moment of truth) was. If the brand didn't win with the shopper at the first moment of truth, it was in serious trouble.

Years before, in 1995, POPAI, the global association for marketing at retail, had produced what could be considered the seminal sound bite of twentieth-century consumer goods marketing, and it supported the importance of the Lafley's first moment of truth. According to POPAI, more than 70 percent of purchasing decisions were made at the point of purchase.[58] It was a striking validation—as if any was needed—that pouring money into stores was a good thing. It was justification for the massive increases in trade spend that consumer goods leaders had signed off on for years. Now there was proof: the store was where it all happened.

Since then, many highly credible studies, like those prepared by Deloitte and by Booz & Company, have presented findings that back up the idea that a significant number of purchasing decisions do happen in-store—59 percent, 71 percent, 75 percent, and so on. In 2012, POPAI updated its own number to 76 percent.[59] These numbers all make it clear that the first moment of truth cannot be ignored, but the original POPAI number is the one that resonated, and still resonates, through the industry. Virtually every article on shopper marketing today seems to use it as part of its introduction to the topic, and every shopper marketing—related agency, designer, or provider seems to use it as the opening salvo in their pitch.

But before we jump on the bandwagon, let's hold back for a moment and dissect exactly what this statistic means. We think the reality behind this number is far more complex than most realize.

The first question that springs to mind is basic: What do we mean by a "purchase decision"? Arguably, buying anything at all constitutes a decision to purchase, even if the shopper is merely reaffirming what he decided before entering a store. Following that argument, 100 percent of purchase decisions are made in-store. But we're pretty sure that's not what POPAI meant, so we are left with the conclusion that "purchase decision" means something more than the mere decision to buy.

So, is it possible that 70 percent of all products sold in a store are done so totally on impulse? If that's true, it is a pretty damning indictment of out-of-store marketing. Have all the billions of dollars spent on brand building amounted to a paltry 30 percent of purchases? And if it's true that it takes six to eight impressions for a marketing message to penetrate the mind of the target, how can we honestly say that 70 percent of purchase decisions are made in-store? Many marketers share our skepticism—Rodger DiPasca

58 Cathy Bond, "Point of Purchase: POP Goes the Retailer," May 2, 1996, http://www.marketing magazine.co.uk/news/51531/.

59 POPAI, *2012 Shopper Engagement Study*, accessed March 7, 2013, http://www.popai.com/engage/docs/Media-Topline-Final.pdf.

from Young & Rubicam says it is "poppycock."[60] Unfortunately, POPAI is not completely forthcoming as to what the statistic actually means. Helpfully, Jeff Froud, former head of Shopper and Retail Strategy Planning at OgilvyAction, has tried to break it down and make sense of it. Jeff cited recently that 72 percent of shoppers *made at least one decision* in a store; his data was based on the following:

1. Decided how much to buy in the store: 52 percent
2. Chose a brand in the store: 39 percent
3. Bought a category they did not plan to buy: 29 percent
4. Walked away without buying: 13 percent

But, critically, this data is quoted based on *all* the purchases they made that day. A shopper may be buying several products but may have made a brand decision on only one of these products. Picture your typical grocery shop. Jeff's take on the POPAI statistic is thus: in the process of buying the entire shop (let's say thirty products), 72 percent of shoppers decided something in-store. What this statistic says is that 72 percent of shoppers decided *something* in-store. This would only tally with the POPAI statistic if all of these shoppers only bought one product and only made one decision relating to that product. Jeff's work already identifies four potential decisions. It is clear from this data that the actual number of decisions for one specific category is, therefore, significantly lower. There is a very significant difference between 72 percent of shoppers deciding something in-store and 72 percent of purchase decisions being made in-store. On this basis, the percentage of total decisions made in a store could be significantly less.

Whether or not the POPAI statistic is true—and there are plenty who would dispute it, including Dr. Neale Martin, who argues in his marketing book *Habit* that 95 percent of shopping behavior is based on habit—it seems clear that the 70 percent figure can be easily misconstrued, leading to dangerous marketing decisions and expensive mistakes. Studies suggest that 10 years ago trade spend accounted for around a third of total marketing spend, but that number is now closer to two-thirds. If it's true that about 70 percent of decisions are made in-store, then trade spend is about where it should be. But if the POPAI numbers miss the mark, the industry

---

60 Bizcommunity.com, "9 Tips for Better Shopper Marketing," November 10, 2011, http://www.bizcommunity.com/Article/196/12/66984.html.

could be wildly overspending on its efforts to influence behavior at the point of purchase.

We find that the statistic has two key dangers. First, it is sometimes treated as a universal truth rather than as a rather catchy statistic; second, it oversimplifies the concept of a purchase decision. In our opinion, both of these dangers have encouraged consumer goods companies to make poor decisions about how they allocate marketing dollars, which has thus contributed to the industry's poor performance discussed in Chapter 1. Let's take a closer look at these two problems with POPAI's simplified assessment of in-store behavior.

PROBLEM #1: THE 70 PERCENT STATISTIC IS NOT A UNIVERSAL TRUTH

If it's true that over 70 percent of purchase decisions are made in-store, we have to ask several questions: Is that the same for every shopper? Every store? Every category? When you think about, it certainly doesn't seem likely that number could be true in all cases.

Of course, the nature of shopper decisions varies greatly based on the category. For impulse categories like snacks, shoppers typically make a large percentage of decisions in-store. A shopper may have decided to buy a snack but walk into the store still considering whether to go for candy, chips, a sandwich, chocolate, or something else. Other categories, like baby milk, are very different—in many markets, less than five percent of purchasing decisions about baby milk occur inside the store. These shoppers are far more brand loyal than the snack shopper and have made their choice long before they start browsing the aisles. In this scenario, Danone's Baby Nutrition division, which produces powdered milk formulated for children from newborns to six-year-olds, arguably need not worry much about the in-store environment; all it has to do is make its products continually available. Money spent on anything other than basic availability is likely wasted.

Mark Weir, Director of Customer Insights and Revenue Management at PepsiCo, has firsthand data on how broadly purchasing behavior varies from category to category. Quaker Oats, for example, demonstrates planned buying behavior at the beginning of the winter season but becomes more and more impulsive in nature as the season progresses. Brand loyalty influences shoppers' decisions before the in-store experience. At the same time, the Pepsi brand is open to more in-store influence, with the major shopper decision being package size. The company's Frito-Lay products reflect an even greater degree of impulse purchase.

Let's consider another case: buying a TV set. Based on the research we conducted with Sony in China, it was clear that on the day a shopper finally bought, she had typically decided exactly which brand and model she wanted before entering the store. Virtually no purchase decisions were made in-store—certainly nowhere near 70 percent. It was also clear that most shoppers visited stores many times prior to this with no intention to purchase; they just wanted to gather information on the variety of products available.

It would be wonderful if every purchase in every category were based on the same set of decision points, if nearly three-fourths of shopper decisions could be influenced within the four walls of a store. If shoppers chose televisions with the same ease as a box of cereal, life would be much easier for the marketer. But they don't, and it isn't.

Sadly (for the marketer), a shopper's behavior can change from aisle to aisle. In one category, she may have no idea what brand to buy. In other categories, she may choose between two or three brands. In still other categories, she may know precisely what she wants. Her shopping list might say "vanilla ice cream," but she knows her family will revolt if she buys the store brand instead of the premium ice cream; in that case, her decision was made long before she walked down the freezer aisle. As she moves to the cleaning products, however, she might spend a few moments comparing pricing and features of dish soaps. She may have already determined that she wanted liquid, not powder, but then she notices the all-in-one tablets her friend has been raving about. Same shopper but very different behaviors across categories. How is the 70 percent number reflected in this shopper?

Every study we do reveals massive variations in how shoppers shop—within categories, across categories, from store to store, and from first purchase to second purchase. And our data shows very few categories where the number of shoppers who have yet to make a decision before entering a store is as high as 70 percent. Even though we're arguing that the POPAI number is overstated, the statistic's overall accuracy doesn't really matter: what's important is that it is probably not true for all of your shoppers, all of the time, in all stores. And if that's true, the number is virtually meaningless and certainly valueless.

You may be surprised that we're spending so much time minimizing the importance of what happens in-store in a book that describes shopper marketing as a revolution. We believe in-store behavior is extremely important, but we feel generalizations give shopper marketing a bad name. Consumer marketers would (we hope!) not build their media plans based on the fact that "94 percent of people watch TV," nor would they launch a chocolate variant because "everyone likes chocolate."

The shattering of this 70 percent paradigm is essential if we are to lift shopper marketing beyond a set of activities done in stores and show it for the genuine marketing discipline that it is. The Chartered Institute of Marketing defines marketing as "the management process responsible for identifying, anticipating, and satisfying customer requirements profitably." In the same way, shopper marketing is about identifying, anticipating, and satisfying *shopper* requirements profitably. If we make gross assumptions on how shoppers behave, then it is unlikely we will satisfy those requirements, and profitability will remain a pipe dream.

Lest our message be misunderstood, however, let us be clear: the in-store environment does have a lot of influence on purchasing behavior. We just believe the allocation of abundant resources to in-store efforts without a clear understanding of the target market and its behavior has resulted in waste. Because brand owners do not often possess insight on more effective activities, much of the money is spent on generic activities—mainly promotions and deals—that fit the retailers' agenda instead of the manufacturer's. The intensity of deals has risen to such an extent that the importance of the point of purchase may have become a self-fulfilling prophecy. With so many glittering deals available, why should a shopper make up his mind before hitting the store?

PROBLEM #2: THE 70 PERCENT STATISTIC OVERSIMPLIFIES PURCHASE DECISIONS

Hopefully, we've dispelled the idea that the 70 percent statistic is a mythical, universal constant that applies to every situation. Let us now address the second problem with overreliance on that number: it oversimplifies the concept of a purchase decision.

As we discussed in the previous chapter, consumers and shoppers are different, and we've already argued that, as such, it is important to draw a line between influencing consumption and influencing shopping, regardless of whether the consumer and the shopper are the same person. In turn, we must also distinguish between consumption decisions and shopping decisions—we can't just lump them all into the same category.

The decision to take a carton of juice out of the fridge, pour a glass, and then drink it is clearly a consumption decision. Likewise, deciding to pick a carton of juice off the shelf is clearly a purchase decision. But are all decisions so clear cut?

If a shopper browses the Internet for information about the products he wants, the price he should expect to pay, the item's availability, etc., surely these are purchase decisions—but they are happening outside the store. The rise of the Internet clearly demonstrates that more and more of the purchasing process takes place outside a store and that more purchase decisions take place there. More important, one of the most significant decisions a shopper makes is where to shop, in addition to when to shop, or whether to shop at all—decisions that most definitely take place outside of the store!

It's clear that there are a set of decisions that connect the spark of need or desire in the consumer's mind to a final act sometime later when a shopper hands over money for a product to meet that need. This is what we call the path to purchase. Consumption—the second moment of truth—only takes place if that cycle is complete, and your brand is available to consume. As a marketer, understanding this path, how it works, and how your brand performs along it are critical to making the journey toward being a genuine shopper marketer. But all this requires digging deeper into the many types of purchase decisions.

A BRIEF HISTORY OF PATH-TO-PURCHASE MODELS

In the field of marketing, a lot is written and said about the path to purchase. Every self-respecting shopper marketing company, marketing department, or advertising agency has a path-to-purchase model, and many models are quite similar. Many of them are also quite useless.

Good marketers have long been aware that their job isn't done until someone buys the brand. Therefore, they knew they had to understand the "journey" a person took from consumer (note it was a "consumer"—no talk about shoppers in those dark ages!) to buyer. Accordingly, path-to-purchase models, or purchase funnels, have been de rigueur in marketing circles for more than 20 years. Indeed, the idea of such a "path" can be traced back to as early as 1898, to the fabulously named sales and advertising pioneer, Elias St. Elmo Lewis, who created the AIDA (Awareness, Interest, Desire, and Action) model for influencing.

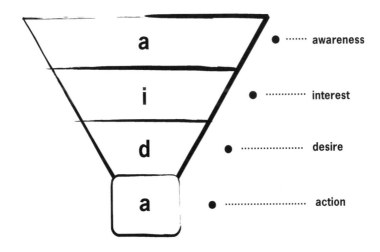

Over 100 years later, most models are extensions of that simple initial model. For example, Marketing Drive—a U.S. promotional and shopper marketing agency—has extended this model into Aware, Attract, Engage, Motivate, Purchase. Here you can see that Lewis's "Action" has been translated into a more specific "Purchase," and the journey to get to that "Action" is now more complicated: from awareness, we now need to attract someone (is this a consumer or a shopper?); engage them; motivate them; and then enable a purchase. Pathtopurchase.com, a usually well-informed blog with lots of input from shopper marketing luminaries, lays out what it calls a "traditional" path-to-purchase model: "Awareness, Engagement, Discovery, Investigation, Selection, Purchase." The model uses different language from the other two and makes the distinction between selection and purchase, which we fully endorse and will discuss further later in this chapter. Pathtopurchase.com then goes on to describe a new "Digital Path to Purchase," in which it separates the process into three broad phases: "pre-shop," which covers awareness and research; "shop," which covers the core purchase decisions; and "post-shop," where people (again, it's unclear whether these people are consumers or shoppers) converse and share their experience. For their part, Ogilvy & Mather talk about a different path: Awareness, Interact, Attract, Interest, Inspire, Engage, Reward, Sell.

There is nothing implicitly wrong with any of these models—they all make sense on their own. And yet, none tells the full story of what actually happens on the path to purchase, nor do any clearly describe what we mean by "path to purchase" and how this differs (if at all) from the entire marketing journey.

The first weakness of these various paths to purchase is that they describe a very generic marketing journey. They assume that whatever the category or brand, the consumer/shopper must go through this same journey, and that can be misleading. How much inspiration or engagement is required for the dullest of commodities or for a brand that a consumer has been buying forever? Although the word *path* conjures up the image of a straight line from Point A to Point B, a person's path to purchase can follow a complicated route that has numerous detours, intersections, and forks in the road.

Their second weakness is that they take little account of an important fact: while the starting point of the entire marketing relationship for a brand may well be need and awareness (i.e., a consumer must have a need or desire and be aware of your brand before the journey starts), this is *not* the starting point for most purchase paths. Tracking back to awareness is hardly practical when a marketer is trying to understand how to change the behavior of a shopper in a supermarket who's buying brands he's known forever.

Third, these path-to-purchase models rarely distinguish between the consumer and the shopper. Although there is clearly a blurring of the roles, it is important that any path-to-purchase model clearly differentiate between the two and focus on the path that a shopper takes in his interaction with the brand or category rather than the steps the consumer takes.

THE LONG AND WINDING ROAD TO PURCHASE

Before we introduce our own path-to-purchase framework, understand that it is simply that: a framework, like the others presented here. We do not suggest that this is a linear journey or that its parts are discrete steps. We recognize that reality is never this simple. But we have used this model across many categories and in many countries, and it stands up to scrutiny. More importantly, it creates a framework that allows marketers to better understand how their shoppers make the decisions they make, and that leads to better marketing and better results for companies.

Our path-to-purchase framework is one that describes shopper behavior, but it begins outside the store, with the consumer. Imagine the path to purchase as a long pipe. Consumer demand pours in at the top, and it should flow through to the bottom, where the perfect products in the right quantities are bought to match exactly the consumer's needs. That is perfection—the shopper marketer's ultimate goal. Unfortunately, this pipe isn't evenly wide in all places. There are "pinchpoints" along the way that restrict the flow, sometimes choking it to a trickle.

The role of consumer marketers is to maximize the flow into the pipe, but the shopper marketer's job is different. She must understand and anticipate the pinchpoints in the pipe and invest wisely in unblocking them to maximize the satisfaction of consumers' demands and keep the flow going to the ultimate destination: the payment transaction, and delivery of the product to the point of consumption. We have identified seven steps along this path, and we'll take a deeper look at each one in the following pages.

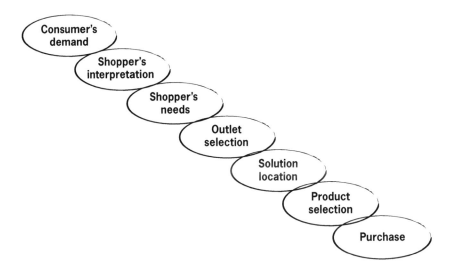

STEP 1: THE CONSUMER'S DEMAND

The journey to purchase kicks off when the consumer sees an ad, listens to recommendations from peers, or wants more of a product he's already tried. It could be highly specific ("I want a slice of pepperoni pizza from Pizzeria Uno"), or it could be vague ("I want a tasty hot snack to eat while I watch the match"). Understanding this starting point is critical to understanding the shopping process that follows.

The specific nature of the consumer's need is of massive relevance to the shopper marketer. Understanding this need helps explain the shopper's mission and gives the shopper marketer the ability to make a brand offer that helps the shopper fulfill that mission. If the consumer isn't sure about what he needs, it may be necessary to clarify it by including some consumer messaging in the shopper's path. For example, Dove soap uses an in-store "skin dryness test" to clarify that a consumer needs not just any soap, but *moisturizing* soap. Had the consumer known that he needed moisturizing soap, this additional communication would have been unnecessary.

STEP 2: THE SHOPPER'S INTERPRETATION

Ultimately, shopping is triggered by the shopper's perception that there is a consumption need to be satisfied. Even in an impulse environment, the first thought is to consumption—"Johnny would love that in his packed lunch," or "That would make Jenny so happy!" The first key question for a shopper marketer relates to this: How effective is the consumer's need translated by the shopper?

Clearly, if the consumer is the shopper, the translation will be very accurate. If the consumer is separate and has a need the shopper isn't aware of, the purchase is unlikely to take place, and a consumption opportunity is lost. No amount of in-store promotion is going to bring that opportunity back.

Poor translations of the consumer's need always lead to problems. If a consumer wants two bottles but the shopper buys only one, consumption could go down. If the consumer wants Budweiser, but the shopper interprets "Budweiser" as "any kind of beer," then the brand choice for that purchase journey is up for grabs. Despite its massive investment in creating consumer demand for the brand, Budweiser is still going to have to scrap it out in the beer aisle with all the other brands. The shopper may very well pick up Coors instead (she's seen her husband drink it, and it's on a promotion). Budweiser may have done a great job of convincing the drinker that Bud was best for him, but there was a break in the path to purchase, between the consumer and the shopper.

And it can happen with everything from beer to Barbie. A seven-year-old girl can clearly articulate exactly which doll she wants (and any parents out there will know what we mean when we say that it's likely to be the expensive one that was just advertised, with all the accessories), but woe betides the parent who just hears "Barbie" and brings home a more basic doll (or worse, a non-Barbie!). The blunder results in unhappy children, anguished parents, and a significant reduction in revenues for Mattel and the toy store. There was a stumble on the path to purchase before Mom even entered the store.

STEP 3: THE SHOPPER'S NEEDS

Regardless of how good the shopper's interpretation of the consumer's needs is, regardless of how specific or vague those needs are, and regardless of whether the consumer and the shopper are the same person, one thing is true: the shopper will consider her own needs before making the purchase. Compared to the complex needs of consumers, shoppers' needs are often far more mundane. How much time does she have? How much money does she have? What else does she need to buy? What mood is she in? What transportation is available? What time of day is it? Is more information required to make the purchase? Who else is with her (kids, friends, colleagues)? The shopper will make trade-offs depending on the weight of her needs and the weight of the perceived needs of the consumer. One of the most important questions a shopper asks when considering these trade-offs is "What else am I looking to buy?" Many consumer goods marketers (and shopper marketers) seem to think of their goods as the sole purpose for a shopping trip, but that's rarely the case. Usually, shoppers must consider many factors—other groceries, other non-grocery items, and other chores—as they plan their shopping trip.

A beautifully created marketing plan and careful investment in the consumer's desire is all wasted if the shopper's desire ultimately comes in first. As Darren Marshall at Coca-Cola said, "There are far more people who love our brand than actually buy our brand."[61] Wouldn't it be a good idea to understand this before we committed the dollars to creating a desire that was never going to be fulfilled?

STEP 4: OUTLET SELECTION

The shopper blends his understanding of the consumer's needs with his own needs as a shopper and makes the first big shopper decision: where to go to make the purchase (yes, this happens outside of the store!). If he is planning a quick dinner, he might choose to check the local convenience store to save time, even though he knows the selection will be limited and he will likely pay more than he would at a supermarket. If budget is important, he may shop around or go to a discount store. If selection is important or he has a long list of groceries, it might be a hypermarket, a large supermarket, or a superstore. Location matters, too: the shopper may be inclined to choose a store close to the office, on the way home, or near a bus stop.

---

61 Darren Marshall (Vice President of Venturing & Emerging Brands, Coca-Cola), in discussion with the author, December 2010.

Availability of a specific brand is typically only a small part of outlet selection. Of course, this varies from category to category, and from shopper to shopper (for a single, high-ticket item, availability of a particular product may be so important that shoppers will call around to find it). The one common truth about selection of the outlet is that it is based on shopper needs as well as consumer needs, and shopper's needs often outgun the consumer's ("I know you wanted Häagen-Dazs, darling, but I only had 10 minutes and this was all the store had").

Of course, there are consequences for your brand if it isn't available in the outlet the shopper chooses. If we don't know which shoppers go to which stores, how can we hope to have an efficient and effective in-store campaign? If we get this wrong, it's not just our trade spend and in-store marketing efforts that are wasted—it's potentially our entire marketing budget.

STEP 5: SOLUTION LOCATION

Once the shopper chooses the outlet, she then has to locate the solution to the combined needs of the consumer (as interpreted by the shopper) and the shopper herself—this means finding various items she wants within the store. Depending on the store's layout, this task could be easy, but it could also be so frustrating that the shopper leaves without making the purchase or buys another brand instead.

Imagine a shopper looking for pizza in a superstore. She could buy it chilled, frozen, or freshly made. If the part of the store she chooses to visit doesn't have your brand, it might as well not be in the store. Trade funds are wasted, as is all the money spent persuading that consumer that your brand is the best for her.

The big question is "What is the shopper looking for?" The answer lies in understanding the needs of both the shopper and the consumer. If the answer is "frozen pizza," the shopper knows where to go. But if she wants non-frozen pizza, it might be found in various spots in the supermarket: hot meals, ready-to-heat prepared meals, baked goods, or in a case near the deli meats to remind the sandwich eaters that pizza is an easy alternative. If this shopper just wants pizza in some form and the first section she finds is chilled, she'll buy chilled. If your brand is in the freezer section—and even if she wanted your brand specifically—you're likely to lose a sale. You can't assume she will walk across the store just to fulfill a consumer's request, even if she's the consumer.

Increasingly, shopper marketers seek to meet consumer and shopper needs by providing entire gondolas where everything needed to complete a meal is consolidated. This trend recognizes that often shoppers aren't looking for categories but for solutions to broader consumption needs. For example, the shopper may just need to buy a lunchbox treat, not really caring whether it's chocolate or cookies or chips. The difficulty is that for every shopper who wants lunchbox treats, there is another who wants cookies and finds it very frustrating to have to hike around the store to find a product. If retailers could put all products of a kind together—all the pizzas, all the cookies—it might be a better solution for shoppers, but the logistics of chillers and freezers prevent this, and some shoppers want "something for the freezer" anyway. This is one of the major limitations of the traditional brick-and-mortar store: it's hard to put products in more than one location (a problem that, as we'll see later, creates many opportunities for online retailers).

STEP 6: PRODUCT SELECTION

Once the shopper has found the right in-store location, he now has to find the right product, and this is where all the industry's efforts make life harder for the shopper. He has to work his way through possibly hundreds of products, many on promotion, to make a final purchase decision. Here the marketer starts asking questions frantically: Will the shopper buy my brand? Will I need an extra inducement to close the deal? What was the behavior I was targeting again? Trial? Purchase of multiple pies? Or just maintenance of loyalty? Let's hope we worked that out before implementing our in-store marketing campaign!

Once the shopper has found the right place in the outlet, he will blend his own needs with those of the consumer. Depending on whose needs prevail, the shopper may look a little harder for the right product—or even go to another store if necessary—or he may just buy a different brand. (And, again, these conflicts occur even when the shopper is the consumer!)

STEP 7: PURCHASE

The final step, occurring once the choice has been made, is the purchase. Let's not assume that the product is automatically purchased once it's been selected. There can be barriers: a long queue, a lock on the display case, or an unexpected out-of-stock notice. (An out-of-stock on a shelf in a supermarket is quoted as one of the biggest frustrations for shoppers, yet marketers continue to create promotions that increase the chances of shortage.)

An Anecdote from Mike

These frustrating barriers in the supermarket rarely match the frustration shoppers face in electronics stores. For example, in the Sony store in Bangkok, I spent 20 minutes trying a video camera, with help from a very friendly Sony salesperson. I explored every feature—testing, filming, and reading all the features. Convinced this was what I wanted. I got out my credit card, only to be told that the product was out of stock. The result? Lost revenue for Sony, and a knock to my perception of the brand.

Through much effort—in advertising, salespeople, signage, display models, securing space in-store—the marketer has guided the shopper to the point of making a purchase, but barriers like this can cause us to fail at the very last step. We need to ensure that there are no barriers to purchase even after the shopper has made the decision to choose your brand.

* * *

Now we've seen the entirety of the path to purchase and the roles the consumer and shopper play in it. By understanding where the pinchpoints lie along this path, we can better understand which shopper behaviors we need to change and where we can influence them. Let's now look at two examples, revealing that shopper marketing can work both inside and outside the store.

CASE STUDY: SHOPPER MARKETING OUTSIDE THE STORE

In China in the 1980s, only about six percent of the estimated forty million children under the age of two were wore disposable diapers. Procter & Gamble looked at this situation and saw a great opportunity to promote its Pampers brand. After doing some research, they learned that moms in urban areas were more likely to value Pampers' benefits than were their rural counterparts. These urban moms liked the hygienic value of disposable diapers and found them less messy. Pampers were readily available in local outlets, making the issue of outlet selection an easy fix in urban areas.

Rural mothers, on the other hand, presented a very different path-to-purchase challenge. Their popular choice for their children was *kaidangku*—split pants that expose a child's bottom and make it easy for him to go to the bathroom anywhere (often on the street!). When rural Chinese mothers did use disposable diapers, it was for special occasions or long journeys, making even the affordable value packs inappropriate for this market. Because there was little peer pressure on rural moms to use a more sophisticated solution like Pampers on a daily basis, P&G had to overcome a sizeable problem.

Seeing the differences in consumption needs, P&G recognized that there were differences in shopper needs, too. Rural consumers only needed diapers occasionally and had low disposable income. Thus, P&G needed to sell affordable packs containing a low number of pieces. In response, the company developed small and single packs of Pampers. This solution made it easier for the parent to use Pampers on occasions when a bare bottom was inappropriate (*the shopper's interpretation*). By reducing the size of the package, P&G could offer a more affordable price for those shoppers with limited cash (*the shopper's need*). They made the new packs available at a wide range of local stores in rural areas (*outlet selection*). The stores were small, so solution location was easy for the shopper (though P&G did invest in "hanger strips" to ensure that the product was easy to see from anywhere in the store). The small pack and low price point ensured that Pampers was selected (*product selection*). By 2009, Pampers had acquired 31 percent of China's diaper market, and P&G's range of products was distributed across towns and villages throughout the country.

CASE STUDY: SHOPPER MARKETING INSIDE THE STORE

Tropicana Twister, a Pepsi product, is an ambient drink that contains five percent juice. It was first launched in markets where Tropicana juice couldn't affordably be imported. Twister is packaged in bottles and should be stocked with other ready-to-drink juice drinks, whether ambient or chilled. The company invested heavily in advertising to promote the product. Naturally, shoppers would look for such a product in the juice section, in the chiller. But in one global chain store in Thailand, Twister was stocked with ambient cordials that needed to be diluted with water, a feature not required for this particular drink. It also was featured in the chiller cabinet near the cold meats. Placed well out of its category, the brand tanked in these stores. It wasn't the product that failed but the solution location—or in this case, solution mislocation! During the launch period, sales of Tropicana's key competitor shot up—perhaps due to all those shoppers who couldn't find Tropicana and went to buy Splash instead. Quite a contrast to the Sunny Delight case discussed in Chapter 4!

BREAKING DOWN BARRIERS IN THE PATH TO PURCHASE

When you understand your shopper in terms of the potential value she represents, and when you understand the barriers in the path to purchase, you can then evolve your strategy on a channel-by-channel basis.

Let's say there's a dairy manufacturer that produces an added-value milk product at a price point that is higher than standard milk, and it wants to increase sales by driving consumption among standard milk drinkers. The process needs to begin with the target consumer, an adult who perceives the value in the higher price point: this milk has added nutrients and is worth more. One target market is women at risk for osteoporosis, because they will benefit from the nutrition boost by drinking this enhanced milk once a day. By convincing them of this, the company will increase its market share.

The company also recognizes the potential to increase its sales within the existing market. It could convince current consumers of the added-value milk that, based on medical advice, they could benefit from drinking more of this product.

But one barrier to consumption this manufacturer faces is the perception that these enhancements negatively impact the flavor of the milk. If the consumer isn't convinced, the shopper is not going to pay more for a premium product.

Increasing product visibility by buying gondola ends each month isn't the solution, nor is couponing. The biggest barrier isn't in-store location or price; it's the assumption that the added-value milk isn't palatable. If this company were to do shopper marketing research, it would find that the solution is in-store trial, potentially combined with a coupon, to disprove the flavor myth.

CASE STUDY: A BRANDING WAKE-UP CALL

A coffee manufacturer was doing well in a particular market, consistently owning the number two spot. The brand owners saw the potential to increase market share through shopper marketing. The first step was to separate the shoppers into two categories: current buyers and potential buyers. The potential shoppers were then broken into two more groups: those who had bought the coffee in the past and those who had never purchased the brand.

And that's how they looked at the world, simple and compact—and while the data is accurate, it isn't really helpful.

This coffee performed well in supermarkets, hypermarkets, and convenience stores but poorly in traditional outlets. The manufacturer perceived the problem resulted from limited distribution in those under-performing channels. The product just wasn't available in enough stores. So a plan was developed to invest loads of money into getting the coffee into more sales outlets. To a sales team, this is an obvious, if expensive, solution. It assumes that the problem lies in outlets—in path-to-purchase parlance, it lies in the "outlet selection" phase. The brand simply isn't available in the outlets the shopper selects.

Armed with a full path-to-purchase model, however, it is possible to consider other alternatives. What if the brand happens to appeal to the people who are shopping in those stores where the brand already performs well? What would be the implications if the shoppers in those traditional outlets were shopping for consumers who are not attracted to the brand? What if the shoppers are ignorant of the consumers' desires, or if the shoppers have different needs? Do we know how to influence shoppers in these outlets once distribution is in place? Simply put, are we sure that outlet selection is the biggest, most important, and only pinchpoint in this path? If that's not the case, investment in distribution may merely be putting product in front of a shopper who has no interest in buying it—extending distribution to stores with none of the right shoppers would lose millions.

As we explored the path to purchase, we discovered that distribution was indeed a barrier but a very small one. Other barriers posed a much larger obstacle, including price, product performance, and brand appeal. Building out more detailed analytics helped them understand exactly what the obstacle to growth was, and they used this knowledge to identify potential strategies for unlocking the growth opportunity.

The biggest barrier turned out to be that shoppers believed that the product didn't taste good. Some were consumers and had tried the product—but many weren't. They merely perceived that the brand didn't taste good. Others based their decision on a negative brand perception. Adding this up, it rapidly it became clear that 80 percent of the opportunity had nothing to do with distribution at all! Research showed that the company's biggest problem was that the majority of shoppers did not feel the brand was appropriate for them (either in brand image or product delivery). And putting more units on more shelves was not going to fix it, because the biggest barrier was the brand itself, not the depth of distribution.

As a result, the shopper research and analysis showed the brand owners that the coffee's marketing challenge needed to fall back in the hands of the consumer marketing team. Until the team could successfully change the market's view of the brand, little that happened in-store would make a difference in the sales and market share—or at least not with the majority of shoppers who didn't buy the brand.

It turned out that the challenge was a brand experience problem. Sure, with increased distribution, the coffee sales would show a slight climb simply because the availability was heightened, but the company would not see a proportionate return on its investment simply by shoving the coffee into more outlets.

The challenge could not be addressed by distribution alone. It required action from the consumer marketing team, as well as those responsible for shopper and trade. The company worked on addressing the brand's relevance to consumers in these areas and developed a new line extension to create a flavor that worked. With these in place, distribution could then be extended, supported by activity such as sampling to reinforce the new taste of the product.

GUIDING THE PATH TO PURCHASE

Retail space can be expensive, and the cost will continue to increase, so it will become even more imperative that we make better use of trade funds by truly understanding shoppers and their path to purchase. Where possible, greater insight and interventions earlier in the path to purchase should be used to avoid an expensive dependence on promotions in the last mile. This gives us greater influence on shoppers, inside and outside the store, and increases the channel choices that are most profitable for you.

Unless marketers take a step back and think about the shopper as an entity that exists before she sets foot in the store, and unless they then manage the entirety of the path to purchase, this dependence on the point of purchase will continue. In the same way that consumer influences stray into the store, shopper influences extend to outside the store. Who is the shopper, and how can you grab her? How can you ensure that the hard work you've done to get a consumer to love your brand results in the shopper correctly translating the consumer's desire?

95

There is no superhighway to purchase. The paths are as diverse as the consumers who use your brand and the shoppers who buy it. Generic models and sweeping statistics won't work here. The purchasing path can vary from category to category and from brand to brand. Increasingly, shopping decisions are made in complex ways, and the more marketers invest in understanding these decisions, the more they can understand where and how to influence them. It's a big challenge but also a big opportunity.

The way people shop changes all the time. Online channels and mobile technology are significantly affecting the way shoppers make purchasing decisions. From blog reviews to Facebook fan pages to mobile apps, your shopper has many influencers along the path to purchase. To be most effective, shopper marketers must invest in new knowledge—not just of the product selection stage but also of all the motivators that drive the shopper to the final point of purchase.

To accept blindly the theory that 70 percent of decisions are made in-store is counterproductive, at the very least. The chances of this being true for your category are small. The chances of it being the same for all stores are tiny. And what of the chances of it being the same for all shoppers? Hopefully, we've shown that's nonsense.

If you presume that in-store is the biggest purchase influencer within your category and you presume wrong, what does that cost you? Quite a bit, we say.

CHAPTER 6

THE TRUE COST OF DISCOUNTING

n the previous chapter, we argued that the path to purchase is a complex road: it varies by category, by shopper, and by market. We saw that at the beginning of this path is the consumer who has a desire to be met and that different people may be involved in different stages of the purchase journey. The consumer is influenced by shopping concerns ("I won't consume that bottle of wine today, as it was expensive; I'll save it for a special occasion"), and likewise, the shopper is often influenced by consumption issues ("I won't buy that; she doesn't like the taste"). Picking a way through all this is difficult but essential for the shopper marketer: True marketing success comes from a deep and complete understanding of the path to purchase, and then using this to create a change in shopping behavior, which fuels a positive change in the consumption of your brand.

On top of the complexity of the path to purchase, the advance of ecommerce and mobile technology has further blurred the lines between consumer and shopper; it has presented marketers with incredible new opportunities for influencing shopper behavior. And although there appears to be plenty of excitement about influencing consumers through digital media, much activity targeted at shoppers is still one-dimensional. For decades, consumer marketers have leveraged a rich and complex marketing mix in their attempts to win the hearts of their targets, but in the land of shopper marketing, there appears to be a strong skew toward a simpler mix—and a strong dependence on promotions and discounts. Even at the vanguard of mobile marketing, the "heroes" of digital shopper marketing are price-comparison and digital-coupon sites such as Groupon.

Journeying down the aisle of pretty much any store anywhere in the world, a shopper is hailed by myriad labels, tags, banners, boards, and stickers—each proclaiming an offer or enticement. This is nothing new, but even with the rise of digital—which one might legitimately expect to reduce dependence on discounts—the intensity with which these offers are thrust upon shoppers has increased dramatically. The reliance on price promotion—driven by retail consolidation, media fragmentation, and excitement about the "first moment of truth"—shows no sign of letting up. Recessionary pressures have further increased the number of promotions. There was a time when, in our experience, the percentage of products on promotion hovered around 15 percent; today, estimates run from 35 percent to 40 percent in some markets.[62]

This wouldn't be a problem if discounts created the desired behavior in shoppers and drove profitable brand growth. But often, as we will see, it does neither.

DESTRUCTIVE DISCOUNTING

Studies have shown that 70 percent of promotions lose money for the manufacturer. Anyone outside the industry must surely, at this stage, be seriously questioning the sanity of anyone who works in consumer goods. But knowing that you are in a hole and digging out of it are two very different things. When we present the 70 percent statistic in workshops and management meetings, we always ask, "Is this the same for you?" The question is usually followed by silence, shuffling, or a nervous laugh. Many don't actually know. Those who do know acknowledge (more times than not) that the failure rate is actually higher for them.

Those who know and those who are ignorant do at least have one thing in common: they all know in their hearts that a lot of their activities lose money. The retailer, ostensibly the manufacturer's "partner in crime" in this, fares a lot better, making money on a full 75 percent of these activities. But try this on for size: 1 in 10 activities loses money for both the manufacturer and the retailer.

---

62 Petah Marian, "Promotional Intensity Reaches 'Record Levels,'" just-food.com, January 10, 2011, http://www.just-food.com/the-just-food-blog/promotional-intensity-reaches-record-levels_id1981.aspx.

It would be easy to criticize the managers who continue to spend money in a way they know to be unprofitable. But it's not easy to stop. Their addiction is driven by retailers who act as though they have a right to receive deals and promotions; by senior managers who demand ever-increasing sales from their teams without considering how those sales are to be achieved; and by a lack of any other credible solutions. We know what it's like. We've been there. We've been faced with a target, based on last year's sales results. Last year's results were driven by a big promotion; this year's sales have to be higher—so how is a manager to achieve them? Another promotion of course! While targets are merely an inflated replication of last year's reality, it is incredibly difficult for shopper marketers and salespeople to hit their results without replicating last year's activity. Just for a second, think about it. Last year we ran a massive promotion that quadrupled sales but lost money. Both facts—the sales uplift and the loss, are enshrined in last year's numbers. The loss may be hidden, but it is accounted for. This year's numbers—well—where do they typically come from? You guessed it—last year's (plus a bit!). So the targets passed down from the boss encourage and legitimize continuing with activity that loses money.

And the alternatives? Well, realistically, many operational marketers have no time to think of alternatives. They have no time to develop a better understanding of how else to hit the numbers. They have little funds to spend on research and little time to develop insights to understand shoppers better. Why? They are too busy managing more and more promotions!

Not just the manufacturers are feeling the pain. While shoppers love deals, the side effects on the shopping experience are less than desirable. There are dangers to retailers, too, as we will highlight later in this chapter. An overreliance on discounting is arguably the biggest single challenge facing the future of the consumer goods industry. All of this points to a real urgency to create a new way of marketing to shoppers—one that does not rely so heavily on promotions, discounts, and deals. But first let's consider why this happens in the first place.

THE ANTECEDENTS OF DISCOUNTING

Even before there were shopper marketers—marketers even, let alone a marketing mix—business owners understood implicitly the huge importance of price: if a product was priced too high relative to the value perception in a customer's mind and within the competitive context (i.e., what could a customer get from a competitor), then the product wouldn't sell. If the price was too low, then the product may well sell, but profits would be poor. Business owners also knew intuitively one other important fact about price. The vast majority of large consumer brands that grew up in the late nineteenth century were built on a quality promise—Cadbury, Nestlé, Lever Brothers: their brands offered a promise of quality and pure ingredients. If the price was set too low, then there was a danger that consumers would cease to believe in that promise, judging the offer too good to be true.

Put simply, business owners (and subsequently marketers) have understood that their job is to create value from their brands, and they do this by maximizing the perceived value that consumers (and shoppers!) see in that brand. They do this by managing an equation of value in the minds of their target—the balance between perceived quality and perceived price. Quality is fantastic and highly desirable but can take a very long time to create. Inventing new technologies, finding new formulations, researching consumer acceptance, commissioning new plants, shelf life testing: all these things can take an enormous amount of money. After a great new, high-quality product has been created, the marketer still needs to ensure that the consumer perceives that value, which is done through advertising and promotions. All this takes time, and as the clock is ticking, the chances that quality can be matched or usurped by a competitor increase.

Unfortunately, the modern marketer doesn't have time. Deborah Cadbury, in her book *The Chocolate Wars,* describes senior family members traveling across Europe for years, searching for new innovative ideas. Today's marketers do not have that luxury. Typically, a marketer will have an 18-month tenure in her position, and her bosses will look to present a return to Wall Street on a quarterly basis. Modern marketers don't have a decade to build their brand. Unfortunately, they need a quicker way to make an impact on their business, and that means a quicker shift in the value equation. If not quality, then price.

To the modern marketer, leveraging price is so desperately tempting. It's easy to do, requires little planning and foresight (no design, product tests, advertising development), and the results are almost immediate. Dropping prices will improve the consumer and shopper value equation, and volumes will rise. Offer the same great quality at a better price. What could possibly go wrong?

However, just as their Industrial Revolution forebears knew, today's marketers know that price is massively important, and that the price lever is not one that should be pulled lightly. Price is hugely important to one's consumers and shoppers; it helps them determine the value that a product or brand offers them. But, of course, price affects something else far more important to the marketer and his business: profit.

Price affects demand, as we have seen, and price also has a disproportionate impact on profitability. A small drop (or rise) in price can have a huge impact on profitability and, depending on the margins in the business, can require huge volume increases to compensate.

For simplicity, imagine a business selling 100 units for a dollar each and making a net margin of 25 percent. That equates to $25 profit. Now, if the company drops the price by 10 percent to 90 cents, what happens to the profit? It drops to 15 cents a unit, or $15. A 10 percent reduction in price equates to a 40 percent decrease in profits. To move profit back up to $25, the company would need to sell 167 units—a 67 percent increase in volumes just to stand still!

But what net margins do consumer goods companies actually make? The top 250 consumer goods companies turned $2.8 trillion in 2010 with a net profit of around $240 billion—that's a net margin of 8.5 percent.[63] Let's look at the previous model—a company selling a hundred units at a dollar a piece but this time making a net margin of 8.5 percent, so making a $8.5 profit. At that margin, reducing prices by 10 percent makes a loss, so let's look at the impact of just a 1 percent price reduction. As the price drops to 99 cents, profit per unit drops to 7.5 cents. A price reduction of just 1 percent now translates into a profit reduction of almost 12 percent! Looking at this another way, the company now needs to increase volumes by over 13 percent just to cover the cost of reducing price by 1 percent!

How to get the rush of sales that a price cut gives without undermining long-term profitability? Enter the price promotion. On the surface, price promotions are an excellent tool for marketers: they are an easy-to-implement, fast-impact way of altering the value equation, and they therefore drive increases in volume without having to mess up long-term profitability by changing the price. With the ever-hungry retail machine asking for more, this becomes simply too easy for many companies to resist.

---

63 Deloitte, *Global Powers of Consumer Products 2012: Connecting the Dots*, accessed February 28, 2013, http://www.deloitte.com/assets/Dcom-Guam/Local Assets/Documents/Global Powers of CP 2012_Deloitte_Web.pdf.

HOW IMPORTANT IS PRICE ANYWAY?

All this activity has an interesting impact on shopping behavior, and not all of it is intuitive. The logic behind most discounting strategies is based on the belief that shoppers actually know how much they pay for products, but they do not in many cases. A *Harvard Business Review* report a few years ago explained a study led by Florida International University professor Peter R. Dickson and University of Florida professor Alan G. Sawyer, in which researchers stood in the aisles of supermarkets. Just as a shopper placed an item in the cart, the researchers asked the person the price. Less than half gave an accurate answer. Most underestimated; over 20 percent did not have a clue. Our own research suggests that shoppers' understanding of real prices depends on the size and frequency of the transaction. Shoppers are more cognizant of high-price items, and they will often know the price of items they buy very frequently. Most shoppers, for example, would have no idea of the price of light bulbs or similar items of a relatively low price that are bought infrequently.

In the confusing mess of the modern retail store, it is hard for shoppers to understand the actual price they are paying and to understand whether that represents value or not. As Herb Sorensen says, "Shoppers know very little about price." The same *Harvard Business Review* research mentioned before showed that the mere presence of a promotion tag suggested value, regardless of the actual price. Other research has shown that in some categories, the presence of the numeral 9 at the end of a price has more of an impact than the actual price. Research has shown that, in certain categories, moving a product's price from $34 to $39 and putting it on display actually increases sales.

THE LONG-TERM EFFECT OF TRAINING THE SHOPPER

As promotional intensity increases, not only does the impact of those activities fall, but also shoppers' perception of the entire category changes. Shoppers may not know the price of every product in a category, but they do have some broad benchmarks, and when these change, they see the whole category differently. Take, for example, the soft drink category. A benchmark product might be a six-pack of Coke. A shopper may judge the prices on offer by their relationship to Coke. Cheaper than Coke, more expensive than Coke. But what happens when Coke gets promoted? With the benchmark shifted, the shopper isn't sure how to judge the relative prices of other products in the category.

Occasional promotions are unlikely to change these category-wide perceptions, but frequent promotions of category benchmarks fundamentally shift behavior. Now that the promotion price represents good value, the standard price is expensive. Because the regular price feels too high, shoppers, if they can, will simply wait for the next promotion.

So the short-term returns from discounting are poor at best, and the increasing intensity of these activities is likely to reduce the already slim returns of manufacturers. Discounting usually delivers only a short-term boost in sales, and sometimes not even that. In some parts of the world, manufacturers are only able to measure sell-in (that is, the volume of product a retailer buys from them) rather than sell-out (what is actually sold to shoppers). Retailers will always buy more because they want to build stocks against potential demand and because stacking product on a floor display requires a lot of product. But this behavior can hide the true trend of demand. By measuring only sell-in, it is impossible to say how much of the promotional peak in sales was driven by shoppers and how much by retail buying. To make matters worse, some canny retailers will deliberately overbuy during promotions so that they get more stock at a better price, which they can sell to shoppers for a higher margin after the promotion has finished.

A promotion's impact on short-term sales varies dramatically by category. Products that are by nature substitutional—existing in a category where one product is easily replaced with another—often perform very well on a promotion. Promoting cherries, for example, may yield very high increases in sales but may have a negative impact on other fruits—shoppers come to the store with "fruit" on their lists or in their minds, and the promotion triggers a purchase of cherries, rather than, say, strawberries. More impulsive categories, such as chocolate, can also create huge uplifts on deal.

The longer-term effect of promotions also varies by category. The key driver in all this is whether the change in shopping behavior driven by the promotion has any significant impact on consumption behavior. Let's consider cherries again. Perhaps the shopper is looking for some nice fruit, sees a great deal on cherries, and buys them. That night, the family consumes the cherries after dinner. That purchase—that change in shopper behavior—created a change in consumption behavior. Cherry consumption grew. If you were a cherry farmer, you'd be reasonably happy with that (assuming the costs of the promotion didn't outweigh the benefits). As a retailer, you may be less happy (as you might have lost sales on strawberries), which is why you will have insisted that the farmers pay for the deal, probably for the display space, and for the cost to feature the product in the mailer. Next, let's consider chocolate. A shopper buys a bar of chocolate impulsively because she saw a deal. It is consumed in the car on the way home. Again (assuming the deal is broadly profitable), the manufacturer should see real sales growth, as the change in shopping behavior created a positive change in consumer behavior. The retailer will also be happy, as he got an extra sale (increased basket size).

Some categories are less likely to have the same positive effect on consumption. If you're like most people, when you buy more chocolate, you will eat more chocolate. But stocking up on laundry powder is much less likely to encourage you to wash more clothes! Consider a major toilet paper manufacturer in Australia. The company sees an 800 percent uplift when its bathroom tissue is on offer. Is this an effective promotion? Not really. All that is happening is that sales are dropping between promotions. The benchmark price for the brand (and perhaps the category) has changed, and the promotional price has become the norm. Shoppers stock up while the deals are on and stop buying the rest of the time. In effect, the "standard" price of the product, in the eyes of shoppers, is the promoted price. The non-promoted price is not seen as good value and is ignored by shoppers, who have been trained to stock up when a deal is on.

An Anecdote from Mike

Case in point: Colgate toothpaste seems to have been on promotion for the better part of 15 years, which might be some sort of record. As a Colgate loyalist, I would buy the toothpaste even at full price, but no matter what country I travel to, I manage to find it at a discount. As an industry insider, I know that these retailers aren't eating the cost of the promotion; Colgate is picking up the tab. As long as the retailers continue to garner their desired margins, they are happily selling Colgate at a discount. And what Colgate-Palmolive has done is to condition shoppers not to pay full price. The company has effectively lowered the price of its brand. I know better than to buy the toothpaste when it is not on sale—a situation I rarely encounter.

In this way, entire categories can be poisoned. The phenomenon is particularly common where products have a long shelf life and can thus be stored at home for a long time. We've heard estimates that up to 40 percent of toothpaste is sold on sale globally. Manufacturers are training shoppers to buy on sale. The frequent cycle of promotions driven by both manufacturers and retailers means that a canny shopper can stock up with enough shampoo to get her through the next few months until the kind manufacturer offers a new deal. That shopper can be highly loyal to the brand, but she knows that she is likely to be offered a deal. This type of shopper can wait, knowing that the worst that will happen is she may have to buy some product at full price. But with the frequent, predictable cycle of promotions, the chances of this happening are significantly reduced.

One thing is clear: discounting merely lessens the brand's value in the eyes of the trained shoppers—and often trains them to only buy on discounts. With this practice, we create more bargain hunters, which is not a sustainable practice for the industry. In the long run, discounting only prompts shoppers to stock up, decreasing their needs later. So, when "later" comes along, the retailer experiences another drop in sales. What's the solution? Drop the price again. And the cycle repeats.

These twin drivers of discounting behavior—short-termism in the boardrooms and retail's hunger for a deal—have driven the intensity of promotions up. Shoppers are bombarded with messages and deals in mailers, in newspapers, in phone apps, on websites, and in every aisle of the store. But because there are so many messages, shoppers often struggle to see them all. If a typical hypermarket stocks forty thousand products, and 30 percent are on special, that's twelve thousand promotions. Shoppers see big displays in the main aisle, promotional areas in some stores, and several deals on every end cap. All of these deals add more complexity to the weekly shop—something that for many is already a complex task. How do shoppers cope with all of this complexity? Our data finds that they ignore it.

In one category we studied in Thailand, only 6.7 percent of shoppers even noticed a particular in-store promotion; 91 percent of the shoppers only looked at one brand in that category; and 99.5 percent purchased the brand they came to the store intending to buy. So if many shoppers ignore promotional messages, who actually buys promoted products? Manufacturers and retailers sometimes report stellar uplifts when products are discounted, so somebody must be buying them, right?

WHO ACTUALLY BUYS PROMOTED GOODS?

Clearly, discounts are appealing to shoppers. One of the most mind-numbingly daft questions asked in shopper research (and asked many times, we are sad to say) is, "Which type of promotions do you prefer?" Time and again, shoppers say that they like discounts. Yes—shoppers are quite keen on paying a little bit less than they usually do for a product. So far so good. But which shoppers actually get the benefit?

Data shows that up to 80 percent of promoted volume is bought by only 20 percent of a category's shoppers. The number varies from chain to chain, category to category, and country to country. But as a rule of thumb, a significant amount of product is bought by what we would call a "deal buyer." And to marketers, deal buyers are really, really scary.

Many of you, especially those of you in the United States, will have seen a show called *Extreme Couponing*. The show focuses on individuals who build their life around discounts in the form of coupons, which turns out to be a lucrative pastime. Extreme couponers collect thousands of coupons, catalogue them all, and plan their shopping trip with meticulous detail. In one episode, a shopper named Joyce manages to buy over $200 worth of groceries for around seven bucks. These shoppers are indeed extreme, and though they make for great TV, they represent a tiny minority of the population.

The dreaded deal buyers are not quite so extreme, but there are lots of them, and they eat up a significant share of promotional funding from manufacturers and retailers alike. Deal buyers focus on promotions in stores, and aisles are full of them, all choosing brands because there's a deal running that week. Some deal buyers will just buy the cheapest on display (in many markets, they buy private label unless a branded product dips low enough to tempt them), but many deal buyers' decisions are more complex. Many have a portfolio of brands that they like—perhaps a range of three mid-priced beers. They may not stray out of this portfolio for anything (they wouldn't drink private label, for example), but they will switch between these brands, depending on the deals. Either way, these deal buyers swallow up the vast majority of the money that marketers spend on promotions.

The problem with the deal buyer is that the value accrued by the manufacturer is limited to one sale. Deal buyers are, by definition, not brand loyal. They'll switch between Coke and Pepsi without a second thought based purely on which brand is running a deal. So while they may be buying your brand this week, they'll be buying someone else's on the next shopping trip. Your deal hasn't created any long-term behavioral change or any long-term value.

And what of the other shoppers who benefited from the promotion? Of the remaining 20 percent of volume not consumed by deal buyers, the majority typically goes to brand loyalists or shoppers who saw the promotion and "brought forward" purchases they planned to make in the future. This may have value to the retailer, but the value is harder to identify for the manufacturer. In highly elastic categories such as confectionary, this unplanned purchase may lead to unplanned consumption, so the gain may be truly incremental. In less elastic categories, however, bringing forward a sale merely mortgages the future—a loyal shopper stocks up on a brand at a discount and does not need to buy for some time in the future. And because many of the shoppers were planning to buy the brand anyway, the net result of the promotion is that these people bought what they were already going to buy but got it at a discount.

Of course, some of the shoppers who bought on a deal may well have some legitimate value for the brand owner. Some of them may usually buy a competitor's product—in which case, share has been taken. Perhaps the brand will be used and preferred by the consumer, and long-term value will be created. Typically, however, this is a small proportion of the total buyers.

Promotions benefit many shoppers. Much of the benefit, unfortunately, falls into the hands of the deal buyers—and that does not benefit manufacturers. And yet, most promotional evaluations don't even cover who bought the product; they merely look at what was sold. Even the promotions that might be deemed profitable against the simplest benchmark (sales) may not be quite so attractive when the person who bought the product is also part of the evaluation.

THE HIDDEN COSTS FOR THE RETAILER

The pain of the promotions cycle is felt primarily by manufacturers—partly because their funding insures retailers against losses and partly because retailers have fundamentally different goals when it comes to a shopper. When a shopper stocks up and there is no increase in consumption, the manufacturer will lose out. The retailer, however, may not. Retailers know that shoppers are promiscuous and that next week's shopping trip may not be to their store. Retailers care less about whether the product is consumed—they merely want shoppers to buy more on the day. But this intensity of promotions does hold some dangers for retailers, as we shall show.

What about the long-term impact of discounting on the retailer's business? How defensible is a brand built primarily on price? Marketers in other industries seem to recognize that a brand built only on the promise of low prices is vulnerable to attack, and the success of hard discounters in many countries seems to suggest that retail is no exception—only one player can be the cheapest. The reality is that the price difference between retailers is often more perceived than real. The fact that discounting doesn't necessarily threaten retailers' profits (as their suppliers fund much of it) has allowed them to stray into untested waters. Promotions are often used indiscriminately rather than strategically, and we're seeing a dangerous rush toward what is largely a zero-sum game. In the UK, Asda and Tesco compete heavily on price. Still, the perception is that Tesco is "upmarket" and Asda is "down market." A recent comparison shop of 1,500 items at both stores revealed that the difference in price was a measly 74 cents. Clearly, in some categories, the upmarket Tesco was actually lower in price.

A similar truth exists with Walmart and Target. In recent years, Target has aggressively promoted its brand, brilliantly leveraging its trade spend to feature brands in its commercials, while also supporting strong brand visibility. Walmart continues to focus on low pricing. In reality, the price difference between the two stores is not much greater than the Tesco-Asda variance. But Target is perceived as upscale.

There is no sustainable competitive advantage in price if your competitors can match it. So while shoppers tell Nielsen researchers that they do consider price and discounts as their top priority when considering where to shop, this needs a little interpretation. If most big retailers have the same price, this data becomes moot. It doesn't explain the myriad shopping trips that shoppers make to stores that aren't the cheapest and that don't offer the most discounts (convenience stores, for starters). Nor does it explain why hard discounters in Europe have less than 100 percent share. They are cheaper, so what is going on? When shoppers are asked what is important to them, they answer based on their perception of their behavior rather than their actual behavior. No one would ever shop at an upmarket store or a convenience store if it were all about price.

The reality is that the Nielsen data is misleading (or can be when translated into sound bites). Typically, price is only a clear differentiator when all else is equal. With two stores that are exactly the same, equally close, and with the same range of products—for sure, I'll go for the best prices. But if one store didn't stock the products I wanted, was much further away, or was a much nicer shopping environment—maybe not. Data like this is misleading an entire industry and encouraging retailers to pursue a one-dimensional strategy that is destroying their business.

The fact that price is even a factor suggests that retailers have failed to differentiate themselves on anything else in the mind of their consumers. Despite decades of private label development, billions of dollars of advertising, and sophisticated store design, it appears that this isn't making much of a difference to shoppers. Clearly, this can't be true. But the fact that retailers can play the price card so heavily and so frequently with little profit impact has led them to become over-reliant on price in their marketing mix.

The impact of this overreliance, and the subsequent training of shoppers, on the retailers' business has had limited impact on the surface until recently. Manufacturers' funding has shielded them from their own discount excesses, but this has led to the creation of weak retail brands that are over-dependent on price. The recent rise of Amazon, however, shows the potential weakness in such a model. Amazon delivers on price but trumps this with a better range and more convenience. If all you have to compete on is price, it is only a matter of time before someone finds a way to do what you do—only cheaper.

STRAIN ON THE SUPPLY CHAIN

A promotion is not merely a strain on the manufacturer's gross margin. It also drives supply chain problems. Out-of-stocks plague retailers—and shoppers. Too many out-of-stocks contribute to the brand erosion we discussed, as shoppers learn not to rely on a retailer, in spite of advertising price cuts to lure them in.

On a recent audit at one of UK retail giant Asda's stores in the industrial town of Slough reported a 12 percent out-of-stock rate; 85 percent of those products were on promotion. So shoppers were unable to obtain the sale items they came for. Asda, a subsidiary of Walmart, is the third-largest retailer in the UK and known for its low pricing. What does the out-of-stock situation do for Asda's highly touted value offer? What perception do shoppers leave the store with, having experienced this level of unavailability? Is Asda creating long-term value or diminishing its brand? And the manufacturer who paid for the privilege of discounting his product in Asda—for the gondola end, mailers, etc.—is certainly not gaining any points with shoppers who can't get what they want, leaving them to either shop elsewhere or choose a competitive brand. For a moment, let us consider what else happens to a retailer's business when discounts are applied. Retailers recognize that it takes more than price to keep shoppers happy. Shopper satisfaction is a difficult measure to pin down, but "keep the customer satisfied" is a mantra that has lasted for a long time. And what frustrates shoppers most? Long queues for sure, and out-of-stocks. And what causes out-of-stocks? Well, many things—bad forecasting, ineffective shelf planning, and yes, you guessed it: discounts.

Promoting lines has two major impacts on in-stock management. First, it is significantly harder to predict demand for short-term promotions: sharp spikes in volume may be brought on by the discount, making out-of-stocks more likely. Dual location of stock also makes things harder, as store systems typically show a total stock position. The product may be in stock on the aisle-end, but out of stock on the shelf.

Promoting products may attract shoppers, but if the shoppers can't actually buy the product when they get to the store, what happens to their view of the store in the long term? And, of course, given that sales of promotional lines are hard to predict, this also means that there are many cases of overstock, which drives cost into the retailer's business—another hidden cost of promotion.

Poor forecasting, limited allocations, store overrides, the proliferation of multiple promotions pinching the retail space, and lack of trust in computer-based planning models can all contribute to the out-of-stock problem. Manufacturers need to be aware of the causes and guide the retailer into planning to avoid out-of-stocks—and disappointed shoppers!

The massive increase in promotional intensity puts even more strain on the supply chain. Manufacturers pay for the privilege of discounting their products, risking the integrity of their brands. They increase the costs of their own production by driving overtime and downtime as they create artificial peaks and troughs in demand. They risk disappointing high-value, loyal shoppers who can't find the brand because it's out of stock due to promotional demand. Store operations teams around the world acknowledge that despite all of the investment in supply chain systems and decades of supply chain initiatives, keeping products on the shelf is the toughest retail challenge. Longer opening hours haven't helped, but the dramatic increases in promotional intensity have clearly contributed. There has to be a better way.

Small price reductions can have a huge impact on profits, and huge volume uplifts are required just to stand still in profit terms. Of course, the reverse is also true—a small price increase can deliver the same profit increase as a large increase in volumes. Marketers know this, or at least the CFOs in their businesses know this. And as raw material costs go up, so does commercial pressure to increase prices. So what is a marketer to do? Step-changing real quality by improving the product is expensive and time consuming. Building more equity in a brand through marketing communication is likewise expensive, time consuming and, as argued earlier in this book, less effective than it used to be. What else can a marketer do to quickly impact the value equation positively without affecting long-term price and therefore destroying long-term profitability? The answer lies in creating a finely tuned and balanced marketing mix, one that does not rely so heavily on price.

GETTING OUT OF THE PIT, ONE STEP AT A TIME

Unfettered and indiscriminate use of promotions clearly has multiple negative effects on the consumer goods industry. It destroys the profitability of brands in the short term and reduces brand equity in the long term. Entire categories can be devalued as shoppers are trained to buy and hoard, and they are re-educated on what a fair price is to pay for a product. Deal buyers soak up promotional volume, while out-of-stocks frustrate store and brand loyalists in equal measure. Shoppers are increasingly being trained in new shopping behavior in the face of the onslaught of offers. Yet marketers are trapped in a pit of their own invention. It's easy to blame big retail for the mess that brands find themselves in, but there is little evidence to support the sole culpability of retailers. Large retailers have surely accelerated the trend by demanding promotions and making them devilishly easy to execute, but manufacturers were using promotions to hit short-term numbers long before. Go back to the turn of the century in China, when retail was completely fragmented and no retailer had more than a couple of percent market share: promotions were in every supermarket. Manufacturers are just as culpable in the creation of this monster. For many, decades of underinvestment in innovation and brand equity has created a vicious cycle that threatens their very existence.

Discounts are here to stay, but do we need so many? As manufacturers, we need to offer alternative, value-changing strategies. Yes, retailers love discounts! But we need to help them see other ways of attracting shoppers.

Shopper marketing can help by urging marketers to consider the impact on both the consumer and the shopper prior to planning activity and by considering alternatives to discounts that will still achieve the commercial goals set by the company and the retailer. When shopper marketing activity is focused in the right way, it can drive growth for brand owners, deliver a significant return on investment, and support retailers at the same time. Chris Hoyt has suggested that introducing shopper marketing into the planning and execution of in-store activities turns a typical ROI of 0.65 into an ROI of 3.5.[64] Discounts and promotions play a part in this, but they work best when used with a touch more precision and as part of a broader, more holistic marketing mix, as we shall see. Activities that change the behavior of the target shopper in a way that fuels future consumption growth are far more likely to drive profitable growth.

FINESSING THE PATH TO PURCHASE

Clearly, every situation is different, and situations are changing all of the time. But time and time again, our path-to-purchase model helps identify the key "pinchpoints" that are preventing purchase and subsequent consumption of brands. Further, by identifying these alternative blockages, the dependence on activity (promotions) at the shelf is often reduced, leading to greater profit opportunities for manufacturer and retailer alike.

And one last thought—if winning at the shelf is so difficult and expensive, shouldn't every possible attempt be made to win elsewhere (earlier) in the path to purchase? The chances that the brand will have to scrap it out in a promotions war at the shelf are diminished if the consumer's need is closely associated with your brand, the shopper is convinced and completely clear on what the consumer is after, the brand offer meets all of the shopper's needs and more, and the brand is available in the right stores and located where shoppers are looking for it.

This overreliance and the subsequent training of shoppers has thus far had limited impact on retailers; the manufacturers' funds have shielded them from their own discount excesses. The recent rise of Amazon, however, shows that retailers can't get away with this forever.

---

64 Hoyt, discussion.

AN IMPERATIVE FOR CHANGE

Shopper marketing offers a solution to the destructive and unsustainable dependence on discounts, but it requires radical change. We know it's not easy to make radical change—to give up on a habit as addictive as this, to change behavior that is so entrenched. We've felt the temptation, the desperation, and the pressure from a retailer who is a huge part of your business. We understand you have to make numbers this quarter. We know that everything can't be perfect and that sometimes we have to use short-term tactics.

We're not advocating that all marketers and corporations go cold turkey and quit discounting overnight. That would create a shock to the system that could be very painful in the short term. But please, do you need to promote all the time? What can be done to inch the needle in the right direction? To move from a 70 percent failure rate on promotions to 65 percent? And to CEOs, chief marketing officers, and marketing and sales directors—where is the strategy to break this habit so that in five years, we truly look at shopper marketing for what it could be—an investment in our brands—rather than a necessary cost that keeps getting bigger and bigger? That, we believe, is a revolutionary step.

CHAPTER 7

THE NEW BRAND MANIFESTO

W e are on the cusp of a revolution. The consumer goods industry has a choice to make. Profits are not growing; growth is becoming more and more elusive, and competition is getting ever tougher. The modus operandi of building brands that consumers love and then paying retailers large amounts of money to put those brands in their stores does not appear to be delivering the right results. As media becomes personal and competition intensifies, creating meaningful, lasting bonds with consumers will get harder and more expensive. Large retailers seem likely to continue to grow their share of the market, and as they grow, their bargaining power will grow, too, meaning that deals will need to be sharper and prices (to the retailers) lower. And while the strategy to win with shoppers remains dominated by discounting, shoppers will continue to be trained, discounted prices will become the norm, and profits will continue to be drained.

It appears to us that this is not only unsustainable, it is also unnecessary. There is an opportunity for the industry, rather than plunging into the void, to soar upwards on a new trajectory. But like turning a supertanker, this change of direction will require a significant shift in many ways.

Marketing needs to change. Not just in the way organizations approach the in-store world but in the way businesses think about their target market. Winning with consumers is no longer enough; shoppers need to be won over, too. And through this process, a new dialog with retailers must be forged. Companies cannot expect retailers to change their way of working unless this new approach offers attractive alternatives for them.

Marketing teams must consider three customers: the consumer, the shopper, and the retailer. And these efforts cannot be considered in separate silos. More than ever before, there needs to be an integrated way to approach these three stakeholders. The world of the consumer blurs into the world of the shopper in so many ways that it should be unthinkable to target one without also considering the other. And despite the promise of digital, a significant amount of shopping will take place on someone else's turf for virtually all brands and categories. To influence shoppers there and to change their behavior requires the support of the owner of that space—be it Target, Amazon, or Tesco. Configuring marketing in this way will drive improvements in efficiency and effectiveness, as investment can be managed better and focused on the critical blockages that prevent brand growth. Synergies can be developed and interventions can be aligned along the complete path to purchase.

This has some significant implications for the way consumer goods companies currently work, which will be addressed in part three of this book. But this new world has a massive implication for the way these companies think about arguably their biggest assets—their brands.

Brands lie at the heart of the value-creation model for a consumer goods business, and this is a fact that has long been recognized. Brand consultancy Interbrand values the Coca-Cola brand at almost $80 billion, potentially half the value of the total company (and that valuation only includes the Coca-Cola brand itself, not the rest of the portfolio, which includes Sprite and Fanta).[65] A similar analysis suggests that the McDonald's brand accounts for over 40 percent of its shareholder value.[66] Since the late twentieth century, in some European markets, "brand value" can be added to the balance sheet as an intangible asset. But recognition of the value of brands is nothing new; over 100 years ago, John Stuart, chairman of Quaker, said, "If this business were split up, I would give you the land and bricks and mortar, and I would take the brands and trademarks, and I would fare better than you."[67]

---

65 "Coca-Cola," Interbrand, accessed March 7, 2013, http://www.interbrand.com/en/best-global-brands/2012/Coca-Cola.

66 "McDonald's Corp. (MCD) | Enterprise Value (EV)" Stock Analysis on Net, accessed March 14, 2013, http://www.stock-analysis-on.net/NYSE/Company/McDonalds-Corp/Valuation/Enterprise-Value.

67 Jwalit Vyas, "Brand Building: Companies Deriving Business Value from Intangibles," *The Times of India*, October 26, 2010, http://economictimes.indiatimes.com/features/et500/brand-building-companies-deriving-business-value-from-intangibles/articleshow/6809770.cms.

What is a brand? Like most marketing terms, this one has various definitions. The American Marketing Association defines a brand as a "Name, term, design, symbol, or any other feature that identifies one seller's good or service as distinct from those of other sellers." In *Kellogg on Branding*, the marketing faculty of the Kellogg School of Management offers this definition: "A set of associations linked to a name, mark, or symbol associated with a product or service," the focus here being on what the target market associates with the mark, design, or symbol rather than the symbol itself. Advertising guru David Ogilvy put it simply as "the intangible sum of a product's attributes." Whatever the definition, the brand and what it means to its audience ultimately creates value for the organization.

While the concept of brands has been around for a very long time, the way it has been used has changed dramatically. The origins of branding are as a symbol of ownership—originally of cattle (the word comes from an Old Norse word, *brandr*, meaning "to burn"). As the Industrial Revolution transformed manufacturing of consumer products in the late nineteenth century, people moved from buying products made in the locality toward products made in large, centralized factories. The origins of products were harder to trace, so brand names were used to help the public know that what they were getting was genuine and of a specific quality. Consumer goods companies led the charge, and the arrival of television ushered in the era of modern day marketing. TV met the need to take messages to a mass market. It spurred companies to invest more and more in making sure that consumers around the world knew their brand offered a differentiated product performance. Better taste, whiter whites, or longer lasting results: each brand attempted to entice consumers with promises of better and better performance.

But as competition increased, marketers needed to work hard to find points of distinction, things that were valuable to the consumer and that the competition didn't offer. Marketers found that competitors could often easily replicate functional points of distinction, and as products became ubiquitous through better distribution, consumers could easily be tempted away. Marketers realized that they needed to create different, less tangible connections with consumers if they were to keep them loyal. Soap manufacturers, for example, might have found that while clean clothes were indeed a great benefit to offer consumers, it was a claim that everyone could make. Each subsequent claim (whiter whites, brighter colors) could equally be claimed by many competitors, if not today then perhaps tomorrow.

117

But if there was trust developed, an emotional connection was built—the housewife trusts that this brand not only helps her get the laundry done but that it also helps her care for her family. A brand like that is trusted, for sure, but also becomes personified as an entity that understands the consumer, understands her world, and understands what is important to her. A relationship is formed, which is arguably more than the sum of the parts of what is functionally going on, and a relationship like that is harder to break up.

Marketers recognized that to forge these bonds, they had to get really close to their target, the consumer. Departments that had been called merely "Marketing" gradually became known as "Consumer Marketing"; the word *customer* was phased out or reserved for retailers. This focus on the consumer was critical to the success of many of the household brands we know and love today, and it has formed the focus of marketing activities for the last 60 years. As with any discipline, marketing and branding professionals created their own language. As brands evolved, they developed personalities—became personified. Models were created to try to capture what a brand was all about, a blueprint that helped marketers ensure that the brand, however and wherever it was presented to the consumer, stayed true to that relationship. Various models have come and gone, but all have one purpose: an attempt to document the brand, the target consumer, and all of the elements that make up the relationship between the two. Very large organizations develop their own individual models, and they come in an endless variety of shapes. Among them are helices, circles, keys, or even "brand temples" complete with pillars. Lipton, at one stage, used a model that was shaped like a leaf. Models often use different language, and some have substantial differences, but most have many things in common.

We use what we call the "brand diamond."

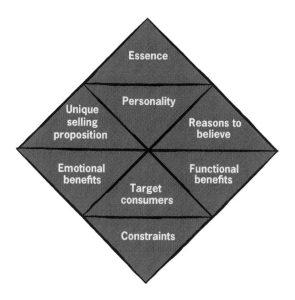

Understand that we are not advocating this model over other consumer models; but we like it, it works, and it is very practical. This diamond integrates the basis of the brand with the variable aspects, from the perspective of the consumer's needs and desires. Look at the diamond as two triangles joined at the base. The top half consists of four brand traits: essence, unique selling proposition, personality, and reasons to believe. These represent the fundamentals of the brand, those traits that do not change:

1. **Essence.** The essence of a brand is made up of the words that describe its central meaning. Branding Strategy Insider (BSI) calls it "the heart and soul of the brand." BSI quotes Starbucks' essence as "Rewarding every-day moments." Note that the word coffee is not included—Starbucks is not about coffee per se. Yet these three words powerfully describe the Starbucks experience. The Starbucks essence must be rewarding, yet simple and accessible enough to be "everyday." It is a moment rather than an occasion. Hallmark's essence, according to BSI, is "Caring shared"—again elegantly describing what Hallmark, in whatever in-carnation, must always reflect.

2. **Unique selling proposition.** The unique selling proposition (USP) is essen-tially what makes the brand different from any other brand—e.g., "Only this brand . . ." The USP must be distinctive enough to be a discriminating point that has real value to the consumer. Subway may position itself as

the "only fresh fast food"; Contac, the cold remedy, claims uniqueness in its ability to bring relief over a long period of time.

3. **Personality.** The personality is usually built up of adjectives that describe how the brand feels and looks. For example, is the brand fun or serious, easy-going or uptight, conventional or whacky? Clearly, the personality of the brand must be one with which the target consumer wishes to be associated.

4. **Reasons to believe.** These are the "truths" about the brand that make the USP believable. For example, "Dove is the only brand that leaves your skin moist and soft [USP] because it's made with one-third moisturizer [reason to believe]." Subway might point to the fact that every sandwich is made fresh in the store every day as a reason to believe their freshness USP.

The top part of the brand diamond is sacrosanct and theoretically should endure. In every articulation or incarnation, these things must always remain true.

The inverted triangle in this diamond contains the variable aspects of the brand. This half presents more flexibility.

1. **Target consumers.** This is a specific definition of target consumers—not as generic as, for example, "women over 15," but something that describes precisely whom this brand is targeting. Subway might be targeting people who are more health conscious but still busy (hence, fresh fast food); Contac might be targeting cold and flu sufferers, etc.

2. **Emotional benefits.** These are how the brand meets the desires or aspirations of target consumers. How does it make you feel? Does it affect your emotional state (happier, calmer, livelier, or more confident?)

3. **Functional benefits.** Functional benefits are how the brand meets the practical need of target consumers. It's quick, easy to use, makes you smell better, or makes your clothes whiter.

4. **Constraints.** Constraints consist of what the brand should never do or where it should never go. Would McDonald's put a store in a casino? I'm not sure, but with a brand that is all about family, what message would

an adult-centered location send? With these constraints, McDonald's restaurants should be in malls and family entertainment venues.

The bottom half of the diamond has more flexibility, which is the key reason we like this model. One brand may appeal to more than one target market. An architecture of brands can and does exist. Gap Kids is a sub-brand of Gap. It should have exactly the same top half to the diamond (things that must always be true to Gap)—but the bottom half can flex. New consumers = new benefits. When you change the core (the top half of the diamond), you are moving to a new brand.

When you combine the eight small triangles that make up this brand diamond, you have a complete picture of your brand and its relationship with the target consumer.

THE TOTAL MARKETING BRAND MODEL

Branding models like these are valuable—to an extent. The standard brand models stop short because they all filter down to the brand's relationship to the consumer, but they neglect to reflect that brands need to foster relationships and add value to shoppers and retailers. As marketing teams focused their attention on intimate knowledge and relationships with consumers, they neglected to consider how that brand might need to deliver for shoppers and customers. We are not suggesting that shoppers were not thought of (benefits such as value for money or easy-to-find placement are clearly shopper benefits), but by focusing single-mindedly on the consumer and not specifically on the shopper, brands run the risk of not developing strong relationships with these important parties.

Consider a men's fashion brand—one positioned as distinctly "for men." With a brand focused entirely on the consumer (men), the brand could legitimately become very masculine; store environments tuned for "real men." But in many markets, men's clothing is often bought by women; even if the man is present, it is often the wife or girlfriend who drives the shopping process. If the store was too masculine, the guys might love it, but the girlfriend may not be so keen. So there is a need for an integrated brand model that reflects the additional attributes that a brand must have to deliver to shoppers and customers. If the brand doesn't work for all three parties—consumer, shopper, customer—it cannot be fully optimized.

Therefore, while this brand diamond is a great start, it is not the end. Here's the Total Marketing approach to the brand model.

The core brand diamond is still at the heart of this model. Fabulous shopper marketing or great retail relationships are unlikely to deliver much unless the brand works with consumers. Developing brands that deliver for consumers is still at the heart of success for consumer goods companies. However, on the left, we've incorporated a brand model that addresses the needs of the shopper; the right side integrates the target customer's brand needs; and they all fit together in an integrated pyramid rather than a single diamond.

The **shopper pyramid** within this overall model identifies the shopper's needs that are met by this brand and guides the in-store marketing mix that will influence her buying behavior. The top triangle in this pyramid identifies the profile of the target shopper; for example, female shoppers buying shampoo for themselves and their families.

Next, we have the **behavioral change** for this shopper. This covers both the current behavior and the desired change. For the shampoo shopper, let's say we determined she buys a major brand in a one-month supply. The marketer wants her to also buy an equal amount of conditioner every time she purchases her shampoo.

Insight refers to the evidence that drives a belief that this behavioral change is possible. In our conditioner example, perhaps we have data that states that most consumers want to use conditioner but forget to buy it because their shampoo purchases are very habitual. This insight drives the shopper marketing activity that would then be used to act on this insight, to create behavioral change.

The **in-store mix** represents the tools used within the store to influence the desired change. The mix is a combination of availability, communication, and offer (as we'll discuss more thoroughly in Chapter 11, "The Marketing Mix"). Brand *availability* would mean that the conditioner is visible to the shopper, easily accessible (not out of reach), and stocked in quantities equivalent to the shampoo. *Communication* refers to the way the marketing message is delivered in-store—signage or in-store TV being used to send a specific shopper-oriented message to encourage purchase. The *offer* could link the shampoo purchase to the conditioner—e.g., "Buy both and save."

On the opposite side, the **customer pyramid** targets the unique needs of the retailers, and the features and benefits that the brand delivers to them. Why should they promote one product within a category over another? Remember that their goal is not to sell more of a particular product if it merely steals market share from the other brand in the same category. There is a need to demonstrate more "What's in it for me?" than that. Retailers would want to know that more shoppers will buy more product more frequently—this is the heart of a strong customer or retailer proposition.

Target customers are those customers that represent the priority channels for the brand. **Features** are the tangible aspects of the brand. **Advantages** are the product benefits that differentiate this product from others within the category. And **Commercial benefits** answer the question of how the brand will meet the customer's needs. Will it increase category sales?

As with the brand diamond, the top of the brand pyramid is sacrosanct—but the bottom may vary. A brand can work for different retailers and different shoppers in the same way it can work for different target consumers—and each may require different attributes—but we see the top of the pyramid as fixed.

CASE STUDY: CLINIQUE AT THE AIRPORT

Clinique is a premium brand of skincare and cosmetic products, and the company has effectively built the brand's value to the target consumer (women). And in most cases, the consumer and shopper are the same person. But here's an interesting channel challenge: the duty-free shop at the airport. The products in this store already reflect a good value because of the lack of goods and services tax. These stores are configured to make shopping fast and simple, with highly focused inventory—in other words, ideal for a man!

Say you call your wife from the airport and she asks you to pick up a particular Clinique moisturizer at the duty-free shop. You walk in there, tell the salesperson what you want, make the purchase, and head out in about four minutes. That's one shopper. Now if your wife were to have gone into that same store, the salesperson might have suggested other products for her. She would have sampled, sniffed, and smoothed on lotions, perfumes, and elixirs that have functions you can't even fathom. There are different emotional and functional benefits for your wife as the shopper, as compared to yours. Your wife experiences the feeling of pampering herself with a premium product and luxuriates in the opportunity to engage in conversation and a sampling experience. You wanted to get in and get out, so availability was the major attraction. The functional benefit is the immediacy of delivery; you don't have time to mess around. The emotional benefit you get is the reassurance that you are buying the right product at the right price for your wife.

The brand model could be adapted for Clinique to address the male shopper. A marketer might want to get any male shopper to buy a cleanser with a lotion, or a lotion with a perfume. If sales are tracked by gender, the marketer can tell whether he has been successful in influencing that change by the increase in unit sales. The customer (the duty-free shop) needs to recognize opportunity here, too. How much could it increase sales of Clinique products by more actively merchandising to the male shopper buying for the female consumer?

BRANDING FOR THREE CUSTOMERS

When we are building a brand for shoppers, we must recognize that the brand must understand the needs of its target consumers and its target shoppers—even if those people are the same. Taking this step ensures that the functional and emotional benefits for one are differentiated from the functional and emotional benefits of the other, because they each behave differently when given different stimuli. The comprehensive brand model should demonstrate an understanding of how each of the three customers relates to the brand. As such, it is the job of the consumer and shopper marketers to build the brand model. Each group needs to ensure that the needs of its customers are met by the brand.

Taking the time to work through this extended brand pyramid ensures that the marketer can articulate the key characteristics that will drive the brand's success to all of the company's customers. She creates for herself a brand that is built on the needs of her consumer, shopper, and retailer. With such a comprehensive brand model, she has the necessary structure in place to differentiate the brand and influence the shopping behavior she needs for success. This new way of thinking, articulating, and developing brands represents a fundamental shift in the ways consumer goods are marketed. It recognizes that while the consumer is still at the heart of what companies are doing, branding and marketing does not start and finish with the consumer marketing team. The consumer is massively important, but all of our marketing must be integrated and aligned to ensure our brands deliver to three target markets. On paper, it all looks rather simple, but the implications for implementing this in the real world are significant. As Chris Hoyt puts it, "marketing, insight development, customer teams, and agencies each . . . [must] know the rules and work together to achieve a single objective . . . They all know what that objective is, their role, and how they interrelate."[68]

If brands are to change in this way, new insights and data will be required. An intimate knowledge of consumers will no longer suffice; marketers will need to develop an equally intimate knowledge of shoppers and retailers if they are to deliver. Marketing techniques like segmentation, essential to creating a clear definition of a target market, will need to be adapted and adopted in the world of shoppers and customers. The need for alignment and integration will force organizations to adopt different processes and practices; which will in turn require different organizational structures and responsibilities. This new way of marketing will have its own metrics; businesses will need to measure different things in different ways. And managing all of this will add complexity, creating new requirements for technology. This new approach represents a fundamental shift in the way brands are marketed in the consumer goods industry and will have a profound impact on all the individuals working for consumer goods companies, as well as on the relationships these companies have with their retail partners. That is why we call this the Shopper Marketing Revolution.

---

68 Hoyt, discussion.

PART III

THE REVOLUTIONARY'S HANDBOOK

CHAPTER 8

UNDERSTANDING SHOPPERS

At the end of part II, we outlined the significant changes that this new way of marketing will require companies to undertake. In this section we get "down in the weeds" with practical steps and guidance as to what specifically is required and how this can be achieved. We will explore how to decide which outlets should be focused on, what marketing activities should be used, how to invest in retailers, and how to persuade them to support your efforts and collaborate with you. But first, we will explore what lies at the heart of this revolution—shoppers, and how to understand them better.

An opportunity to step out of the discount-led world of modern retailing shimmers on the horizon, but marketers need to understand how to change shoppers' behavior to get there And that requires a really good understanding of how people shop.

Marketing professionals have long understood the value of market research as a way of understanding how consumers think, feel, and act. The purpose is to create an understanding that can be leveraged to create competitive advantage. As early as the 1900s, companies were providing market research services, focusing on understanding media usage and advertising effectiveness. Nielsen, the world's largest market research company, was founded in 1923 (then as AC Nielsen); by the 1930s, Nielsen offered a range of research surveys and products.

Fast-forward to the last few decades and you'll see that the industry has been transformed. The Honomichl Top 50, the authority on the topic, estimated that the top 50 U.S. market research agencies turned over $8 billion in 2010[69]; globally, the number is $33.5 billion[70]. Market research has ballooned from simple surveys of closed "yes or no" questions to encompass myriad techniques. Qualitative approaches use open questions to explore the motivations behind behavior; quantitative techniques ask tighter sets of questions to larger groups of people to find statistically solid evidence of behavior and to predict behavior under new circumstances.

And although the recognition that it is important to understand shoppers is growing, the proportion of that $33.5 billion spent on doing so is still tiny. Given that the scale of the funds thrust into shopper and in-store activities is so large, it seems strange at first that so little money is spent understanding them. In researching for this book, we've struggled to find any data on exactly how much money is spent on shopper research (a fact that is telling in and of itself), but informal discussions over the last few years with research contacts suggest that for many of the big research houses, shopper research represents less than 10 percent of total revenue. Among the clients we work with, a significant majority just embarked or are about to embark on their first bespoke shopper research project. Considering that one of the very first market research products was the Nielsen retail audit—a measure of shopping (what was bought) rather than consumption—it's ironic that today so little effort is put into understanding shoppers.

That's not to say, however, that the shopper research industry is not developing fast. Methodologies have evolved rapidly through adaptations of consumer marketing techniques (interviews, questionnaires, diaries) and through the development of shopper-specific techniques. Shoppers are observed, recorded, tracked, and questioned throughout their shopping journey. They can now be asked to wear special headsets or glasses that track their eye movements and tell researchers what they actually looked at in a store. Shoppers can be invited to visit virtual stores so that researchers can rapidly check how they might respond to different layouts. Neuroscience is applied to understand how the brain is processing data during those few seconds in front of the shelf.

Still, there is a disparity: given the amount of money spent on shopper marketing versus consumer marketing, one would expect significantly more

69 Jack Honomichl, "The Honomichl Top 50 Report of U.S. Marketing Research Firms," June 10, 2010, http://www.marketingpower.com/ResourceLibrary/MarketingNews/Pages/2010/6_30_10/Honomichl_Top_50.aspx?sq=honomichl.

70 http://www.esomar.org/uploads/industry/reports/global-market-research-2012/ESOMAR-GMR-2012_Preview.pdf.

expenditure on shopper research than actually happens. While most leading manufacturers would not dream of launching a new product without exhaustively testing what consumers think, that diligence does not seem to be transferred to activity (and associated expenditure) focused on shoppers.

The reasons behind this are complex and perhaps require a little explaining. The world of shopper marketing (and the need for shopper-specific understanding) is relatively new. In comparison with a consumer marketing discipline that has, in its modern form, been in existence for six decades, the world of shopper marketing is new. This creates natural barriers to investing in something that is "unproven" and means that perhaps shopper research techniques are viewed with more suspicion than the more familiar consumer research methodologies. Shopper research is often perceived as expensive, too—partly due to the complexity of the studies that companies conduct. Shopper research has intricacies that consumer research doesn't (for example, the need to research at stores rather than at a convenient central location). The range of current technology certainly creates a buzz and excitement, but the equipment required for eye-tracking, for example, is not cheap. To test a consumer's response to a new product, little more than a product sample is required, but to test his response to a new store layout, some manufacturers find themselves going to the expense of constructing an entire test store to recreate "reality" in a test environment.

Often, too, those individuals responsible for shopper-related activities in nascent functions are not from a marketing background. In many organizations, responsibility for the activities that take place in stores falls to a trade marketing team, which is typically part of a sales team. Sales leaders may not have exposure to research or believe in its value; most critically, they may not have a budget for research. The abundance of technology and the level of complexity may also be off-putting to (consumer) research managers who are used to more familiar consumer methodologies. Research managers may shy away from techniques seen as "too technical." And, indeed, the fact that often agencies focus on their new "toys" in their pitches may inadvertently contribute to this problem.

The lack of a marketing background or research experience in these individuals leads to what we believe is the biggest and most pernicious reason for the lag in adoption of shopper research approaches. A lot of the research we see is poorly conceived, poorly executed, and badly analyzed, and therefore does not yield value. We'll mention no names, but the vice president for Europe at one major multinational we work with has banned shopper research, calling it "a waste of money." We certainly don't support that position, but we can empathize a great deal!

The lack of quality, in many instances, can be attributed to factors that are diminishing as more and more organizations and individuals gain experience in the world of shopper marketing. However, those factors serve as a warning to any would-be marketer in this space and thus warrant inclusion here. The inexperience of practitioners on the client side is often matched within the agency world. A highly experienced researcher who has little experience in shopper projects can often miss both the obvious and the subtle differences between consumer and shopper research. In some situations, this creates a situation of "the blind leading the blind," and fundamental problems with research structure are not spotted until the data is being analyzed.

In addition, and in part because of this, research briefs are often hopelessly vague or broad. The fact that organizations have little or no existing formal research in the area of shopper marketing encourages them to overreach and try to understand everything at once. In most large consumer goods companies, their understanding of consumers has been built piece by piece through successive studies: periodic usage and attitude studies, interviews around the brand, tracking studies, product concept evaluations, etc. All of these compound to create a much more complete understanding of the consumer than any one study could achieve. It is therefore unrealistic for a company to hope to match that depth with one shopper study, and it is equally disingenuous for research companies to accept briefs that ask for the impossible.

There are many reasons that managers within organizations find themselves unable to persuade their business to invest in shopper research. It would be simple for us to dismiss these as a lost cause—how is it possible to market to anyone without an understanding of that market, after all? The good news is that there is hope. Many actions can be taken to improve understanding of shoppers without spending a fortune, and we shall discuss that towards the end of the chapter. We will also make suggestions about how to persuade others that shopper research can add enormous value. But for now, let us focus on how to ensure that when shopper research is conducted, the investment accrues maximum value.

CONDUCTING GREAT SHOPPER RESEARCH: WHERE TO START, WHAT TO KNOW

This is not designed to be a complete and comprehensive manual on how to conduct shopper research and glean high-value insight. Rather, we have attempted to condense the key factors into one place to help individuals avoid the most common pitfalls and create better results from their research work. The starting point of any research project, any voyage of discovery, is clarity about what it is that we wish to know and how that is valuable to business. Having persuaded the company to back an investment in understanding shoppers, the last thing a marketer wants is the resulting outputs to be low value or generic. Gathering shopper data is relatively easy. Many businesses already have some data, and gathering more is straightforward. There is, therefore, little competitive advantage in data. As little as 20 years ago, organizations had a limited data set to play with, but today's marketer typically has many sources and, from our experience, not much of it is ever used. When commencing an assignment with a client, we usually review the client's existing data. Regularly, clients challenge us later in the project wanting to know where we sourced the data!

Research agencies are fabulous at analyzing data. The experienced ones can turn data upside down and present it in ways that make it easy to digest. But research agencies are not exclusive, and well-presented data is still data. To create real value, you need insight, and insight isn't valuable unless you can implement it. As Chris Hoyt, founder of Hoyt & Company, explains, "Insight is a conclusion based on the facts and findings, based on intensive research. The better the research, the better the insights."[71]

Insight is an overused word. It is also poorly defined. Manufacturers, research houses, and academics each have their own definition of the word, though there are many common themes. An insight is knowledge, deep understanding, inspiration, or revelation. But more than that, it must be actionable. A true insight is a deep truth about something that leads to action. Lisa Klauser, VP of consumer and customer solutions at Unilever, says: "An insight is a penetrating understanding that can lead to a business-building opportunity. A shopper insight focuses on the process that takes place between that first thought the consumer has about purchasing an item, all the way through the selection of that item."[72]

---

71 Hoyt, discussion.
72 Lisa Klauser, "Team Unilever," *The Hub*, accessed March 14, 2013, http://hubmagazine.com/html/2008/may_jun/unilever.html.

How the insight is derived matters not one jot, and in our experience, it is an unquantifiable blend of inspiration and perspiration, but what emerges must be actionable. If there is no "so what," then it is just an interesting fact. A shopper insight is therefore a new understanding of shoppers and how they behave, an understanding that leads to action that will create a new behavior in those shoppers.

So, where to start? What exactly do we need to know about shoppers? The starting point, perversely, isn't even the shopper. In the same way that the path to purchase and our Total Marketing model both start with the consumer, our understanding of the shopper needs to include knowledge of the consumer that the shopper is endeavoring to serve. Once the marketer has clarity about the consumer, he needs to understand the shopper; who she is, what motivates her, and how she behaves. The marketer must know where she shops, what she does when she gets there, what actually happens in-store, and how she interacts with the various stimuli she finds there.

The following list is not exhaustive but serves as an excellent checklist of the types of information a shopper marketer should consider gathering about the consumer, the shopper, the outlet, and the in-store world. We are not recommending that an attempt be made to gather all of this data in one go; nor are we suggesting that this should be necessarily all be gathered via shopper research. Much of this data may already be available within the organization (see the later section on data sources on page 143).

ABOUT THE CONSUMER

- **What opportunities exist to drive additional brand/category consumption?** Ultimately, as argued elsewhere in this book, driving sales that do not lead to additional consumption results in, at best, short-term growth only. A clear understanding of the consumption opportunities creates many advantages. First, it creates focus: by knowing which consumers are being targeted, the question of which shoppers are of interest becomes in principle quite simple—they are the shoppers buying for the consumers we are targeting. Second, by using this as a starting point for research, the chances of the insight, and therefore the resulting actions, being aligned with the actions of consumer marketers increases dramatically. If, for example, the consumer team is focusing on driving penetration among urban teens, a shopper solution that targets the same group is likely to be much more aligned than one targeting pensioners (unless of course the pensioners are purchasing for their teenage grandchildren!). Finally, if these consumption opportunities are quantified, then this can and should be an important input into prioritizing research options and the subsequent activities.

- **How elastic is category consumption?** In other words, if more product is purchased, is more consumed? If the category consumption is highly elastic, then driving additional purchase is more likely to increase consumption (e.g., candy). If not, then driving purchase may merely fill the pantry (e.g., detergent).

- **What occasions exists where a consumer could consume the brand/ category but currently does not?** On which of these occasions would the brand/category have been consumed had it been available at the point of consumption? If consumption is to grow, then the product must be delivered to the point of consumption. Shopping is merely a process of ensuring supply to this point. The more we understand about the consumption need we are targeting (when it occurs, where it occurs), the more likely we are to devise an effective shopper solution that will fuel that consumption. If the consumption occasion occurs in the home, then perhaps targeting shoppers on their regular weekly trip to the supermarket might be appropriate. If the consumption occurs at lunchtime at the workplace, though, the shopping behavior required may be different; perhaps convenience stores near business districts would be more appropriate.

ABOUT THE SHOPPER

- **How do shoppers interpret and articulate the needs and desires of consumers?** The accuracy and specificity of the "brief" that the shopper begins his journey with helps us understand the challenges that might lie ahead as we attempt to influence his behavior. If there is a gap between the consumer's specific needs and the shopper's interpretation of these needs, then opportunities might be missed and investment might be wasted. For example, if the consumer specifically wants Pepsi and Lay's but the shopper is looking for cola and chips, the battle has to be won all over again. If our marketing has successfully persuaded the consumer of the merits of our proposition but that hasn't been transferred to the shopper, the work has to be done again, and the shopper may stray.

- **What are the shopping missions?** Shopping missions are closely aligned to the interpretation of the consumer's need, as explained previously. These missions are a difficult yet important concept for manufacturers to understand. Marketers are often very absorbed in their business, their brands, their categories, and their shoppers, creating a paradigm that is fundamentally different from the world shoppers actually inhabit. Shoppers are often not looking for product categories or brands as marketers articulate them. Pepsi might occupy a category called carbonated soft drinks, but we rarely find that written down on a shopping list. Often the shopper's mission may be "something for dinner" rather than a specific category. Understanding this language and what the shopper might be looking for within this framework is critical to getting inside the head of the shopper. It's also important to check whether you've overinflated the importance of a particular category or brand. To the marketer, it is the most important thing in the world; for a shopper, it is often one of many priorities for that shopping trip.

- **What do shoppers do currently?** By mapping the shopper's current path—what he does, where he does it, how he does it, and what drives that behavior—it becomes possible to understand where in that journey it is necessary, and also possible, to exert influence. Without a clear understanding of the current path to purchase, the ability to exert influence on that journey is obviously diminished.

- **How much can be gained from changing this behavior?** Following on from (hopefully) a quantification of the consumer opportunities, it is important to understand the value that might be accrued by changing shoppers' behavior. Understanding what happens currently, what might happen in the future, how many shoppers would change, and what other purchases would be affected are all critical inputs to this. For research to be an investment rather than a cost and to ensure that future activity yields a return, this analysis is impossible to avoid. Further, given that retailers are likely to look for an economic rationale for implementing the proposed activity, this understanding paves the way for the creation of a motivating story to use with retail partners in the selling process (see Chapter 13, "Motivating Retail Customers").

- **What exactly is the shopper looking for?** Understanding specifically (or broadly, as the case might be) what shoppers are looking for is fundamental in achieving the goal of helping them buy it. It is also critical if the goal is to encourage them to change their purchase behavior. It guides what and where and how they may be influenced. Sunny Delight (see Chapter 4) clearly used an understanding that shoppers were looking for healthy products to develop the strategy of locating the brand in the chiller with juice.

- **What is preventing the shopper from buying what we want them to buy?** If shoppers' behavior is to be changed, then we must understand the barriers to making this happen. If consumers don't like the taste of the product (and the shopper is aware of this fact), high-profile displays aren't going to change their opinion or their behavior. Nor, in most cases, would a 10 percent discount.

- **How urgent is the shopper's need?** Urgency can create fundamentally different decisions. If the shopper perceives that there is no urgency, then he may be more risk averse, choosing to delay purchases of a new or untried brand, or choosing to research further before purchasing.

- **How does your shopper view and define the category of your brand?** Stepping beyond the language of the industry and into the language of the customer is important in any relationship, and the same goes for shopper marketing. Employees of Kimberly-Clark may think they work in "paper goods," but their shoppers buy toilet tissue. More specifically, understanding how shoppers divide products within the category (segment) is also important. Segmentation is a crucial input into how product should be laid out (merchandised) on the shelves. Making it easy for shoppers to find what they want to buy is a core principle of shopper marketing.

ABOUT OUTLETS

- **To which outlets do target shoppers go?** Though this question might at first appear obvious, and relatively easy to answer, that isn't always the case. The sales data an organization already has can give an indication of what is bought where (which is a useful proxy for the number of shoppers), but the subtlety here lies in the word *target*. Just because a store is packed full of shoppers, it doesn't necessarily mean it is also full of the shoppers who are of interest to us. Further, if the primary goal is to persuade shoppers who currently do not purchase the brand or the category to do so, then the presence of current shoppers in that outlet is potentially irrelevant.

- **In which of these outlets could the target shopper be most effectively influenced?** Just because your target shopper is present in a particular outlet or environment does not necessarily mean that she is open to influence. This will vary by outlet, category, and indeed the shopper (and her particular mission). A shopper may be uninterested in switching her cola brand in a convenience store—preferring just to grab and go. That same shopper may be open to switching to a different candy bar in the same outlet within a few seconds of having picked up the cola. Some shopping occasions are so pre-programmed that interrupting shoppers is close to impossible; under other circumstances, shoppers are actively looking for engagement, advice, and input.

- **How does this behavior vary by segment?** Different shopper segments may visit different stores for different reasons (see Chapter 9, "Segmenting Shoppers"). Being able to map shopper segments onto stores allows future shopper marketing activity to be much more focused.

ABOUT THE IN-STORE WORLD

- **Where do shoppers go in the store, and where do they buy?** Understanding where a shopper goes in a store, or on a website for that matter, is fundamental if we are to influence what they do. Rarely do shoppers walk every aisle of even the smallest stores; and shoppers certainly do not visit every page of a website. Therefore, understanding where they go creates an idea of where they can be engaged. The choice is then between taking a message or product to that location or attempting to persuade the shopper to go somewhere else.

- **How does the shopper decide what to buy, and what influences this?** Understanding what the shopper planned for this shopping occasion, what actually happened, and what influenced the shopper lies at the heart of shopper marketing. We have already argued that in a store with perhaps twelve thousand promotions, most of them don't get noticed. As marketers, if we can cut through to really understand which media, which messages, which items, and which locations get noticed, then the opportunity to influence increases, as does the opportunity to stop doing activities that shoppers ignore.

- **What do shoppers actually buy?** Ultimately understanding what, if anything, was purchased in this environment is important—after all, driving purchase is the goal here! A measure of who buys what and where, and whether this departs from their plan, is critical to assessing the effectiveness of the shopping environment being tested.

Clearly, the list of potential findings is large, and it is unlikely that uncovering all of this in one survey would be possible or even desirable. The challenge is therefore to focus research investment on what is most likely to deliver the best return to the business. In our experience, three techniques help shopper marketers in this endeavor: setting objectives, developing hypotheses, and prioritizing hypotheses.

SETTING OBJECTIVES

A client once called, excited to inform us that a budget was allocated to do the company's first piece of shopper research and that he wanted to work with us to make it happen. Our first question was to ask him the purpose, the objective of the research. His response? "To understand shoppers."

With a brief like that, a marketer is guaranteed to be disappointed. Understanding shoppers is, to some extent, an easy aspiration to meet, but to completely understand everything about them? Unlikely. With an objective that broad, the chances of developing useful or beneficial information are slim.

As with most activities, having a clear purpose before commencing will improve enormously the chances of success. Objectives should be focused on a clear business issue or opportunity—perhaps launching a product, driving the growth of a brand, or improving the effectiveness of promotional spend. It is perfectly acceptable to have a number of objectives; indeed, in our experience this is desirable. One study can support multiple insights, and the returns will be higher if the organization can benefit in several ways from the research investment.

The qualities of good research are the same as the qualities of any other objective: *specific*, *measurable*, and *actionable*. Clarity and a lack of ambiguity ensure that everyone is on the same page, including third-party agencies. Measurability ensures that it is possible to judge the effectiveness of the project. And if the objective isn't actionable, there is little point in pursuing it!

DEVELOPING HYPOTHESES

The use of hypotheses has proven to be one of the most useful approaches to gleaning real value from research findings. Yet from our experience, their use is rare to say the least. Perhaps due to ignorance or misunderstanding of how hypotheses help—or, more likely, how they should be used—the majority of research briefs do not contain a clear set of hypotheses. A Google search (nonscientific, we know) for "research brief examples" yields not one example or template recommending the use of hypotheses. Granted, hypotheses are not necessary for all research; some research is, by nature, exploratory. However, far more research, particularly in the shopper space, is not; hypotheses in this type of research can be extremely useful.

The *Oxford English Dictionary* offers two definitions of a hypothesis: first as "a proposition made as a basis for reasoning, without the assumption of its truth," and second as "a supposition made as a starting point for further investigation from known facts." The second definition is largely the way hypotheses are used in commercial market research. In generating insight from research data, hypotheses can often be used more in the way of the first definition, a point covered later in this chapter.

Hypotheses statements, therefore, are suppositions, or predictions, about what we expect as the outcome of the research. In statistical circles, the hypothesis that is a statement of what we expect as a result of the research is often known as the "alternative hypothesis," and is denoted as H_A or H_1. The opposite of this (i.e., the prediction being wrong) is typically known as the "null hypothesis," denoted as H_0. For example, suppose we predict that displaying products on an end cap will drive category penetration. There may be many alternative hypotheses, in which case they are usually numbered (H_1, H_2, H_3, and so on). The primary alternative hypothesis in this case may be phrased something like this:

H_1: "Positioning the brand on an end cap makes new shoppers buy the brand for the first time."

The null hypothesis might be:

H_0: "Positioning the brand on an end cap does not make shoppers buy the brand for the first time."

Hypotheses are incredibly useful in research for a number of reasons. They create clarity about exactly what the research should be able to prove. First, and most obviously, this creates a simple way of holding agencies accountable and ensuring that they deliver the research outcomes the business needs rather than just gathering data. Hypotheses help the agencies design the research, in particular in defining the sample size.

PRIORITIZING USING HYPOTHESES

Most important, however, hypotheses help prioritize research. Formulating a clear statement of the expected outcome (and indeed the alternative outcomes) enables an assessment of the implications of the research and how they might help generate certain business results. By considering the likely results, the marketer can consider the potential value to be accrued from implementation of the findings and consider the likely barriers to implementation that could occur.

A simple case study illuminates this. Some years ago, a company that manufactured alcoholic beverages carried out some research. The research manager wanted to understand the attitudes of the consumers buying in supermarkets (this manager hadn't caught on to the difference between shoppers and consumers at the time); in particular, he wanted their reaction to the temperature of products bought for immediate consumption. The research showed that consumers valued a cold beverage more and may be persuaded to pay more for it. Excited, the research team approached the sales team and the retailers with this fantastic data, only to be pushed back. The operational implications were clear. How would the retailer manage to have the same product at two different prices in the same store? It would require different barcodes—essentially different products—which would mean stocking two separate items, doubling stock holding. It was clear that this was not going to fly. Would a hypothesis have helped? Perhaps there would have been an opportunity to give more consideration to the implications—something they didn't get with the rather woolly research objective "to understand attitudes to price"—if the researcher had formulated a clear hypothesis, such as *Shoppers purchasing for immediate consumption in supermarkets would pay more for a chilled product than an ambient one.*

Hypotheses are built from what is already known about the situation being researched. If nothing or little is known, then exploratory research can be used to help build hypotheses. A qualitative phase of research may be used to frame the hypotheses used in a later quantitative phase. By using the broadest set of inputs, the marketer or research manager ensures not only a better quality hypothesis, but also ensures that the research is not focusing on something that's already known. Most organizations have existing research, and while it might be in the realm of consumer marketing, this data is a great source of existing knowledge. Consumer research often hints at shopper behavior, and many usage and attitude studies include questions about shopping behavior. While this data may not prove or disprove a point, it creates a great starting point, a great hypothesis. Alternative data sources—sales data, scan data from retailers, retail audits, household panels, focus group reports—can be used to discover and subsequently hone a list of hypotheses down to a focused, valuable list of predictions that need to be proven. And while overreliance on the wisdom of experience is dangerous, experience or expertise from your category or other categories can and should be used as inputs to hypotheses. In this way, hypotheses and subsequent research into them can be used to disprove the myths on which businesses often run. An opinion from an experienced manager can be challenged to see if there is any existing data that either supports or disproves it. Research can be used to remove these myths and create new strategies based on fact rather than belief.

The process of hypothesis development has one other benefit: it forces, or at least encourages, a thorough review of secondary data available to the business. There are many potential sources in most organizations (see sidebar). Here we discuss some of the most useful and common ones. Although we strongly endorse thoroughly reviewing secondary data sources, these should also be treated with a degree of caution. Things change quickly, so it's important to ensure that the data is current. There is no absolute benchmark for this, but any data more than a couple of years old should be viewed with caution (though may be excellent for hypothesis building). Understanding the context of the data collection, the sampling technique, and the sample size is also important. One manager told us recently that all the consumers of a certain product bought the product themselves. What is more, the brand manager said that he could prove it and went on to produce a report showing that 100 percent of respondents (consumers) bought the product themselves. We were shocked for a moment, until we checked the sample: "consumers who are the primary purchase decision makers." Suddenly, the data became clear: 100 percent of the consumers were also the shoppers . . . but to qualify to be in the sample, they actually needed to be the purchase decision makers. It was a self-fulfilling prophesy. Anyone who consumed but didn't decide what to buy was excluded from the sample. What had been seen as fact in the business became myth—and became a hypothesis for subsequent research.

Beyond this, sensible checks on the source of the data, its reliability, and the errors inherent in the analysis and the technique should all be checked. Data drawn from secondary research is a great resource, but it should be treated with the same scrutiny as any primary data. With that disclaimer, let's look at some sources of secondary data.

RETAIL AUDITS

Nielsen and GfK are in the business of gathering and selling consumer and shopper data. Together they monitor more than 250,000 households in many countries and maintain technology that collects sales and price data from nearly every major retail chain around the world. Their

SECONDARY DATA SOURCES

Consider these resources for finding potentially valuable information that is already available to you.

- Existing shopper research in your markets, which could be available from a research firm

- Research in other potential markets, also from research firms

- Consumer research, which could contain useful shopper-related questions

- A retail audit, such as those from Nielsen or GfK, that collects data from in-store scanning of product codes and store visits

- Purchase panel data, which can reveal purchasing behavior such as penetration, buying rates, loyalty, purchase frequency, and demographics

- Articles in business newspapers or magazines that may report general trends or insights of local shoppers (do a keyword search)

- Market reports, such as ones obtained from Euromonitor

- Point-of-sale (scan) data from retailers

- Sales data from your team

- In-store audit reports

- Price-monitoring reports

- Internal activity evaluations (e.g., your in-store promotions)

143

research reports can provide general data about behaviors within certain market segments, channels, geographic locations, and shopper groups.

LOYALTY CARD DATA

Encoded loyalty cards contain troves of information about the cardholder or shopper. But the best thing about these loyalty cards is that they track purchases for an individual shopper, enabling the marketer to understand *who* buys over a specific time. It is possible to learn where and how often a particular shopper purchases a specific product, and by cross-referencing this data with what was in-store at the time, it is possible to build hypotheses based on the correlation between in-store stimulus and shopper behavior.

Global marketing firm Dunnhumby, a company owned by Tesco, is very good at interpreting data gathered from loyalty cards. Dunnhumby creates analyses that enable their analysts to predict the behavior of different groups of shoppers in a specific environment. However, data from loyalty cards provides only a narrow window of shopper behavior. Despite the name of the card, shoppers aren't loyal to retailers in that way. So when you are looking at the loyalty card data on shopper behavior for your brand in Tesco, it is important to bear in mind two facts. First, it is not a representative cross-section of shoppers. It is limited to one retailer and limited to those who carry a loyalty card. Second, for those shoppers, it is limited to tracking their behavior in that chain. Data that shows purchases being made every two weeks means that the shopper buys in that chain every two weeks. Whether they purchase at other stores in between is not known but may form the basis of a hypothesis.

PURCHASE PANEL DATA

Research products such as Kantar Worldpanel track the products that enter a household over time. If this is available, it can create a useful basis for understanding which products enter a household, how frequently, and at what price. This is hugely valuable, as it drives penetration, frequency, and weight of purchase data across what is usually a large and representative panel. Again, there are some caveats: The data relies on humans scanning the products they buy, often when they get home. Products such as snacks and beverages may be consumed before they are scanned. And data we have seen suggests that the "pick up" (the percentage of purchases captured) is significantly lower in convenience stores than in supermarkets. The implication is that panel members are more diligent in scanning their major shops, but "top-ups" often get ignored. The last weakness in this data is the inability or inaccuracy in terms of which household member actually purchases. Often this is not tracked, or the data skews towards the main shopper of the household.

ACTIVITY EVALUATION

Every week, marketers put activity in front of shoppers, and those shoppers respond. Retail is a fabulous test ground, but those tests only have value if they are evaluated. Using the resulting patterns of activity creates ample opportunity for hypothesis creation: if the same activity works in Target but not in Walmart (or works less well there), what might be causing that? Is the shopper profile different? These questions can form the basis of a hypothesis.

A great hypothesis drives highly valuable, highly actionable insight. It must be clear, simple, and single-minded. Quality hypotheses avoid multiple elements. A hypothesis such as "Signage and pricing drive trading up" has multiple potential answers and half answers (what about signage on its own?). Consider separating this into two separate hypotheses unless the test is specifically regarding the impact of a combination of two elements— though, even in this case, listing out separate hypotheses in addition to the core one is more informative and less likely to mislead an agency.

Beyond this, a strong hypothesis will be answerable (i.e., the likely response can be articulated), researchable (hopefully your research agency will challenge here), and of course, as stressed earlier, valuable.

MANAGING SHOPPER RESEARCH PROJECTS

With clarity around what insight is desired, a research manager is well placed to take the shopper research project forward. Many of the steps included here are common for any research process, but a number of significant differences exist between consumer research and shopper research that are worth special attention.

The prime differences revolve around the role of the retailer in both conducting the research and implementation of the findings. As will be discussed in greater detail in Chapter 13 ("Motivating Retail Customers"), consumer research findings are primarily used to guide and support decision making within the manufacturer, while shopper research findings from research conducted by a manufacturer need to be used to persuade retailers to support their action. The retailers themselves are more fortunate, being in a position to implement many of their own research findings, but even they may find that cooperation from their suppliers may be required to optimize the returns from their findings.

Given that a significant proportion of shopping trips involve some retail environment, the retailer may also need to be involved in the research process. When trying to understand shoppers, interfacing with them as close to the actual shopping experience as possible is critical. As mentioned in Chapter 6, many shoppers have no idea about the price of an item even a few seconds after purchase, so proximity to the point of action is critical. For researchers, this may mean going to where people shop rather than bringing them to a central location, as is often the case with consumer research. To observe shoppers or question them as they are shopping will require permission from a retailer (at least in physical stores). In some cases, retailers simply refuse; others are happy to comply. Sometimes retailers want guarantees that they will be able to share the data; sometimes they insist on influencing how the research is conducted. In all cases, getting retail permission is important, and it can take time, so allow for that in the research process.

Beyond permission, research also has implications for the recruitment of respondents. Recruiting for consumer research is relatively straightforward, but the total quantity of target shoppers in a particular store needs to be factored into the planning of shopper research. For high-frequency, high-penetration categories (for example, shampoo), recruitment is typically straightforward. But for categories with low frequency or low penetration, recruitment may be challenging. Categories such as air fresheners or light bulbs may have only a few hundred shoppers per day per store—and that's in a large store. If the target of a survey is, say, a segment representing 20 percent of category shoppers and recruitment only picks up about 10 percent of shoppers approached, then a store may yield only two respondents per day. To hit a sample size of 100 would require 50 store days (number of stores multiplied by the number of days), which might take weeks to complete.

PARTNERS FOR RESEARCH

Selecting the appropriate partner for research and briefing them fully can make or break a research project. A quality brief clearly scopes the project, creates transparency around expectations, and forms part of the agency's legal obligations. Constructing a quality brief takes time, but our experience has been that it saves time—and a lot of heartache—in the long run.

The most important elements of a research brief are the objectives and hypotheses, as discussed previously. The brief needs to explain why the research is being done; beyond the research objectives and the hypotheses, you must explain the business situation to ensure that the agency has a clear understanding of the context of the research. The brief should also summarize other research findings to date or be linked to additional research reports. Beyond the hypotheses, other data that must be collected should also be detailed here.

The research brief should also explain the mechanics of the research, such as where and when it needs to take place, when results are required, and the format of those results. Particular attention should be paid to festivals, holiday periods, or seasonality, as each of these may have a big impact on shopping behavior. Stores change at festival times, as do the attitudes and behaviors of shoppers. Unless understanding Christmas shopping behavior is the goal of the research, then researching any time in December or early January is not going to yield anything of value (and, by the way, is unlikely to be sanctioned by a retailer, as this is such a busy time for them). Likewise, if a category tends to be seasonal, the researcher should consider in which season to conduct research. If there is a clear budget, it should be detailed, as should any suggested or mandatory methodologies. It's often tempting to leave this up to the agency, but if results need to be compared or contrasted with other data (e.g., in other categories, channels, or markets), then using similar methodologies may be mandatory. Which shoppers and which stores must be clear.

In selecting the right partner, experience is paramount: the depth of experience in shopper marketing, the category (or similar categories), and desired methodologies. It is important to beware, in these formative years of shopper marketing and research, that while the agency itself may have conducted a particular type of research, the team in your country may not have, and therefore the quality and experience of that team should also be considered. As proposals are evaluated, consider whether the proposal actually responds to the brief or is largely generic. Finally, do a sense-check—does the agency have credibility within your business and the market in general, including with retailers? Without credibility, using the outputs becomes that much harder.

Once the project is underway, the agency should drive much of the activity, but the shopper marketer cannot leave it in the agency's hands entirely. It is her responsibility to keep the project on schedule and ensure that fieldwork can take place in stores. Rarely can the agency help much here.

The market research firm will need to build a questionnaire that outlines the questions to ask the shoppers. The questionnaire is the basis for collecting required data. If the right questions are not asked or the respondents don't interpret the question in the way it was intended, the responses will be of low value.

While it might be tempting to assume that designing a research questionnaire or discussion guide is something that an agency can easily manage, our experience suggests otherwise. Questionnaires are often badly conceived, with poor questions or sometimes the wrong questions. It is not the responsibility of the marketer to develop the questionnaire, but she will be held accountable for its outputs, so diligence here pays back—and once the fieldwork is over, it's too late to make changes.

To gain qualitative data, the questions should be open-ended, not satisfied with a yes-or-no answer. The goal with this research is to explore the in-depth aspects of a particular issue. To get the full value of the survey, questions should be phrased so that respondents are encouraged to explain their answers and reactions. For example, "Why did you decide to come shopping at this store today?" Follow-up questions should be used to probe further.

When reviewing the questions, consider what kind of results will be obtained from the responses. How useful will the answer be? If it's not useful, is this because of the way the question is phrased or because the question adds no real value to your objectives?

We also recommend asking the agency to prepare a spreadsheet that will show you how each question connects to the research objectives and hypotheses outlined in the brief. Use this as a checklist to ensure that the full scope of the objectives is addressed in the questionnaire and to identify any questions that are potentially of low value. In our experience, the quantity of questions desired far outstrips the time available to ask them. Shoppers will often not want to stop for too long, and the duration of

ELEVEN MISTAKES TO AVOID IN SURVEY QUESTIONS

To make the questionnaire as useful as possible, invest enough time to get each question right. Here are 11 things to avoid when phrasing questions.

1. **Double negatives.** Think positively. Don't ask: "Without a discount coupon, would you still not buy this brand?" Do ask: "Would you buy this brand if you had a discount coupon?"

2. **Double-barreled questions.** Give respondents one question at a time. For example, don't ask, "Can you remember the pack size and price of the product you bought in your last shopping trip?" Break this into two questions.

3. **Conjunctions.** Similarly, don't pack two separate thoughts into one question, such as "Do you like shopping in supermarkets and convenience stores?" Separating the two thoughts into individual questions allows for a clearer analysis of the responses.

4. **Jumping ahead.** When posing a question such as "What will you buy from this store next week?", the implication is that the respondent will be coming to shop in this particular store next week. First asking, "Would you come shopping here next week?" and then following up will create a more reliable answer.

5. **Leading the witness.** The goal is to gather honest responses. Pushing thoughts into the minds of respondents reduces the chances of this happening. Rather than posing a thinly veiled statement, like "You will buy this brand whenever it is on promotion, correct?" try phrasing it without the not-so-subtle lead: "Would you buy this brand if it were on promotion?"

6. **Overly general questions.** To get the most relevant and specific responses, avoid generic questions such as "Do you like shopping at this store?" At the very least, consider follow-up questions such as "What is it about this store that adds to your enjoyment of shopping here?"

7. **Difficult, confusing, or unfamiliar words or frames of reference.** Words and phrases that could be hard to understand (e.g., industry-specific jargon or acronyms) or subject to personal interpretation by respondents should be avoided.

8. **Long sentences.** Questions should be kept simple so that the respondent does not get lost in a tangle of words.

9. **Extreme words.** Terms like *always* and *all* are very broad, so don't ask questions such as "Do you always buy all of your products from this store?" Instead, questions should ask for specifics, such as purchase frequency of products this shopper buys.

10. **Halo effects.** Respondents tend to answer questions based on their perception of what is generally accepted practice. If you ask, "Do you agree that unhealthy products should not be advertised to children?" who is going to answer no?

11. **Implicit alternatives.** If you asked a respondent, "Would you prefer not to wait in the checkout line?" most would answer yes. But if you phrased it differently, you will gather more valuable information—for example, "Which of these would you prefer more: (A) Waiting in the checkout line, or (B) Using instant payment shopping carts but paying a small premium on the products bought?"

the questionnaire needs to fit with this. Ask questions for too long, and there's a danger that shoppers will not complete the questionnaire or will rush through questions without giving due consideration to the answers. There is no hard-and-fast rule as to duration, but it appears to depend, in part, on the type of shopping trip. On a quick trip to a convenience store on the way to the office, where the shopping trip takes no more than two minutes, it is unlikely that a respondent would submit to more than five minutes of questioning. In a furniture store, as part of an hour-long trip (and without kids), a respondent may well be happy to contribute for up to 30 minutes. In either case, an understanding of how each question relates to the research objectives and hypotheses makes the process of editing the questionnaire significantly easier.

CONVERTING DATA INTO INSIGHT

Typically, the agency will present its findings once the fieldwork is completed. Almost always, there will be questions leading to follow up and perhaps a second presentation. The job is not completed here, unfortunately. Now, what the agency has presented must be converted into that valuable insight.

Agencies can be insightful. Unfortunately, in many cases, their lack of understanding of the industry leads to impractical solutions and a lot of great insights left undiscovered. The biggest job of the shopper marketer kicks in once the agency has left (hopefully leaving the data tables and raw data behind them)—she must now generate insight.

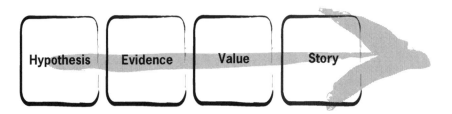

The process of developing insight starts with a familiar concept: a set of hypotheses. These hypotheses may be the same as those researched, or they may be new ones resulting from the research. For each hypothesis, evidence is gathered to support (or disprove) it. The evidence should be gathered from all available data sources. As evidence is gathered, more hypotheses will be created; each new question or assumption becomes a new hypothesis. In this way, the insight process becomes a journey of discovery, of hypothesis-based questions and evidence-based responses. Insights are formed by looking at data again and again from different points of view.

The next step is to clarify the value of the insights. To the company or retail partners, how big is the prize for implementing each one? In this way, the various insights can be prioritized in much the same way that hypotheses were prioritized earlier in the process.

The final step of the insight process is to create the insight story: the narrative that will be used to persuade both the company and any retail partners to support the initiative. The story contains much of the information garnered already through the process: the size of the prize, the insight and data that supports it, the result of the activity being implemented, and a clear description of what must be done to ensure that the prize is realized.

NO RESEARCH, NO INSIGHT?

Although we are massive advocates for researching shoppers, we recognize that not every marketer in every business has the opportunity to conduct studies of this nature. Fear not: that does not mean insight cannot be created. And the process for creating insight from any source is comprised of exactly the same steps: beginning with hypotheses and ending

THE RECIPE FOR AN INSIGHT STORY

- The size of the prize
- Why should the retailer listen?
- What will be the impact on their big issues (usually sales or profit)?
- The insight
- What are the consumer and shopper issues?
- Why should they believe in the opportunity?
- The expected results
- What will be the impact on the retailer's sales, profitability, share, and operations?
- What needs to be done?
- What will the company do to support the initiative?
- What must the retailer commit to?

in a story. In many ways, the process is easier without a full research initiative, as there is less data to churn through. What is important is to work secondary data really hard, and include any supporting evidence that can be found. Without a research budget, evaluating activities becomes even more important: observing and spending time in stores and finding cheap or easy ways to gain even a little data. In-store staff, merchandisers, and students can all be used to gain some basic knowledge and to survey stores—perhaps not leading to the same level of science as a full bespoke study but significantly better than what companies are doing now, which is making decisions with no data at all!

CHAPTER 9

. . . .

SEGMENTING SHOPPERS

. . . .

Segmentation of customers is arguably the most fundamental concept in marketing. Without segmentation, it is not possible to target; without targeting, positioning will be generic. Dr. Philip Kotler calls this process of segmentation, targeting, and positioning "the essence of strategic marketing."[73] The recognition that all of a company's customers and potential customers are not the same marks the move from broad mass marketing (Kotler quotes Henry Ford, the father of mass production, speaking of the Model T: "You can have any color, as long as it's black") toward target marketing. How many cars would Ford sell today if they were all the same? The vast differentiation of product seen in every category in every store is testament to this principle of marketing. Markets are not homogeneous: if they were, why would companies like Procter & Gamble have more than one detergent brand? People are different in many ways, and therefore if one particular brand is going to "win" with a particular customer, it needs to meet the needs of that customer better than any other product. Consumers are heterogeneous—each one of us is different. Clearly, creating individual products for each customer is a tricky proposition for most companies; segmentation is the compromise between unique products and mass markets. To work for an organization, a segment must be sizeable enough, or at least have enough potential, to make marketing the product to them cost-effective and ultimately profitable.

---

73 Phlip Kotler, *Marketing Management: Analysis, Planning, Implementation, and Control* (Englewood Cliffs, NJ: Prentice Hall, 1994).

Segmentation is defined as the division of a market into differentiated homogeneous groups. Segmentation gives companies the opportunity to place a different marketing mix before each segment and tailoring it to match a segment's needs more perfectly than a generic approach and better than any competitor. In any circumstance, there are many ways to segment; but for a segment to have any value, it must be measurable, reachable, substantial, and profitable. From a marketing point of view, there is a further consideration: it should respond differently to a particular marketing mix. If the response in one segment is precisely the same as in another, then for the purpose of this situation (i.e., marketing to them), the differences are irrelevant. We will come back to this final point later in this chapter.

Given how fundamental segmentation is to marketing, it is somewhat surprising that it was as late as 1956 that Wendell R. Smith, an American professor in marketing, first introduced the concept. If, as the Chartered Institute of Marketing in the United Kingdom insists, marketing is defined as "the management process responsible for identifying, anticipating, and satisfying customer requirements profitably,"[74] then marketing without segmentation is possible only when the entire market has the same need. When Henry Ford invented the motorcar, the needs of the population (in relation to motorcars) were pretty homogenous. But as the market developed, that was clearly no longer the case. The same happens in all markets as they develop.

Whatever its beginnings, the need for and the application of segmentation has grown rapidly in the intervening years, driven by many factors. Market maturation drives the need for less obvious growth opportunities, forcing marketers to dig deeper to find new gaps. The nationalization and then globalization of markets create a scale by which a relatively small segment in share terms can still be sizeable. The creation of mass media, somewhat ironically, made marketing to small niches much more possible, as did the fragmentation of media discussed in previous chapters. Fragmentation allows for targeting, which makes it possible to focus media dollars on a specific group of consumers. The Internet takes this further, reducing the cost of access to markets. Niches that may have been small on a regional scale have become significant, and therefore viable as segments, on a national or global scale; the Internet makes influencing them cheaper and easier.

In broader marketing circles, the benefits of segmentation are widely

---

74 The Chartered Institute of Marketing, *Marketing and the 7 Ps: A Brief Summary of Marketing and How It Works*, accessed March 14, 2013, http://www.cim.co.uk/files/7ps.pdf.

accepted. Segmentation allows companies to understand, and then better meet, the needs of their customers. With effective marketing, this will clearly lead to sales growth. It can also lead to higher loyalty, because the customer feels a closer bond with brands that seem to understand his needs. Profitability can be enhanced by focusing product design only on features that the customer values, designing out superfluous and potentially costly features, and focusing marketing communication on media that works for a particular market rather than having to rely on expensive "catch-all" campaigns.

Segmentation can help create new growth opportunities, both by trading people up to higher-value offers and by using lower-value offers to entice customers locked out with current products. Segmentation helped Coca-Cola identify the need for Diet Coke (or Coke Light) by understanding that there was a group of consumers who were put off by Coke's sugar content and later the need for Coke Zero by identifying a group of consumers who were health conscious but for whom Coke Light was "too feminine."

Segmentation allows for targeting, and that allows you to create a more effective marketing mix by closely matching your offer with what the target wants. This also drives massive improvements in efficiency. Marketing efforts can be focused on a smaller group of individuals, reducing waste. In the world of consumer goods, media can be focused on the channels used by the target segment or on the shows they watch.

SEGMENTING SHOPPERS

As argued previously, segmentation is indisputably of high value to the marketer as a way of understanding how a large, heterogeneous group of consumers can be split into smaller homogeneous groups, against which we can leverage a more targeted marketing mix. This, in turn, creates the opportunity for our marketing to be both more effective and more efficient. The application of this thinking has fueled the growth of consumer goods companies for 50 years: as growth slows, as profits are threatened, and as more and more spend is piled into inefficient (and often ineffective) in-store activity, it is not surprising that leading companies, both manufacturers and retailers, are looking to apply similar techniques to shoppers. Indeed, we would argue that this is essential and that the application of effective segmentation is one of the key differentiators between shopper marketing and what went before it—what we call largely indiscriminate activity. Our definition of shopper marketing deliberately talks about changing the behavior of the *target* shopper, and it is not possible, as Doctor Kotler argues, to target without first segmenting.

To create value from shopper segmentation, an appropriate segmentation must be constructed first. Each segment must then be evaluated and prioritized. From there, clear objectives can be set, against which strategies and plans can be created.

HIGH-VALUE SEGMENTATIONS

For a segmentation to create value, it must satisfy a number of criteria. It must be:

- **Measurable:** The segment must be identifiable using criteria or characteristics that can be measured (at a justifiable cost).

- **Sizeable:** The segment must be large enough to represent a significant sales or profit opportunity. Over-segmenting can create very clear, differentiated groupings, but if the value they represent is unlikely to deliver a return, then combining segments should be considered.

- **Homogeneous:** All members of the segment should be the same or similar across a clear set of criteria.

- **Differentiated:** The segment must be clearly different from the rest of the population across one or more clear, measurable criteria or characteristics.

- **Actionable:** It must be possible to approach each segment with a particular marketing mix and elicit a positive or desirable response from it—one that is different from the response you'd get from the general population.

In recent years, there has been a rush of shopper-segmentation models. Research agencies, looking to find a common approach to analyzing their clients' data, have created their own shopper-segmentation models. For example, Ipsos has developed a segmentation model that it uses globally to analyze data. The model identifies five shopper segments: "Brand Lovers," who spend money on expensive brands and are more likely to value convenience; "Price Driven" shoppers, who are more likely to make shopping lists, compare prices, and go to discount stores; "Indulgents," who are more impulsive, love new things, have great taste, and will typically pay more for brands; "Responsible Planners," who have a fixed budget, compare prices, often shop online, and have changed their habits to shop in a sustainable way; and "Bargain Hunters," who hunt for deals, are not necessarily constrained by price, are often impulsive, and are less likely to buy online. Marketing agencies, too, have their models. G2/Grey, part of WPP, identified four key shopper segments in Asia: "Loyal Listers," "Whim Indulgers," "Engaged Info Seekers," and "Passive Value Fans." According to Grey, 44 percent of Japanese shoppers are "Whim Indulgers," to whom shopping is an unplanned adventure.

Manufacturers, too, have developed their own models (Coca-Cola launched a global shopper-segmentation model in 2008), but retailers, with their huge databases of shopper transaction data, have arguably made the most effort in the shopper-segmentation area. According to Deloitte, "all leading retailers (e.g., Safeway, Walmart, Kroger, Sam's, CVS, Best Buy) use segmentation models to understand the different types of customers that they are targeting, and develop strategies to appeal to them." Ahold, a Dutch international retailer, segments shoppers into six different classifications: "Urban Seekers," "Traditionalists," "Quick Fixers," "Good Lifers," "Deserving Diners," and "Budgeters."[75]

Standard segmentation models have many upsides—they create a common language throughout an organization and, in particular, between manufacturers and retailers. Manufacturers who do not understand how their retail customers look at shoppers will increasingly find it difficult to gain traction for their initiatives. They create significant levels of efficiency, too, and avoid the need to crunch data through multiple statistical models to find new segmentations. The difficulty, however, with all of these segmentation models lies in exactly how to apply them. Shoppers do not typically behave consistently. As Herb Sorensen puts it, "A great deal of segmentation is misguided, because shoppers move from segment to segment with disturbing regularity."[76] Someone who is highly planned in one category may be impulsive in the next; brand loyal on a Saturday but buying a competitor on a Monday. It is difficult to understand what a

75 Chris Hoyt, "Chain Reaction," *The Hub*, July/August 2007, http://hubmagazine.com/archives/the_hub/2007/jul_aug/the_hub19_hoyt.pdf.
76 Sorensen, discussion.

manufacturer of floor cleaners would do with the knowledge that 44 percent of Japanese shoppers are "Whim Indulgers." These models are useful and are a step forward from thinking in terms of a homogeneous, generic shopper; unfortunately, standardized models rarely create competitive advantage. If marketing guru Michael Porter is correct that "the greatest opportunity for creating competitive advantage often comes from new ways of segmenting, because a firm can meet true buyer needs better than competitors or improve its relative cost position," then relying on a standard model created by an agency or using a model that was designed to support another organization's competitive advantage is perhaps not the best idea.

There are many segmentation options available to the shopper marketer—the challenge is to find which ones are most useful and valuable. In our experience, this requires a fair amount of trial and error, but the rewards are high. After all, it is from effective segmentation that true insights can be gleaned. Segmentation is merely a grouping—real advantage comes from selecting the right grouping. In a focus group for cookies many years ago, respondents were asked to sort products as they saw fit (a simple but effective segmentation exercise). The respondents grouped the products not by ingredients or flavor or what they were used for but by the color of the packaging. To be fair, that *is* a segmentation—just perhaps not the most useful one!

The most commonly used segmentations fall into three categories based on the shopper's profile, behavior, and psychographics or attitudes. *Profile* includes demographics, socioeconomic class, or where the person lives and shops. *Behavior* covers the person's shopping behavior (including where she shops) and the consumption behavior of the consumer whom the shopper is servicing. It may also include other marketing-related behaviors, such as media consumption, technology usage, or vehicle ownership. *Psychographics and attitudes* covers the shopper's general lifestyle and attitude, her attitude to shopping, the brand, or the category in question, or her needs and mission as a shopper.

Segmentations are built up by overlaying a number of differentiators. There is no golden rule; however, the following differentiators, in our experience, have typically yielded high value:

- **Demography-based:** This approach segments shoppers based on their demographic profile, such as their age, gender, marital status, educational background, or household income. While demographic segmentations are commonplace, they can be extremely useful. Presentations from research agencies will often cut data by age group or socioeconomic class, but these steps are often skipped in shopper work. In the kids' milk category, we found that educational level was a valuable segmentation—those with a high level of education appreciated and understood the complex information on a pack, while those with a lower level of education could not.

- **Geography-based:** Where people live and shop can be important differentiators. In a coffee study we worked on, there was a significant difference in behavior between shoppers who lived in more rural areas and those who lived in urban areas, even though they shopped in the same out-of-town hypermarkets. Hypermarket shoppers were segmented and targeted with different activities on this basis.

- **Consumption opportunity–based:** This is one of the most powerful segmentations available. Too often data refers to the behavior of a generic shopper; however, brand growth comes from the shoppers who can unlock additional consumption. If the identified consumption opportunity is to encourage switching from a competitor brand, then segmenting based on the brand currently bought may be useful. If the consumption opportunity is based on driving on-the-go consumption, then segmenting based on those buying for now versus later may be valuable. If the key purpose of segmentation is to isolate data about the most valuable group of shoppers, then using the consumption opportunity to segment is often very powerful.

- **Barrier-based:** Segmenting shoppers based on the reasons they do not buy can be extremely powerful. When you understand the reasons they passed up your product, the solution often becomes clear. This segmentation approach saved a client of ours millions in wasted distribution costs (see Chapter 5).

- **Channel- or retailer-based:** Segmenting shoppers based on the channel or retailer they shop in has many benefits. The insights from this type of segmentation are simple to apply, since the entire segment can be targeted through the corresponding channel. And because retailers will wish to see data based on their shoppers, it's likely that data would need to be analyzed at this level anyway. Shopping behavior typically varies dramatically by channel, so analyzing data based on this segmentation should be considered mandatory.

- **Mission-based:** Different shoppers come to stores with different missions; segmenting based on these criteria often yields interesting results. Shoppers looking for one item may respond very differently to those completing an entire grocery store trip, for example. Shoppers looking to buy an entire meal may respond to meal solutions, whereas these may be less effective for shoppers searching for one item for the cupboard. Separating shoppers based on whether they have a purchase plan (for a product, a brand, or a category) often creates very different marketing challenges, as does separating those who are buying for themselves from those buying for someone else. For a beverage manufacturer, introducing a new product via wet sampling (i.e., providing the product ready to drink in the store rather than in a packet) is likely to be more effective if the shopper is the consumer than if the consumer is not the shopper.

- **Hypothesis-based:** As stressed in the preceding chapter, carefully structured research objectives and hypotheses improve the value of research outputs considerably. In addition, each hypothesis becomes a potential segmentation. For example, a hypothesis that point-of-sale material did not affect brand switchers suggests segmenting shoppers based on whether they switched brands. A hypothesis that the consumer is always the shopper may lead to a segmentation of shoppers who also consume the product versus those who do not.

All of these factors may be elements in a segmentation; multiple factors are often used to create meaningful and valuable segments that can then be targeted.

Typically, these factors can be analyzed individually using spreadsheets or databases; using cluster analysis, you can create discrete segments based on a number of differentiators relatively easily.

PRIORITIZING SHOPPER SEGMENTS

The prioritization of shopper segments is done by understanding the potential value that the segment represents and the relative ease or difficulty of realizing that potential. The segments at the top of your list should be those that represent the biggest opportunity and are relatively easy to influence. Large opportunities that are harder to influence should be the second priority.

Shopper segmentations create a new way of looking at data and, if completed correctly, create a clearer way to see the potential value of each segment to the manufacturer. This is most easily done when the segmentation itself is actionable (one of the previous segmentation criteria). One of the reasons marketers get frustrated with standard segmentation models is that they are not always actionable: by tailoring the segmentation using some of the differentiators suggested here, the segments will be tuned to the brand or the category in question, making potential action (and therefore valuation) easier. For example, we helped a cooktop supplier segment shoppers based on their attitude to the brand. A simple analysis helped us understand shoppers who preferred one brand over another, and those who might at least consider buying a particular brand versus those who would never consider buying it. The data was quantitative, so it was simple to understand the potential value of converting sales, but the segmentation also helped us understand the relative ease or difficulty of that conversion (it would be far simpler to convert a shopper who already preferred the brand than one who was not aware of it). In this particular case, the brand was failing to convert even shoppers who were considering it; therefore, we agreed to prioritize shoppers who already preferred or considered the brand, and the rest would be de-prioritized. If the brand could barely convert someone who was actively considering it into a buyer, what chance was there to convert a shopper who rejected or did not consider the brand? With a clearer vision of the target shopper now in place, further segmentations could be made, focusing just on these shoppers rather than looking at all shoppers. Shoppers were segmented based on how they shopped and how they gathered information, and this was analyzed by channel to create more effective in-store communications tuned to the target shoppers. We found that while 24 percent of total shoppers consulted in-store staff, this number leapt to 41 percent for the target group, a significant shift in the importance of this in-store tactic.

In valuing a segment, it is important to consider the long-term and the short-term value of the desired behavior. The value of creating one purchase is significantly lower than the value of changing long-term behavior. Again, understanding the consumption behavior behind the shopping trip is critical in this valuation. Shopping behavior that creates additional consumption is of high value; if it only creates stock in a cupboard at home, then its value is lower. It is impossible to value shopping behavior accurately without fully understanding the consumer behind the shopper; therefore, any shopper-segmentation model that does not include this differentiator is harder to prioritize.

This is one reason we assert that manufacturers should not rely solely on retailer segmentation models. Retail models care little for consumption. Consider the Ahold segmentation model mentioned previously, which segments shoppers into these groups: "Urban Seekers," "Traditionalists," "Quick Fixers," "Good Lifers," "Deserving Diners," and "Budgeters." These segments don't give any clue as to the potential value of the shopper to the manufacturer. Retail models should not be used to drive a brand's shopper strategy; rather, they should be used in selling and executing. Referring to the Ahold model again, understanding how many of a target group were "Traditionalists" may help target activity at a tactical level (and using this language would be sure to impress Ahold, too!).

The potential value of a segment can, therefore, be calculated by understanding the value of its members' current behavior and the value of their future or desired behavior. To calculate the real value this represents, the research sample needs to be mapped against the total population that it represents. This allows a marketer to quantify in dollar terms, which is essential for calculating a return on investment.

The other dimension of the prioritization is to consider how easy or difficult it might be to realize an opportunity for a given segment. This cannot be calculated in a purely quantitative way; however, the following factors should be considered:

- **The scale of the barriers.** The bigger the barriers, the harder it will be to create the desired behavior. Quantification of this can only be done based on either previous activity or experimentation in a test environment. For example, if a barrier is linked to perceived taste, then data from previous sampling (how many shoppers with a negative taste perception were converted) might help. Unfortunately, the data would also need to be segmented in the same way (only shoppers with a negative taste perception would be of interest), but at least it might give a directional indication, or an additional test could be set up subsequently. As a rule of thumb, barriers based on personal experience tend to be harder to overcome than those based on word of mouth. A shopper who knows that they do not like the taste of the product is likely to be harder to persuade than one who merely perceives this.

- **Strategic fit.** Opportunities that require a significant strategic shift will be harder to realize than those that do not. In the coffee case discussed in Chapter 5, the biggest opportunity was with the segment of shoppers who rejected the brand. These shoppers were aware of the brand, understood it, but rejected it. Winning them over would potentially require a significant strategic shift and could risk alienating current shoppers and consumers.

- **Channel fit.** Shopper segments that require entry into new channels will typically be harder to influence.

- **Shopper versus consumer.** A shift in shopping behavior is generally easier to achieve if the consumer is present at the point of purchase. Certainly, if the consumer is an important part of the decision-making process, then influencing a change in behavior is much harder when the consumer isn't present. This is particularly true for new products or to generate trial for existing products.

- **Retail strategy fit.** If the shopper segment is not important to the key retailers, then implementation may be more difficult. This is not a reason to reject the opportunity; it merely makes it harder. Easier opportunities should be prioritized.

With clarity on which shopper segments are to be prioritized, it is possible to develop objectives and use them as an input to channel prioritization (see the next chapter) and to creating shopper strategies and tactics. These objectives should describe the behavioral change required and should be quantified, as in this example: "To convert 26 percent of moms planning to buy our brand into actual buyers, every month from July 2012." This creates real clarity for the rest of the organization as to what must be achieved and should ensure that any activity is focused on this specific goal.

CHAPTER 10

FROM BRICKS TO CLICKS:
THE CHANGING WORLD OF RETAIL AND HOW TO PRIORITIZE CHANNELS

Regardless of you the vehicle you use, when you've segmented shoppers correctly, you will have identified the groups of people most likely to help drive consumption. Clear shopper segmentation enables you to define exactly which shoppers buy your brand now and which of these can be encouraged to spend more or buy more often. And it helps you identify who *doesn't* buy your brand and what stops them from doing so. At the end of this part of the process, you'll have a clear view of which groups to prioritize, what you want them to do, and how much your business might grow from encouraging this behavioral change.

In order to realize these opportunities, you need to encourage actual behavioral change. You need to get your shoppers to do something differently. As we've seen in our analysis of the path to purchase, we can encourage people to do things differently along the entire shopping journey. We know that the messages shoppers receive passively through traditional advertising and communication channels can have a significant impact on the decisions they make. But shopper marketing comes into play when shoppers are actively engaged in the process of shopping. To date, the industry has placed the bulk of its attention on the physical environments where this engagement happens: the millions of shops around the world where the vast majority of goods are bought. But the dawn of the age of the shopper coincides with the explosion of virtual environments, all of which shoppers can also engage with. Global, twenty-first-century shopper marketers need to understand clicks *and* bricks, as well as their importance to their target shoppers and the opportunities they represent, and therefore, where they should invest their time, effort, and money to change behavior.

In this chapter, we'll explore how to segment these environments into shopping channels effectively, how to prioritize these channels, and what you need to consider as the physical and virtual worlds become more intertwined and future technology influences the decisions we make.

MILLIONS OF ENVIRONMENTS—A WORLD OF DIFFERENCE

The world is full of stores. There are simply millions of them—so many in fact that nobody really knows how many there are. We know that retail, in all its shapes and forms, is probably the biggest employer on the planet. In 2010, Walmart employed 2.1 million people—the third-largest employer after the U.S. Department of Defense and the Chinese army.[77] We estimate that the world's top 10 retailers employ over 4.5 million people—but this just scratches the surface. Nielsen estimated in 2010 that there were over 13.3 million outlets selling packaged consumer products in Asia Pacific alone, 13.1 million of which were independently owned retail stores.[78] This excludes clothing stores, consumer electronics stores, and bookstores; and given that expenditure on apparel and other consumer goods (home furnishings, personal care, and tobacco) in the United States largely matches expenditure on food in the home,[79] these outlets could potentially account for at least two of every five stores. We know that from the heights of the Himalayas to the heart of the Sahara, there is no corner of the populated world where you can't find retail outlets of some form or another. If we simply extrapolate Nielsen's estimate using population as a guide, we could easily assume that there are over 40 million shops in the world selling consumer goods.

And that's just physical shops! What about online? It's still too early to gather the statistics, and without the need for a physical infrastructure,

---

77 Matthew Bishop, "The Great Mismatch," *The Economist*, September 10, 2011, http://www.economist.com/node/21528433.

78 Nielsen, *Retail and Shopper Trends Asia Pacific 2010*, August 2010, accessed March 7, 2013, http://hk.nielsen.com/documents/APACRetailandShopperTrendsReport2010.pdf.

79 US Bureau of Labor Statistics, "Consumer Expenditures in 2010," August 2012, accessed March 7, 2013, http://www.bls.gov/cex/csxann10.pdf.

online traders can open and shut every minute. According to comScore, Inc., a source for digital business analytics, U.S. shoppers spent $256 billion online in 2011.[80] What's true today, though, is that with nearly 25 percent of the world's population connected to the Internet and with nearly two-thirds of the population owning a mobile phone,[81] the opportunity for shoppers to engage with online environments is quite literally in their pockets.

Here's the thing, though—all these environments have one thing in common: they are all completely unique. Not one store is identical to another; even outlets that look similar serve a slightly different micro-community. They all have tiny variations in configuration and slightly different products available. This massive diversity in outlets makes retail remarkable. Ask a Western shopper to describe a store and the first he'll describe might be a drugstore, a hypermarket, or a supermarket. Then he might talk about a clothes shop, an electronics retailer, a health food shop, or if he's from the UK like us, a corner shop. But an African shopper or Asian shopper will describe an entirely different set of outlets.

Shoppers in the Philippines will immediately talk about *sarisari* stores, which literally consist of a little hole in a wall that is covered with bars and features a slot just about big enough to fit a shoebox through. Behind that slot, you'll find a tiny shop. A sarisari generally stocks cigarettes, alcohol, shampoo, soap, toothpaste, and maybe rice—but not much more than that. It is about the smallest type of outlet we've ever come across, but some estimates suggest there might be around fifty thousand in the city of Manila alone.

Travel to India and you'll find hundreds of thousands of *kirana* stores where groceries and everyday goods are sold from behind a counter. These stores often offer local shoppers the opportunity to buy on credit to help make ends meet. In Taiwan, the convenience store is ubiquitous, with a Family Mart or 7-Eleven on almost every street—and more than one on many! Go to Nigeria and you'll find "sitting" wholesalers, whose stalls in traditional markets not only sell goods to passing shoppers but are also the main source of supply for nearby retailers.

In today's world, it's inconceivable to manage this complexity on an outlet-by-outlet basis. Imagine trying to configure the perfect blend of availability, communication, and offer precisely tailored for each individual shop—today this is impossible. Try to persuade a sales team that they need

80 comScore, *2012 U.S. Digital Future in Focus*, accessed February 28, 2013, http://www.comscore. com/Insights/Presentations_and_Whitepapers/2012/2012_US_Digital_Future_in_Focus.
81 Jim Lecinski, *Winning the Zero Moment of Truth* (Mountain View, CA: Google, 2011).

to vary everything they do for every store—impossible. Try to distribute products directly to each of them using your own fleet of trucks—again, impossible! The consumer goods industry has to manage this complexity efficiently, which is why the concept of grouping outlets together into channels is so essential.

Channels are groups of shopping environments that have similar characteristics that enable companies to create consistency within diversity. Channels break up the diverse world into manageable segments and—critical to the shopper marketer—enable one environment to be prioritized over another, simplifying the work of creating a marketing mix in those environments.

HOW CHANNELS ARE FORMED

Enter the world of consumer goods and you enter a world with a whole new vocabulary. It's a world littered with terms that would be unfathomable for the layperson. Managers talk in three-letter abbreviations and make up terms that are never spoken outside the office. This is particularly true when they talk about channels. When was the last time you shopped in a CTN or visited a QSR? How much did you spend when you last visited a CVS or PCS? Did you do your shopping in the "modern trade" or the "general trade" last week? And just how was your last visit to the impulse sector?

For people who don't work in this field, those questions are completely meaningless. But around the world, the thousands of people who work in consumer goods know that a CTN (confectioner, tobacconist, and newsagent) is a great place to buy candies, cigarettes, and newspapers. They know you can get a sandwich and a drink in a McDonald's, which is a quick service restaurant (QSR). Need to stop on your way home to buy a cold drink? Just go to your local convenience store (CVS). Need to stock up on shampoo or aspirin? Go to a personal care store (PCS). Did you shop in a supermarket? You went to the "modern trade." If your local shop is a sarisari, it's in the "general trade." And the last time you impulsively bought a candy bar, you probably bought it in a shop that's in the "impulse sector." Some of these terms are more accessible; for example, many shoppers around the world know that a "hypermarket" is a really big supermarket.

For professionals who work in shopper marketing, clearly distinguishing one channel from another is important; selling a family pack of potato chips in a supermarket makes sense, but selling one in a pharmacy doesn't.

The need to distinguish between retail environments has driven the huge variety of language that helps the consumer goods industry describe the outlets in that sell their products.

How did these terms come about? In most cases, they rose from the historical demands of logistics networks or from definitions applied by companies trading in market share data, such as Nielsen. In many parts of the world, sales teams are organized across two trade sectors—the modern trade and the general trade. Recently, in discussion with a Chinese sales manager, when asked about the rationale splitting outlets into "modern" and "general" he said, "Well, before we had modern supermarkets in China, we sold everything via distributors. When retailers like Walmart arrived, they asked us to deliver direct, so we split the sales team based on whether they manage distributors (the 'general trade team') or manage chain stores (the 'modern trade team')." This "modern versus general" segmentation is a common approach in many parts of the world, and it's driven by how companies *serve* their customers; for example, both 7-Eleven and Carrefour require central delivery and a key account team. From a service point of view, they are similar—the sales team will treat them the same, and therefore manufacturers will group them into the same channel.

So what's wrong with this? Well, let's start with the problems that arise from distinguishing between outlets purely on the nature of a commercial relationship. The first issue is diversity—are 7-Eleven and Carrefour really the same? Some Carrefour stores are huge, dwarfing a 7-Eleven outlet. Carrefour stocks thousands of lines; 7-Eleven stocks hundreds. 7-Eleven's stores are close to home, within walking distance, but a Carrefour hypermarket has a huge parking lot because people have to drive there.

So the shops themselves are different, but so are the reasons why shoppers visit them—and this is the second issue. Shoppers who visit 7-Eleven and Carrefour rarely see these two options as interchangeable. Would you drive to a hypermarket to buy one pack of toothpaste? No. Would you nip in to 7-Eleven on your way home to grab a week's groceries? No. Shoppers know that Carrefour trades on the idea that you can purchase all your household needs for at least a week, and 7-Eleven is there for you when you need something now. Shoppers have different needs when they visit different stores, so if we want to influence shoppers' behavior, we have to market to them in these outlets differently. The range of options we have as marketers is different. You can't ask someone who wants to buy something for immediate consumption to buy a month's supply, nor can you offer someone who wants to buy a month's supply a pack that will last a day. Incredible as it may seem, however, some manufacturers do exactly that!

One global manufacturer of soap powder offered only large packs to 7-Eleven in Thailand because they didn't make small packs available to the "modern trade." The same manufacturer also insisted that store owners running independent supermarkets take only small packs because, according to this manufacturer's definition, independent retailers were in the "general trade." So if you happen to be a shopper visiting a general trade supermarket to buy a pack of soap powder for the next month, you would have to buy twenty small packs. Naturally, this suppressed the sales of the brand in those stores; shoppers either went elsewhere or bought the competitor's large pack.

It's clear that this is folly and it's a rare case, but it clearly demonstrates that for shopper marketing to work, broad channel categories like "modern" or "general" are likely to lead to failure. If we want to pinpoint accurately which outlets to focus on, such large, indiscriminate distinctions are no longer viable. A more appropriate approach is one that looks at the characteristics of shops we can all see. This is the approach that data traders like Nielsen and GfK take.

Nielsen, for example, creates standard definitions of channels based on simple and easily observable criteria. These might include whether the store has a door or not, the size of the store, the number of categories it sells, the type of shelving used, the number of checkouts, or whether shoppers can help themselves to products. By examining these characteristics, Nielsen arrives at consistent channel definitions for the whole market.

In many of the markets where it operates, Nielsen creates a sample of retail outlets in each channel and gathers information about the products those outlets sell. Nielsen then turns around and sells this data to manufacturers and other retailers. For many manufacturers, such data forms the basis of a number of their key performance measures, such as market sales value, volume, and market share.

Where available, Nielsen provides data to the fast-moving consumer goods (FMCG) industry, covering an array of categories, and its samples aim to reflect the retail ecology of the each market. Nielsen offers the advantage of being able to compare performance of competitors in different types of outlets. Because each manufacturer looks at the market in a slightly different way, Nielsen avoids having to cut the data differently for each client by becoming the arbiter of how the data is accessed.

But this, too, can be problematic for shopper marketers. It's best to illustrate this with a real case. In Malaysia, hypermarkets and supermarkets have, in the past, been treated by Nielsen as one channel—data is presented to manufacturers as a combined "supermarkets and hypermarkets" channel. Historically, this was because Dairy Farm International (DFI) operates both hypermarkets and supermarkets under the Giant brand, and they were the leading player in these channels. By splitting the channels, Nielsen would have provided manufacturers with confidential information on DFI's business; hence, the two store types remained grouped together. Such a significant data gap can lead definitions like this to be imperfect, but they are still recognized by the industry, for want of a better solution, so everybody uses them as a point of reference.

Equally, Nielsen's definitions are not as granular as they might be, given that the data is based on only a limited set of differentiators. In Malaysia, 10 differentiators are used. The country has something called "provision stores," which range from about 150 square feet to about 3,000 feet, and there are about 20,000 such outlets in the country.

All provision stores are classified using the same list of 10 differentiators, but a provision store could be a small supermarket or a tiny retailer at the base of a shop house. No shopper would suggest that these outlets have much in common, but for a manufacturer studying Nielsen data, they are all rolled together. Having 20,000 stores, ranging from very small to quite large, in that one channel doesn't give us much to go on when evaluating this set of outlets as an entity, does it? As you can see, these commonly used definitions can be imprecise because they lack granularity.

Granularity is important in shopper marketing because we want to prioritize only those environments where we know we can change someone's behavior. In Malaysia, we've found that shopper behavior can be influenced in very different ways in a hypermarket than it can be in a supermarket. We also know that when people are shopping a large provision store, their behaviors have more in common with supermarket behaviors than the behaviors seen in small provision stores. Our clients in Kuala Lumpur and elsewhere have therefore developed new definitions of the channels they manage.

DEFINING CHANNELS

The recipe for a great channel definition must include a number of ingredients to produce the perfect balance. You need just the right level of granularity to enable targeting without creating so much complexity that management becomes impossible. You need to strike exactly the right balance between specificity for your market and measurability given the data you have available. Definitions must reflect the real world shoppers live in and the commercial constraints within which the business operates. And the marketers who create the definitions need to recognize that someone else—probably on a different team or in a different organization—will execute plans in the environments that are prioritized; thus, channel definitions must be accessible and easy to understand.

We believe the best place to start is the real world with which shoppers engage. Shoppers already define channels in their own terms. Researchers seeking to understand the way shoppers select outlets, will hear people say things like: "Oh, when I'm buying your product I go to my local supermarket," or "When I need something really special, I go to the department store," or perhaps even "I used Best Buy's website to research that product." When shoppers are asked to describe the environment, they'll talk about the physical or online environment in terms of what they could see. We call these physical differentiators. They might include the things they see from outside the store, like store location, store size, store branding, whether the store has a parking lot, and whether it has a door. Physical differentiators inside the store include the look and feel of the store, its lighting, its air conditioning, its layout, and the extent of the categories that can be bought there. Physical characteristics can extend to the types of products stocked, the prices, the merchandising, the service, and the apparent attitude of staff or the level of cleanliness. All of these things help shoppers determine whether this is an environment they want to be in when they buy your brand, and that helps you influence them.

To see how this works in practice, let's go back to Malaysia. Malaysia is an incredibly interesting market: compact, rapidly developing, with amazing geographic and ethnographic diversity. It's easy to believe the country's own marketing slogan—"Malaysia is truly Asia." For shopper marketers, Malaysia is exciting because its vibrant economy supports a high level of personal consumption, while its ethnic mix keeps it rooted in tradition. Malaysia has one of the fastest consolidating retail markets, with Aeon, Tesco, and DFI building stores in competition with strong local chains like Econsave, the Store, and Mydin. It also has a significant independent retail sector, one element of particular interest to many FMCG businesses—the Chinese medical hall. Nearly a quarter of Malaysia's population is ethnically

Chinese, and this population clusters in the nation's capital, Kuala Lumpur; the Island of Penang; and the northern city of Ipoh. In these centers and elsewhere, you'll find medical halls. Originally, these retailers specialized in the herbs, extracts, and elements traditionally used in Chinese medicine. In the past, patients visited practitioners who would diagnose ailments and recommend treatments. The medical halls supplied ingredients as prescribed. In some cases, the halls acted as both clinic and pharmacy.

Today, the tradition of using herbs continues, but the medical hall has moved on—you can still buy herbs, but the store owners have found that FMCG products are a great draw for shoppers of all ethnic groups. To attract more shoppers, many offer a range of branded products, and many of these are heavily discounted in the hope that the shoppers will purchase much more lucrative medicinal products in the same trip. One of Malaysia's worst-kept secrets is that you can get many leading brands in a medical hall significantly cheaper than at the most price-led hypermarket. This presents a problem and an opportunity. The problem lies in managing price points—hypermarket retailers aggressively attack manufacturers who "allow" their products to be sold cheaply. The opportunity is, with so many shoppers having a long-standing relationship with the shop owners, medical halls could be a super-environment in which to influence shoppers. But which medical halls?

Nielsen uses a simple differentiator to identify medical halls: whether or not Chinese herbs are sold there. But the stores themselves are diverse. Some are very traditional, selling herbs and medicines only. These offer counter service and expertise. Others are nearly supermarkets, offering a wide selection of groceries, fresh foods, and other products. Between, there is a whole range of stores. On the more traditional end of the spectrum, shoppers have a specific purpose for their visit; at the opposite end of the spectrum, shoppers of all ethnic groups come for regular grocery needs. It's only by observing the physical characteristics of this wide range of stores that the right distinctions can be drawn.

Working with Nielsen, we audited these stores and looked at all the physical characteristics shoppers used to differentiate between environments—those they used for grocery purchases and those they used for specialist purposes. We were able to cluster these characteristics to create three subsegments, which we then mapped back onto Nielsen's database. We found that the majority of these stores fell into the cluster we named "traditional medical halls"—1,333 stores of the total 2,298. Less than a quarter of these stores sold our FMCG clients' products, instead focusing on herbs and over-the-counter medicines. For the first time, we were able to quantify the traditional end of the spectrum described earlier. The next cluster we found represented the opposite end: the "full-service medical hall," which is closely akin to a supermarket, accounted for 27 percent of the outlets. The remaining 344 stores, or just 15 percent of outlets, fell into a crossover group, not offering the same range of grocery products as the full-service stores while maintaining their focus on traditional medicines.

Few of our clients would wish to establish a specific marketing mix for these 344 stores alone. And with 90 percent of these stores stocking our clients' products, this small part of the market was rolled into the "full-service" segment for practical purposes. This created two polar groups: "traditional medical halls" and "full-service medical halls," accounting for 60 percent and 40 percent of the outlets, respectively. Now, this doesn't sound like a big deal in many ways, but here's the thing—the "full-service" segment sells 20 percent more of our clients' brands a year than all of Malaysia's hypermarkets combined. Suddenly these stores have some commercial weight in the market; it's now much easier to decide where to focus.

Commercially, our clients can now make better decisions about how to supply these outlets, what sorts of trading terms they might offer, the types of people they might deploy to sell to store owners, and—critical for shopper marketing—what marketing mix they should apply to influence shoppers.

Unfortunately, not all channel definitions are as clear-cut as this. Around the world, there are many environments that are similar in physical appearance but with massively different commercial requirements. To explain this, we need to visit a country very different from Malaysia and with a very different type of retail outlet.

In the heart of the United Kingdom is the picturesque market town of Stamford. Stamford offers a wonderful example of the variety of environments available to British shoppers. The high street is full of big-name brands offering clothing, electronics, coffee, health foods, and so on. It has a vibrant weekly market, and all of the UK's major grocery chains have stores in and around the town. The town's 22,000 or so inhabitants are unusually well served.

What's also interesting is that the town has a number of locally owned stores, many of which have weathered the onslaught of chain retailers well, and they continue to do so. One such retailer is Walkers Bookshop, which has a central position on the high street in a beautiful eighteenth-century building. The shop offers an excellent range of stationery, cards, books, newspapers, and magazines, as well as a small range of toys, games, music, and video.

Not far away, on the same street, you will find a very similar store. This one, however, is owned by the WHSmith chain; though the store lacks a little of Walker's charm, it offers a broadly similar range of products in a very similar setting. For Stamford's shoppers, these outlets are interchangeable, at least in their physical characteristics. But for publishers, stationery manufacturers, and music and video distributors, the outlets have very different commercial characteristics.

WHSmith is a major listed multinational company with a highly centralized UK retail operation; all the ranging decisions are made in the head office in Swindon. It operates a hub-and-spoke distribution network that manufacturers service directly; it offers national promotions; and it requires a common price point and centralizes financial settlements. With a network of over 990 stores across the UK, WHSmith is the biggest customer for companies selling goods in several categories. Walkers Bookshop, by contrast, is a chain of only five stores, and the company remains family owned and managed by Tim Walker. Merchandising and pricing decisions are made by Tim or the store's managers. Walkers purchases much of its product from their appointed wholesalers or distributors, not from the manufacturers. It may be physically similar to WHSmith, but there is a huge difference commercially.

While shoppers might treat these two types of outlets the same, manufacturers cannot. Working with retailers like WHSmith requires a specialist sales team. Often this team will include logistics, finance, and in-store marketing specialists working alongside a key account manager, who may have many years of experience in high-level sales and negotiation. Managing the relationship with WHSmith requires careful financial analysis, sophisticated forecasting and logistics planning, and a strong understanding of the chain and its shoppers. In short, working with a chain stationery retailer like WHSmith requires a lot of time, people, and investment.

By contrast, working with independent retailers like Walkers requires a very different approach. Manufacturers need to find an efficient route-to-market to supply their products, as delivering small amounts of product is extremely expensive in the UK. Often, the entire financial and logistics relationship is managed by a specialist wholesaler who may service many other similar outlets. Some leading manufacturers may choose to maintain a direct relationship with retailers like the Walker family, but this is managed by a team of sales representatives who travel from store to store, giving advice on merchandising and promotions in order to influence orders from the wholesaler and explaining how product should be presented to shoppers. Manufacturers may provide a web portal for independent retailers to learn more about the market and how to succeed in it, as Unilever does in the UK, or they may have a small group of people creating generic merchandising plans and materials for dissemination by wholesalers and sales representatives.

Given all these differences between physically similar outlets, it's important to factor in the commercial characteristics of an environment as channels are defined. Commercial characteristics might include ownership and decision-making structures; attention needs to be paid to routes of supply, delivery points, and invoicing requirements. It may be useful to consider the flexibility of retailers in the channel and their investment requirements. Financially, thought may be given to margin requirements, credits terms, and stock-returns requirements. Commercial characteristics should then be overlaid onto the physical differentiators to come to channel definitions that enable the company to manage and prioritize channels effectively. In this way, companies can draw clear distinctions between outlets like Walkers and WHSmith.

There's no doubt that if a company is faced with a relatively simple channel structure today, this re-segmentation is going to lead to a more complex structure. When Coca-Cola did this in the UK some years ago, it concluded that it had over 60 different channels! For almost all the companies we have worked with, this level of complexity is unsustainable. So, before you present your managing director with a proposal to move from 5 channels to 50, consider some key factors.

The first and most important is this question: "Are your new channels likely to be manageable?" If the marketing team plans to increase the number of channel definitions, it will have an impact on the level of complexity the company has to manage. Can the marketing team bear this? Can other teams bear it? Might the existing organizational structure need to change? Does the company have, for example, sufficient skilled people to support this? If the answer to any of these questions is no, we would advise simplifying the approach (unless, of course, the financial gains from this restructuring are so significant as to render the on-costs of scaling up the team affordable). Perhaps the best approach might be to combine distinctions that might exist at the granular level but that might be less significant at the macro one—refer, for example, to the case in Malaysia, where distinguishing between the 15 percent of medical halls at the midpoint between two clear extremes would add unnecessary complexity.

Next, consider measurability. If performance can't be measured, it can't be managed, so avoid creating distinctions that can't actually be monitored. You may have to live with the fact that service providers like Nielsen may be unable to "split data" in a market. Certainly implementing new channel structures will require the support of finance teams to ensure that internal sales data can be split, and—in companies where this is difficult—further compromises must be made.

Lastly, consider the fact that if the members of the marketing team are the only people who understand your channel definitions, the rest of the organization cannot support the goals they might wish to set. It's important to clearly communicate which environments are included in a channel and which are not, with a strong rationale for change, and this should be explained to everyone systematically.

FROM BRICKS TO CLICKS

As online environments become increasingly ubiquitous, new channels are forming. What we love about online is its flexibility and its capacity to inform consumers and concurrently influence shoppers. Starting a retail website is easy: there are thousands of templates available, and the cost of logo and site design tumbles daily. It's now possible to establish a retail proposition on the web in less than a week for less than $1,000. The requirement for physical space and capital—once a significant barrier for budding retail entrepreneurs—has been completely overcome. Payment systems and search applications allow you to run an effective offer from your home. Around the world, fulfillment operators offer the ability for anyone to stock, pick, pack, and ship merchandise with a level of sophistication once available to only the largest retailers. And with affiliate marketing programs like Amazon's, websites don't even need to sell a product to make money from the traffic they attract.

Online propositions have the power to engage shoppers in a whole new way by providing reviews, rankings, and even the opportunity to experience the product in the home through augmented reality. Shoppers can see what their friends and other shoppers "like" and benefit from, thanks to algorithm-led recommendations that range from suggesting the right wine for a meal to information on similar products other people also bought. We can now leap from a recipe suggestion to an order page in one click. All these phenomena are democratizing retail and placing the power in the hands of the shopper.

Of course, it's true that the online world contains some major players. Amazon now dominates not only the world of books but also numerous other categories, and its success has led to the decline of many traditional operators and to the development of thousands of specialists around the world. Some global players were caught napping as Amazon transformed from specialist to generalist and eBay turned individuals into retailers. How many shoe sellers would have thought people would buy a pair of pumps online? Few, probably. But then Zappos came along and removed the risk of ordering footwear online by offering free shipping and free returns—and great customer service. But in the last few years, major retailers and brands alike have wised up to the power of online retail, and all the major global players are steadily rolling out compelling online offers that extend their brand into digital.

This new set of environments creates new channels where microsites, run from the home, can compete with mega retailers. In the world of clicks, this competition can cross borders with relative ease, and the distinction between environments that market to shoppers and environments that market to consumers has become blurred.

This world is likely to change rapidly, presenting new ways to reach out to shoppers. In 2010, Tesco's South Korean affiliate, Home Plus, sought to acquire a leading position online, not through enhancing back links and page ranking but by bring the offer to shoppers directly. In a recent YouTube video, Tesco's agency, Cheil, showed how in the highly connected, time-poor market of South Korea, they brought the shopping experience into a completely new realm. Using billboards in subway stations, they created a virtual Home Plus store. Posters showed life-size replicas of the stores' shelves as they appeared in the real world (or perhaps better than they appeared in the real world, as these shelves never went out of stock!). Commuters were encouraged to scan QR barcodes for the products they wanted, and items were delivered to their homes 30 minutes later. The campaign was a hit, attracting new shoppers to both the physical stores and the online offer.

Defining these channels requires that you stretch the physical and commercial characteristics you apply currently—but these characteristics do still hold true. Distinguishing between a WordPress site and a massively sophisticated mega site remains relatively easy today, and with many e-tailers seeking direct relationships with major manufacturers, the commercial differentiators hold true regardless of whether the outlets are virtual or actual. Today, online might be a small part of a company's sales, but it could have a huge influence on your shoppers. It's unlikely to remain static—40 percent of one global brand's South Korean sales of vitamins and mineral supplements are made online, making it the biggest single channel in the market. There is little left to prevent this happening globally. Online channels can't be ignored, however small they are right now.

THE DIGITAL CHANGE—A GREAT LIBERATOR

In the words of Brian Harris, "There has probably never been in the history of consumer and shopper behavior a bigger change between one generation and the next in terms of the aspirations and the requirements of shoppers and the tools and methods they use to meet their shopping needs." While there are many complicating factors and challenges, we believe that overall the effect is one of liberation, for the following reasons:

- **Unlimited ranges.** While there is a physical limit to how many products can be merchandised in even the biggest stores, there is no limit in a virtual environment. Even before it ventured beyond books, Amazon offered a range well into the millions—far beyond the capacity of even the largest bookstores.

- **Differentiated merchandising.** In a traditional store, each shopper is presented the same basic range and layout. All of the thousands of shoppers who visit a particular hypermarket on any give day see the same range of products laid out in exactly the same way. This is highly limiting. For example, if I want to encourage one group of shoppers to trade up to a more expensive product, I may choose to merchandise them next to each other. While this might create great visibility of the premium product to those shoppers, it also makes the cheaper product visible to those shoppers already buying the premium product. Whatever is done, there is a possibility that some might trade down, thereby reducing the sales and potentially the profit from that shopper. In the digital world, this problem is theoretically removed. Each shopper (assuming we know who he is) can be presented a different layout, a different page of products, and products placed in a different order. While the entire range might be made available to everyone, shoppers who usually buy the cheaper product may have the premium product on their first page, while the cheaper product may be absent from the front page of the premium buyer. The challenge this creates lies in understanding the difference between range, availability, and visibility. Amazon's success is not simply because it has great service and a huge range, but because the site is navigable, and the "right products" are made available.

- **Multiple locations.** In any store, availability and visibility is connected to location. Rarely do shoppers cover the entire shop floor, scanning every aisle. Most shoppers visit less than 30 percent of a store's aisles. Clearly if a brand is in a store location that the shopper does not visit, then they are highly unlikely to buy it, as to them it is "not available." Many manufacturers have attempted to market shopper solutions by grouping products together, putting all of the ingredients for a particular meal together, for example, or grouping lunchbox snacks together. In a brick-and-mortar store, there are limitations to this. For every shopper who wants cookies for a lunchbox, there is someone who just wants cookies; so ideally, there would be cookies in multiple locations. But locating a product in more than one location is expensive (it increases inventory holding for one), so these activities are typically limited to temporary displays—on an end cap, for instance—rather than part of the ongoing store merchandising. Online, however, this limitation is removed. A product may appear on many thousands of pages (cookies, lunchboxes, kids' treats, gifts, with tea or coffee) without increasing inventory holding by one case.

- **Limited offers.** The consumer goods industry uses promotions a lot—too much, we argue. But promotions do have their place in the marketing mix, and if they are discriminately used, then the returns can be substantial. Part of the problem with promotions in the non-digital age was that a promotional deal was offered to every shopper. Loyalty cards and a digital environment change that. Under these circumstances, offers and discounts can be much more targeted and, in theory, deal shoppers can be avoided. This alone could improve the effectiveness of the activity substantially. Imagine if that buy-two-get-one-free Colgate promotion was only offered to regular Crest shoppers? The uplift would not be so great, but the money wasted on giving deals to current shoppers, and on deal shoppers, would disappear.

- **Democratized communication.** In the pre-digital, pre-mobile world, what went on in the store was largely the responsibility of the retailer. Manufacturers who wished to do anything in-store had to gain the permission of retailers who, understandably, may not wish to do things that were not in their interests and who may levy a fee for the privilege of doing so in their stores. The realization that shoppers can be reached out of store allows manufacturers the opportunity to communicate with shoppers in a more unfettered way. Mobile merely takes this one step further. The shopper now has a device that they control. No longer can communication lines be vetoed or subject to levy by a retailer. Brand owners can communicate directly with the shopper right in the store.

INFLUENCING SHOPPERS—THE ROLES CHANNELS PLAY

One of the key reasons we can't ignore online is the immense opportunity it gives us to influence shoppers' purchase decisions—and that is the heart of shopper marketing. Shopper marketers of the future will not add value by grasping that there are millions of environments to influence shoppers, nor by having clever segmentation of those outlets. True magic happens when you understand how shoppers use these environments and what value can be created from changing shoppers' behavior in each.

In his book *Winning the Zero Moment of Truth*, Jim Lecinski describes how digital creates new opportunities to influence shoppers. He contrasts this with the way the analog process worked: Dad sees a TV advert for a digital camera; Dad visits the store and buys the camera. But in the digital world, "Dad still watches football and he still sees your TV commercial. But now he grabs his laptop off the coffee table and searches for 'digital camera reviews.' He looks at comments from users on CNET and two other sites. He goes to Twitter and posts: 'Anybody have a great camera for under $100?' He hits YouTube and searches 'digital camera demos.'

Before the game ends—and before he gets to the store shelf—he's ready to make a decision."[82]

Each aspect of that behavior had a different but subtle influence on Dad's decision making. In truth, he didn't even have to get to the store shelf we mentioned; he could just as easily have bought the camera then on any number of websites and be using it by the following weekend. And the distinction here between Dad as a consumer and Dad as a shopper is also now blurred—when he Googled for camera reviews, was he a consumer exploring his consumption needs and others' consumption experience, or was he a shopper interpreting consumer demand? There's no doubt that what he experienced during the football game will have had a huge influence on his next decision. The mission of shopper marketers is to identify the importance of each influencing factor on the path to purchase and to prioritize them. They need to establish where these influencing factors are most potent so they can ensure that the right activities are happening in the right places, thus influencing the behavior of target shopper groups.

Let's go back to Jim Lecinski's example again—why didn't Dad just buy the camera online? The reviews are good, the demo works, he's decided on the brand—each of these communication channels has done its job. The trouble is, he's not yet shopping. Smart shopper marketers would take up the process from here—asking questions like, "How can we clinch the sale now?" "How can we get this guy to leap straight to an e-tailer?" "Where is he going to next?" and "How do we make sure this guy's intent doesn't dissipate when he walks into Best Buy?" Shopper marketers are looking for channels where they can change intent to purchase rapidly, and—because they are profit minded—how they can secure that purchase at the least possible cost.

Over years of research, we've learned that different shoppers use different outlets in different ways. We know that different retail and e-tail environments have different potentials to influence a purchase decision: by knowing where the highest potential to influence lies, the shopper marketer can identify where to focus his efforts. We've also learned that that potential can lie in surprising places—let's share a personal example.

---

82 Lecinski, *Winning the Zero Moment of Truth.*

A TALE OF TWO SHOE STORES: INFLUENCING TOBY'S BEHAVIOR

Here's a story directly from Toby about his experience with a retailer that really knew how to influence him.

About eight years ago, I got it in my head that I needed a physical challenge—a very large physical challenge. I decided that I would compete in a triathlon. Considering I hated running, this was perhaps not the best choice, but I decided to do it anyway.

With steadfast commitment, I hired a personal trainer. He analyzed the way I cycled, swam, and ran. After this study, he announced that he was going to run with me twice a week for 10 weeks to teach me how to run properly.

At the end of the 10 weeks, I was lighter and fitter but suffering incredible pain in my shins and calves. My trainer advised me to buy better running shoes that offset the imbalance in my stance. Having always used Nike shoes, I went to the Nike store. I walked in and saw an entire wall of impressive looking running shoes. I asked one of the salespeople for help choosing a pair.

"Well, here are 20," he said, pointing to the display and looking at me like I was an idiot for not seeing the wall of running shoes in front of me.

"Which is a good one?" I queried.

"Well, this one is on promotion," he responded, picking up one shoe.

"That's fine, but I need a really good running shoe," I insisted.

He then grabbed another shoe and said, "This is the most expensive."

Clearly, he wasn't understanding my question. I proceeded to explain my problem: the pain in my legs and my fervent desire to compete in a triathlon. I then asked again for a recommendation, to which he responded, "I don't know. I play basketball."

Nike invested a ton of money on the in-store merchandising of this outlet, a place to showcase the power of its brand. And I expect that a lot of basketball players had a fantastic shopping experience here. But I left empty-handed. This unprepared employee lost the sale of not one pair of shoes, but possibly four pairs per year, because long-distance runners go through shoes very quickly. And the salesperson's lack of knowledge—and inability to guide me to the person who had that knowledge—indirectly cost the store additional sales, because I am quite vocal. I shared my dissatisfaction with other runners.

Shortly after this disappointing shopper experience, I was heading to the United Kingdom for a visit with my family, and I decided to get advice from my father, an avid runner, while I was there. He pointed me to a shop called

Advance Performance in Peterborough, a small shop that specialized in shoes for runners. When I walked in, I marveled at the unusual environment. The polar opposite of the sleek Nike store, Advance Performance was cluttered with shoes everywhere and a running machine in the corner. (In deference to my friends at Advance Performance, I have to say they now have two very nice new outlets in Peterborough and Cambridge.)

A rather average-looking man approached and offered his help. Already, my shopping experience was different from my Nike visit. I explained the problem with my legs, and he told me to take off my shoes. He knelt down and looked at my legs and feet. Then he asked, "When did you break your ankle?"

Surprised that he could know about my accident, I answered that it happened about 10 years earlier.

"Did you do any physical therapy?" he asked.

"Not much," I replied.

"It shows," he said, not unkindly. He explained that my feet were pronated and that the injury aggravated the problem. The salesman—fast becoming a trusted advisor—then put me on the running machine and conducted a gait analysis. He watched to see the way my feet hit the ground when I ran. He had me try on six different pairs of running shoes and get on the machine to test each one, videotaping each effort. After viewing the tapes, he prescribed the shoe that would best meet my particular needs. As it happened, the choice was about 40 percent more expensive than the running shoes I had been wearing. I bought two pairs of these godsends and now order online from Advance Performance whenever I need replacements. This salesperson responded admirably to my need. He didn't need the spit and polish of a slickly merchandised store, nor did he sit back and rely on brand performance. He burst through the performance barrier and instilled my faith in the shoe.

Examining Toby's experience, you might begin to see how insight into the roles channels play for target shoppers can be extremely valuable. At the time, Toby was a "novice triathlete"—potentially a valuable shopper for a manufacturer of running shoes. As a novice, Toby was looking for information, and he went first to an outlet in the "showcase store" channel to get that information. When his experience in the Nike store failed to deliver the advice he needed, he turned to a different environment, the "independent specialist"—Advance Performance. Both channels performed the same role for Toby—to provide information and guidance (and Nike didn't do so well this time!). Armed with the shoes and the information, the next time he may buy his shoes at chain sports store like Foot Locker because he knows what he needs, and getting the right shoes at a deal has become important. You see, not only did the "independent specialist" have the potential to strongly influence Toby's buying behavior eight years ago, but its influence continues to the present day, some 20 pairs later.

So which of these three channels—the showcase store, the independent specialist, or the chain sports store—is most important if you want to target "novice triathletes"? Clearly, Toby only bought two pairs of shoes from an independent specialist, whereas he bought 18 pairs from the chain sports store. The sales are bigger in the latter than the former. But without the independent specialist, those sales may never have happened.

What's important here is that different environments influence different shoppers differently, so it's essential to prioritize channels based on the influence they have on target shoppers, not on the value of the sales you make in them. We recently found this was the case in Thailand.

Thailand has a very large market for powdered milk—particularly milk for young children. In this market, mothers naturally take a great deal of care in deciding which product they will use when they choose to stop breast-feeding. The range of products available in the market is very wide indeed, but these products can generally be considered either "premium" or "affordable." This description goes beyond price, with premium products offering more specialized nutritional supplements. Yet, when some premium products go for twice as much as their more affordable counterparts, price is an important differentiator.

What's interesting about this category is the level of loyalty that brands engender; mums rarely change brands, using no more than two brands in the entire time that powdered milk is part of their kids' diet (which could be three years or more). Brand-switching behavior is interesting in itself because it really only happens for two reasons: either the child rejects the product because of taste (often in spectacular style), or mum changes brand when her child is ready for the next "stage"; the milk industry has created products specifically designed for children in different age groups, tailoring them to the differing nutritional requirements of babies, toddlers, and preschoolers.

The major "stage change" happens when kids turn one. They're no longer babies; in many cases, they are no longer breast fed, and their diet has become much more diverse. Milk is still an important element of the diet but no longer the most important one. This time is also a significant period of relief, especially for first-time parents. The things that had once been critically important seem much less so as they realize that their child is still very much alive and growing nicely.

Our research showed that 42 percent of the market switched brands at this one-year-old point. Perhaps most interestingly, in switching, many shoppers who had previously chosen a premium brand now bought an affordable one. Before the switch, just over 60 percent of the market sales are in the premium segment; afterward, the inverse is true. As a result, total sales shrink by over 12 percent.

It's clear that one major way to grow sales in this category is to encourage shoppers not to purchase a cheaper brand when the time comes to change products. Players who make premium products, therefore, seek to keep shoppers loyal to their brands as they transition through stages. Alternatively, players who manufacture affordable brands will wish to be the beneficiaries of switching behavior. In order to grow their sales, they might encourage shoppers to purchase their products when switching. In either case, the winners in this market will be the manufacturers that are most effective at influencing their target shoppers. In order to win profitably, manufacturers need to know where they can have the greatest influence. This is where understanding the role of retail channels is essential.

Thailand, like Malaysia, has a very dynamic hypermarket sector in which two major global players, Tesco and Casino (operating the Tesco Lotus and Big C brands respectively), square off in a high-stakes turf war—with massive stores offering huge ranges of products at deep discounts. For mothers buying milk powder, these hypermarkets are a great place to shop—competition keeps prices low, and stores offer consistently available product. Powdered milk shoppers visit these stores almost twice a month and buy to a plan: more than 95 percent of shoppers have decided what they want before they go to the store, and less than 5 percent of shoppers buy anything other than what they planned to buy. Few shoppers look at anything other than their preferred brand, and most buy exactly the quantity they'd planned to buy, regardless of promotions. This highly planned behavior is very difficult to influence. In short, very few people change brands in hypermarkets, so the potential to influence shoppers' behavior is low. Here the hypermarkets play a very specific role: to service the regular needs of milk powder shoppers and have the hypermarkets deliver higher sales volumes than any other channel.

Pharmacies, by contrast, deliver some of the lowest sales volumes; yet our research shows that for milk powder manufacturers, this channel may be the most important in the country. In contrast to hypermarkets—where shoppers already know what they want when they go to the store—shoppers visiting a pharmacy often do not. Indeed, on the day that mothers switch brands in Thailand, they are 70 percent more likely to go to a pharmacy outlet. Why? Well, Thai law demands that retailers apply for a license to sell prescription medicines, and there must be a qualified pharmacist working in the store. For many Thais, these pharmacists represent a "free" source of medical consultation, and many seek a pharmacist's advice in the diagnosis and treatment of minor ailments. In an environment where pediatric care may be expensive, the pharmacist is always on hand to give a trusted opinion. So when mothers decide it's time to change brands, they visit the pharmacist to get advice. In this case, the role that the pharmacist channel plays is giving product information. Shoppers who are considering changing products visit the pharmacy outlet and follow the recommendation. They then return to their regular store for the next purchase.

Think about the consequences of this: if a mother buys milk powder twice a month from the time her child is six months old to the day the child turns three, there are 60 shopping occasions. The statistics show that shoppers will change products on only one of those occasions, generally around the point at which the child turns one. So she may purchase the first product she uses from a hypermarket 12 times, but she goes to a pharmacy and potentially changes brands on the thirteenth shopping trip. On the fourteenth shopping trip, and for all of the subsequent 46 shopping trips, mom returns to the hypermarket and buys the new brand. The 47 sales of that brand in the hypermarket are directly attributable to the decision made in a pharmacy!

So which channel is most important? The hypermarket, in which 59 sales are made? Or the pharmacy, in which a single sale is made? From a shopper marketing perspective, an investment in changing a shopper's behavior in the pharmacy channel delivers 47 sales opportunities in the hypermarket. By contrast, the likely probability of changing shopper behavior by investing in hypermarkets is significantly lower. A wise shopper marketer would certainly consider over-investing in pharmacies as a result of this understanding.

PRIORITIZING CHANNELS—A SIMPLE MODEL

The whole idea of clustering shopping environments into channels is driven by the need to reduce complexity. Unfortunately, creating a clear channel segmentation is not a panacea for complexity in itself. Many consumer goods companies sell brands and products in multiple categories. In each category, shoppers behave differently; additionally, channels play different roles for the shoppers in each of these categories. The nightmare facing shopper marketers is where to focus. Imagine for instance that your company sells 10 categories and you identify 10 discrete channels. That's 100 different combinations in which shoppers may be behaving differently. In this environment, prioritization becomes essential.

	Category	Category	Category	Category	Category	Category	Category	Category	Category	Category
Channel	?	?	?	?	?	?	?	?	?	?
Channel	?	?	?	?	?	?	?	?	?	?
Channel	?	?	?	?	?	?	?	?	?	?
Channel	?	?	?	?	?	?	?	?	?	?
Channel	?	?	?	?	?	?	?	?	?	?
Channel	?	?	?	?	?	?	?	?	?	?
Channel	?	?	?	?	?	?	?	?	?	?
Channel	?	?	?	?	?	?	?	?	?	?
Channel	?	?	?	?	?	?	?	?	?	?
Channel	?	?	?	?	?	?	?	?	?	?

Managers must use a relatively simple model that enables them to define which combinations are most important to their business. The simplest approach is the prioritization matrix, which has been a common management tool since Boston Consulting Group (BCG) introduced the "Growth/Share" matrix in 1968. These matrices let managers decide where to focus by mapping potential options against two variables. The famous BCG matrix allows marketers to prioritize brands by comparing market share with growth rates. Our channel prioritization matrix takes a similar approach by comparing the relevance of each channel to target shoppers with the relative barriers to implementing in-store marketing activities in each channel:

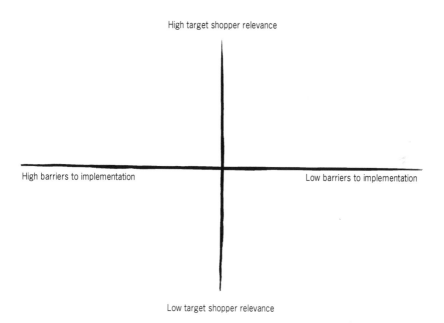

High target shopper relevance

High barriers to implementation

Low barriers to implementation

Low target shopper relevance

In the cases discussed, we saw that the channels with the greatest influence on shoppers should be prioritized. Ideally, one would focus on the environments that attract the largest number of targeted shoppers, that offer the greatest potential to influence those shoppers' behavior, and that already account for a large volume of sales. In these environments, an investment in marketing activities is likely to have a very high level of return. But to be successful, these marketing activities need to be executed on a customer's property.

Years of experience tell us that not all retailers are equally predisposed to changing their in-store environments to fit the marketing needs of a given brand. It's well known for instance that, although centralized hypermarket operators like Tesco or Walmart are highly effective at executing activities across a wide store base, they are rarely willing to act purely on the advice of a single supplier, nor are they the easiest of "partners" in the trade as a whole. So while you may find that the channel in which such retailers operate has huge potential to change the behavior of a large number of target shoppers, there may be significant barriers to implementing the marketing activities that will realize this potential.

Mapping channels into the matrix helps identify which of them to prioritize:

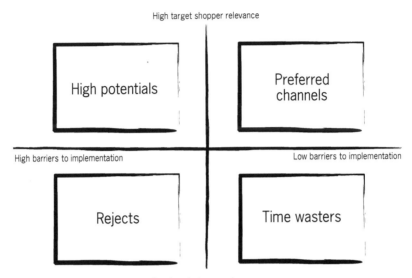

High target shopper relevance

High potentials	Preferred channels

High barriers to implementation · Low barriers to implementation

Rejects	Time wasters

Low target shopper relevance

"Preferred channels" are clearly the highest priority—they offer an abundance of target shoppers in environments where it's easy to influence shopper behavior. Channels in this quadrant represent the best bang for the shopper marketing buck—the potential return on investment is high and with retailers willing and able to execute changes in-store, returns should flow quickly. By contrast, "high potentials" offer the same potential for business growth, but it's likely to come more slowly and at higher cost, as retailers in this space will require higher levels of grooming and investment to encourage them to move.

The lower two quadrants offer less exciting potential. Neither can deliver the number of shoppers or the level of influence that either "preferred channels" or "high potentials" can offer. "Time wasters" may offer a high sense of security, as the retailers in this space are happy to try new ideas and able to execute rapidly. But this is a fool's paradise—these marketing efforts deliver lean results. Perhaps the greatest problem area, though, is found in the "rejects" box. Here, intransigent retailers tie up resources for scant returns. If these channels represent a large volume of sales, the sales team will be challenged to reduce levels of investment while maintaining turnover.

Thinking back to the example of milk powder in Thailand, we see that pharmacies would fall into one of the two top boxes. With many outlets in the channel, fragmentation is an issue, but the store operators tend to be open to investment from manufacturers and, in return for the promise of incremental sales, may well be open to try new ideas. Pharmacies, therefore, may well be a "preferred channel" for some manufacturers.

In the same example, hypermarkets draw vast quantities of shoppers and capture the lion's share of the market. Yet these shoppers are operating on autopilot; research shows that they rarely break with preset plans. Few notice promotions, and almost none switch brands. Clearly, getting a return on in-store investment in these environments will be tough, yet big global players who use price promotions as a vehicle to draw traffic to the store dominate the channel. These retailers have proven difficult to deal with and slow to make changes, especially in favor of single brands. So, this hypermarket channel might be in the "reject" box, but exit would be impossible. Working in this environment, therefore, presents a challenge. As we go on to consider the wider marketing mix, its implications on investment, and how to manage retailers in general, we'll return to this case to discuss what can be done.

IS THIS THE FUTURE?

Before we leave the topic of channels to explore the world of in-store marketing, we think it's important to pause and reflect a little on how retail environments might change in the future and how technology might change the way we view them.

Plenty of developments in 2012 might suggest that traditional offline retailing is in crisis: Over the last decade, online retail has led to the decline and closure of traditional stores in travel, music, video, and—in 2011—in bookselling. In 2012, we saw the consumer appliance retail sector rocked by competition from online: In the UK, Comet filed for bankruptcy; in China, the country's largest retailer, Suning, announced that its existing business model of focusing just on consumer appliances was no longer sustainable. Around the world, electronics retailers struggled with what to do about "showrooming" (where shoppers use a physical environment to check out a product before buying online) and "multi-channel retailing" (the strategy of creating coherent links between physical and virtual environments as a way to secure greater loyalty) became common parlance in the industry.

In the United States, 2012 saw the biggest daily sales online in history, with Cyber Monday delivering $1.25 billion. But the real online story was in China, where Taobao's single-day promotion on November 11 set the world record for online sales in one day, at $3.06 billion *through one portal*, nearly three times as much as Cyber Monday's record. In China, we also saw the greatest evidence that the next battleground between bricks and clicks will be in grocery retail, as global behemoth Walmart acquired online retailer Yihaodian. When retailers like Walmart start acquiring in this space, we should take it as a clear sign that grocery retail is about to change.

Indeed, grocery retailing changed in other ways during 2012. Speaking at the Asia Shopper Marketing & Insights 2012 conference early in the year, Anson Dichaves suggested that hypermarkets are in decline, with fewer trips being made less often in Asia. He also signaled that the more proximate offers of convenience stores and local supermarkets were gaining ground. A major casualty of the year was Carrefour, which completed its exit from Southeast Asia. With its offer struggling in China, too, it may be a matter of time before Carrefour, which once claimed to be the most global retailer in the world, might be again constrained to markets closer to home.

All this suggests that the future of shopping is online—or more accurately, that the future of shopping will have a significant online component. Now that so many have embraced online shopping, it seems unlikely that they will give up the convenience they currently enjoy. It's also pretty clear that no category will remain entirely immune. Let's just look at the history: first, travel went online; then insurance and banking; then entertainment; and now home appliances, computing, groceries, and fashion are all seeing a significant shift. The growth of e-commerce in China proves that this will be a global phenomenon, and it's fair to presume that emerging economies may embrace online faster than developed ones.

For most manufacturers, "online" is still a small share of total sales. This is similar for retailers. Seven percent of UK retailer John Lewis's sales in 2012 were online, and nearly 13 percent of Debenhams' sales were online. But in all cases, the growth in online sales is staggering.

Grocery retail has been affected at much lower levels to date—but this will change rapidly, and we make an unscientific prediction that by 2020, about 20 percent of grocery purchases will be online. This will have dramatic impact on big retailers and leading brands alike. Think about this: if 20 percent of a retailer's sales come from "outside the store," how efficient is the return on real estate? Online retail puts control in the palm of the shopper—quite literally—and in many markets, the explosion of mobile devices and the ubiquity of wireless broadband means that shoppers will inevitably turn to the convenience of online retail. This will require a profound rethink for many manufacturers and retailers alike. Online retail environments are becoming highly personalized, in effect increasing the volume of outlets exponentially as individual shoppers form their own "stores." Shopper marketers will have to take this into account and develop expertise not yet envisaged by most consumer goods companies.

New technology will be required, and greater levels of insight will become essential. Yet the impact of this could potentially be incredibly powerful. Globally, sales force automation and trade-promotion-management systems are becoming more sophisticated and integrated. They offer shopper marketers the ability to target outlets with common characteristics in a far more granular way than is currently possible. As technology that overlays shopper data with outlet data becomes available, the ability to focus marketing activities on specific shoppers in specific environments is becoming a reality. This level of accuracy could have a profound impact, perhaps doing away with the fundamental need for channels altogether.

Until that time, however, a clear segmentation and prioritization of channels remains essential.

CHAPTER 11

THE MARKETING MIX

The concept of a marketing mix has been around for decades and has been revisited countless times during that period. Yet the concept of shopper marketing—and the implications of considering the shopper as well as the consumer in a Total Marketing approach—requires that it be revisited once again. In this chapter, we will propose and describe the components of a shopper marketing mix. We will discuss how such a mix can be developed and how it should be integrated with a consumer marketing mix to create a Total Marketing approach.

The first acknowledged marketing mix—Jerome McCarthy's "4 Ps" model developed in 1960—is still revered by many and used by countless more. There are many variations on the concept in use today, each applying a similar principle—that there is a mix, a bundle, or blend of many things that are brought to bear to achieve a particular marketing goal. Additional "Ps" have been proposed, taking the total up to about 15. And in the early 1990s, Professor Robert Lauterborn proposed a more customer-centric model: the "4 Cs" (this model was later put forward by Philip Kotler, the esteemed American marketing expert). In his version of the model (there are now many more variations), Kotler argues that the original Product, Price, Place, Promotion model is "manufacturer centric" and that replacing these with "Customer need/value, Cost (of ownership), Convenience, and Communication" effectively revisits the same elements from the point of view of the market. In our experience, this model has much to offer—particularly in the realm of consumer goods.

The focus on the value that the customer is looking for certainly creates a clearer view of what is being marketed and allows for a broader definition than McCarthy's "product" perhaps allows. It opens up the possibility of services, as well as the emotional satisfaction or connection that a brand might offer. But most importantly, it challenges the organization to really think about who the customer is: "product" is product (i.e., what is produced), whereas "Customer need/value" requires a definition of customer. As argued elsewhere in this book, the advent of shopper marketing—and with it a Total Marketing approach—centers on the recognition that the customer may not be one person, and certainly not one persona. As consumer goods marketers, we are naturally drawn to the idea that "customer equals consumer." The word *product* does not challenge this paradigm as it focuses solely on the "thing"—the object, the food, the shampoo, the drink. Kotler's model allows for the existence of a customer who is not the consumer and therefore the creation of a mix that will work for the customer, whoever he is, and at any particular place on the path to purchase.

McCarthy's "Promotion" becomes Kotler's "Communication," which—in addition to putting the emphasis on what is heard (rather than what is said)—converts largely one-way messaging into something closer to dialog, which is very important today because of digital connection and social media. The change also clears up the widespread misunderstanding of "promotion"—a word that once had a message closer to "communication" but that has been subverted to largely mean "discounts." Kotler's "Convenience" clarifies what McCarthy meant by "place," in particular, emphasizing the importance of the target being able to find the product on her terms; before, the focus seemed to be mainly on the task of shipping the product to a store. This creates the opportunity to differentiate between the place of consumption (the concept of availability to consume—see Chapter 4) and the place of purchase. Convenience allows the marketer to help the shopper shop, and she then helps the consumer consume. Think of a consumer who will only drink beer if it's cold and in the fridge. The marketer can make it easy for his wife to encourage consumption by making sure that the beer is well chilled and easy to find in the store. Finally, "Cost" opens up an understanding of the total cost of ownership and clarifies the difference between price (often used as the long-term price) versus what is actually paid.

Does the understanding that the target is actually split in two—the consumer and the shopper—have implications for the marketing mix? Yes. We need to market to shoppers as well as consumers in an integrated approach because they are two target markets: the consumer and the shopper may not be the same individual. And even when looking at the same individual through two separate lenses (the shopper lens and the consumer lens), one sees very different things. One consumer might even be different types of shoppers in different stores. Think about how you might be described as a shopper in a supermarket versus in a convenience store—same person, same consumer perhaps, but a very different shopper.

Not only are the target markets potentially different, but the marketing objectives are different, too. The result of consumer marketing activities (the consumer marketing objective, if you will) is to create a desire or need, to drive and encourage new consumption opportunities, and to create engagement with a brand. The shopper marketer's objective, on the other hand, is to create changes in purchasing behavior: predominantly getting people to buy the brand. There may be sub-objectives revolving around propelling them along the path to purchase, but the ultimate goal of shopper marketing has to be purchase.

And while shopping is not an activity that takes place exclusively in stores, a vast majority of shopping behavior takes place somewhere separate from where consumption happens. Different targets, different goals, different environments—it certainly feels like this is a very different marketing challenge. Under those circumstances, would it not make sense to consider a separate marketing mix for shoppers?

TWO DIFFERENT WORLDS MERGED

While the realm of the shopper has a different focus, it also has significant overlap with the consumer realm. If you picture a continuum from the place of consumption to the place of purchase (let's imagine a dining table and a supermarket shelf), you'll see a gradual change in the relative influence of consumer versus shopper as we progress from one side to the other. At one extreme, the point of consumption, the shopper has little influence (assuming that the product is actually available!). The decision of when and where to clean my teeth is driven by the consumption drivers (see Chapter 4) of need, occasion, experience, and availability to consume. But even here, the shopper has influence to a slight extent. The choice to drink a particular bottle of wine depends to a small extent on how much you paid for it or perhaps how easy or difficult it might be to replace it, right?

197

Even deep in the heart of the consumer realm, the shopper has some sway.

And at the other extreme, right at the point of purchase, the consumer certainly has influence. As a shopper in front of the coffee fixture, I might be swayed by the range of products or perhaps by a deal or a "new" flash on a pack—but before I buy, I will almost certainly consider the consumer. Will she like it? If not, then that new product is unlikely to get into the basket.

Laura Ashton, Vice President and Head of Marketing for Lighting in Growth Markets at Philips, likes to think of this continuum graphically:

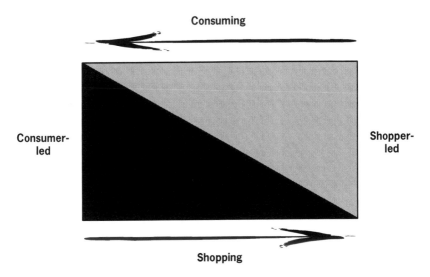

And in between? Digital has ensured that this zone (between the table and the shelf, so to speak) is blurrier than ever before. Individuals can switch between reading product reviews (understanding the consumer experience) and price-comparison sites (deciding where to buy) with the swipe of a finger. An individual can switch from thinking like a consumer to thinking like a shopper and switch back again in the time it takes a page to refresh. Even more disconcerting to the marketer, it is impossible to separate media for consumers and media for shoppers. Even before digital, consumers and shoppers both may have seen your TV commercials in the same way that both consumers and shoppers saw the price slashing in stores. While the blurring was always there, digital has arguably made it worse and certainly made it harder to ignore.

The fact that shopper and consumer marketers simultaneously have two very different targets and goals, yet have a merged "arena" in which to play, is one of the greatest challenges facing organizations that attempt to build this new discipline into the way they manage their brands. Framed in this way, the existing model of consumer goods marketing merely ignores the differences, assuming that the target is the consumer. Our experience would suggest that there is a much more effective way.

To achieve what they want to achieve with consumers, marketers must develop a consumer marketing mix framed by consumption objectives. At the same time, marketers must create a separate and distinct shopper marketing mix designed to affect the behavior of shoppers in a particular way. The final step is to merge or integrate the two marketing mixes and then optimize them. An integrated marketing plan should consider the impact that one plan would have on the other target (and vice versa) and consider whether this is detrimental. There is little point in activity that drives the right shopper behavior but that is likely to be a complete turnoff to the consumer. A discount deal that might make shoppers very excited might make a consumer doubt the integrity of the brand (or indeed its quality). In the same way, a revolution in the consumer offer that doesn't work for the shopper is unlikely to fly.

It is beyond the scope of this book to discuss the creation of a consumer marketing mix—this ground has been well trodden by others, after all. Therefore, we will restrict our discussion to the creation of a shopper marketing mix and how to integrate the two.

THE SHOPPER MARKETING MIX

As we designed our approach to marketing, we hesitated before creating a new language for the shopper marketing mix. We considered whether existing language would suffice, but we concluded that it would not. The primary reason for this was the tendency (in our observation) for things to get lost in translation: we felt that if we used identical language, the differences between the consumer marketing mix and the shopper marketing mix might get lost. Yet, at the same time, we wanted to ensure that the mix was instantly recognizable and that it fit with existing models.

We have, therefore, created a shopper marketing mix that neatly mirrors Kotler's 4 Cs model. The shopper (the customer) is at the heart of our model; it's built out of an understanding of who the shopper is and what her needs are. In addition to this, our marketing mix has three main elements: *availability*, *communication*, and *offer*.

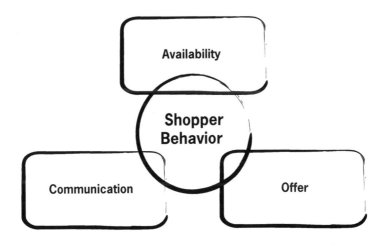

Availability is what makes shopping convenient for shoppers. It is about ensuring that the product can be found wherever the shopper wants it. *Communication* is the language and messaging we use with shoppers. And *Offer* is a focus on the cost to the shopper—what she actually has to pay to achieve her shopping goal.

AVAILABILITY—"WITHIN ARM'S REACH OF DESIRE"

Robert Woodruff's vision for Coke to be "within arm's reach of desire" is fascinating. It demonstrates the company's absolute desire to ensure that its product is completely available—a recognition that, even for a global powerhouse of a brand like Coke, not being "convenient" is highly risky: if the brand is even slightly hard to find, then a sale might be lost. Time and time again, our research and studies demonstrate that for many brands, the biggest barrier on the path to purchase is simple availability. No matter how complex the path to purchase and no matter how sophisticated the web of messages that is laid to guide a shopper toward that ultimate goal of buying the product, the biggest stumbling block is the same as it has been for decades: shoppers' inability to find the brand when they want it. Today, a shopper who really, really wants to buy something can. He may have to trek to other stores, order it online, or perhaps scour every shelf on every aisle of the store to locate it, but the product is theoretically available to him. However, it is not available *enough*. In other words, the process of the shopper trying to get his hands on the brand is simply not convenient.

To be available to a shopper, a product must be placed so that he can find and purchase it conveniently, with a small amount of effort. Too much effort and the sale is at risk. The trouble is, the amount of effort the shopper is willing to put in—the "convenience threshold"—depends on who he is, where he's shopping, and what he's shopping for. It may be perfectly acceptable to go to a specific store to buy certain items (for example fresh produce), but most shoppers would be unlikely to make an additional stop for others (say, a can of peas). If the convenience threshold is, therefore, highly variable, we can be sure of one thing: making it more convenient for the shopper to do what we want him to do is almost universally a good idea!

And that means improving availability. At this point, we forgive you for wondering why we are going to such great lengths to spell out the importance of availability. It would seem obvious to anyone that if a shopper cannot find a product, then he cannot buy it, and that is hardly a good outcome for the shopper marketer and the company that employs her. But given the amount of shopping trips that break down because of this, it is clearly a point worth making.

Many in the consumer goods industry focus their definition of availability on whether the product is "listed" in a store. Unfortunately, this is a long way away from true availability from the point of view of a shopper. A product being "listed" merely means that the store owner or buyer has agreed to make it available to the store manager to order. Key account managers across the world (ourselves included!) have been known to celebrate success immediately following a great meeting with a buyer, only to suffer an awful sinking feeling when the product doesn't appear on the shelf as planned. For a listing to translate to product on the shop floor, it needs to be ordered at store level and then make the journey from the stockroom to the shelf. In our early days as sales representatives, we were both drilled on the importance of going "out back" and pulling product onto the shelf.

But "on the shelf" is not "available," either. Even if our work to date has ensured that we are focusing on the right channels, and even if we've managed to get the product onto the shelf, this doesn't guarantee that it is "available" in the shopper's terms. Look at the problem that Tropicana Twister experienced (discussed in Chapter 5) when the location of the chiller was nowhere near where shoppers expected it to be. They considered it unavailable and opted for a brand that was more visible. The product was in the wrong location in the wrong part of the store—to the shopper, it was unavailable.

Even when a product is in stock and at the right location in-store, this still doesn't guarantee availability from the shopper's perspective. Many categories have hundreds of products, so it is quite possible that a shopper simply won't be able to find or simply won't notice one particular product among the sea of choice. The product is there, but it is invisible to the shopper. It is, from his perspective, unavailable.

The process of shopping is complex: in a typical shopping trip, a shopper may have to find, select, purchase, and pack many products in a short period of time. This needs to be done in a complex, often stressful environment. A modern hypermarket may have tens of thousands of products across many aisles with hundreds of marketing messages. A shopper has to navigate this to find, in among the twenty thousand products, the 30 he is looking for (and at the same time juggle a phone call from the office, bored kids, a shopping cart that won't go straight, and hundreds of other shoppers!). Shoppers use schemata—scripts—to guide them around the store. A movement to a new location on the shelf, not enough space, or a new packaging design can throw off a shopper, disrupt her shopping patterns, and prevent a sale.

What other barriers conspire to make products unavailable (at least from a shopper's perspective)? Gillette, in many markets, has a tremendous challenge because its razor blades are deemed to be of high value and are frequently targeted by shoplifters. Some retailers lock them up in protective cases or keep them on a shelf behind a counter. They are visible but not accessible. Depending on the loyalty factor (or how urgently a blade is needed), the shopper may or may not seek out a store employee to assist with getting the desired razors. If the product isn't bought, what happens to consumption? The shave is lost. An old blade will be used for an extra few days, and even if the blade is eventually bought, the purchase is retarded forever. If that happened just four times a year, with a delay of a week each time, Gillette would lose the equivalent of four weeks' blade usage, which translates into an almost eight percent drop in sales. That is quite a price to pay to reduce theft.

Next, let's consider the "unavailable avocado." Avocados are wonderful, and for most of us, they are imported. This means they must be picked before they are ripe to allow for the shipping time. But too often, they are plucked so early that you find them still too firm as you stand squeezing them in the produce section of your store. Sure, you can take some home and wait for them to ripen, but what if you want to eat your avocado right away? In effect, what the shopper wants—ripe fruit—is unavailable.

The final issue is possibly the biggest. As discussed in Chapter 6, an out-of-stock means that your product is, unfortunately, unavailable. You put in all that effort to get a shopper to the point where she's convinced to buy your product, and then it's not available.

To achieve availability is to achieve it on the shopper's terms. That means the right product in the right place and in the right pack size. The shopper has to be able to find it and then buy it on her terms. Product in a stockroom or on a lower shelf that's out of sight of a casual glance may seem available from the point of view of a marketer examining a planogram or from the perspective of a supply-chain clerk examining inventory levels. But to a shopper, it isn't available.

The cost of this unavailability depends on what happens next. How does a shopper react to a product not being available? This will depend on whether she was searching for that product or not, but her actions can be categorized into three key possibilities: either she will defer the purchase of that object until another shopping trip; she will buy something else; or she will buy nothing at all and continue with the rest of the shop. The following figure shows these three possible shopper outcomes; it also includes a fourth possibility: that the shopper buys what she intended to buy in the case of the product being available.

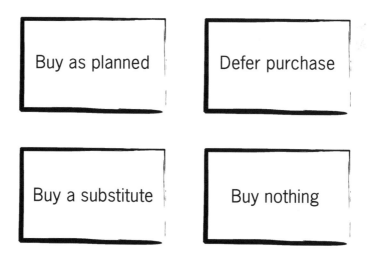

A shopper who *really* wants a specific product may defer a purchase to another trip. That's not all bad news for the brand owner, as the purchase will eventually be made (or may be made). Yet, there is always a chance of the shopper "cooling off" in the time between this disappointment and the next time she shops, and there is always time for a new message from a competitor to interfere and perhaps persuade her to buy something else.

The cost of this delay may also impact consumption. If the deferred purchase is for a product still available to consume (for example, there is still shampoo at home), then the delay will not impact consumption at all—the consumer will have enough product to continue for some time, hopefully long enough for the purchase to be made. While a short-term sale has been lost, long-term consumption continues. Ultimately, if consumption is not interrupted, *there will be no long-term loss of sales to the manufacturer.*

If, however, the product is not in stock at the point of consumption, then the risk is high. If the consumption occasion is for a carbonated drink and there is no stock at home, what will the consumer do? The shopper may be unprepared to switch to a different brand of soft drink, but the consumer almost certainly will. A consumer faced with a fridge devoid of Pepsi is unlikely to go thirsty. He'll drink milk, water, or juice. *The brand has lost the consumption occasion forever!* If the consumer usually drinks a can a day, he is unlikely, after all, to drink two the following day to make up for the missed soda. You can't get that volume back; that volume is gone—and that means that over the long term, the amount bought will likewise be lower.

As you can see, when evaluating the shopper marketing mix, understanding the consumption behind the shop is critical. Further, the deferred purchase potentially costs a retailer more. While retailers bombard shoppers with loyalty-laden offers, the reality is that most shoppers use many stores in a week to satisfy their needs. There is a good chance that the deferred purchase will take place in a different store, and potentially one owned by a competitor. The retailer stands to lose much more from the deferred purchase, on average, than the manufacturer.

All retailers hail the switcher shopper. When a shopper decides to switch brands or products in the face of in-store unavailability, then things look brighter for the retailer. At least the retailer makes a sale, even if the manufacturer didn't. The switched product might even be more expensive or more profitable to the retailer! Of course, there's just as much chance that the shopper will switch to a cheaper or less profitable product, but at least a sale is made. More damaging to the retailer is that the shopper's image of the store may be damaged by the out-of-stock—and if it happens consistently, the shopper may well question the wisdom of shopping in a store that habitually lacks some of the products she wants to buy.

To manufacturers, the switched purchase is a terrible situation. Not only do they lose a sale today, but consumption of their brand is likely to be replaced (and therefore lost forever) with consumption of a competing brand. Worse, a (potentially) loyal consumer is now going to try that competitive product and may well like it—or even prefer it. A relationship with a loyal consumer, built up with potentially millions of dollars of marketing, could be destroyed by a simple out-of-stock. With this in mind, it really is hard to fathom why so many marketers do not pay closer attention to what happens in stores.

So, faced with unavailability, the shopper may defer purchase or switch to a competing offer. But she may also make the third potential choice—she may simply buy nothing. When this happens, both parties lose. A purchase is lost, and the brand is not available for consumption. Clearly, the need to buy wasn't that great, but the chance to get a sale in the short term—and the opportunity to nurture a relationship in the long term—has vanished. The consumer marketing mix may have been very effective, but the ball was dropped in this crucial part of the shopper marketing mix.

Managing availability

So how does a marketer ensure that the product is available? Further, how does the marketer use an understanding of availability and how shoppers shop to maximize sales and returns?

The starting point is an understanding of who the shopper is, and where and how they shop. The challenge is to ensure that the product is available and visible. Further, if we consider that we, as shopper marketers, are trying to change shoppers' behavior, we must ask ourselves how we can maximize the opportunity to influence shoppers, to actually disrupt their shopping trip and enable them to do what we want them to do—buy our product in a certain quantity. Putting it another way, managing availability is about striking a balance between making it really easy for shoppers to do what they want to do (i.e., convenience) and making it easy for them to do what we want them to do. These two concepts are bound together in the two core elements of availability: *ranging* (the decision about which products will be stocked in a particular store) and *merchandising* (the decisions about how and where these products will be displayed). Some models of in-store marketing separate these two. Indeed, they are two distinct concepts, but it is impossible to plan where products will go in a store without first being aware of which products are included. In the same way, it is impossible to finalize the range of products without first knowing how they will be displayed. At the simplest level, the amount of space allocated is a major limiting factor on the range that can realistically be held by a shelf. Thus, it is impossible to separate the two in practice.

The challenge is to choose which products should be made available and where to place them so that you achieve the dual goal of making it easy for a shopper to do what he wants to do and making it easy for him to buy what you want him to buy. This challenge is made more complex by two other considerations. First, the retailer will want to optimize the situation financially. From a retailer's point of view, the goods it stocks can often be the single biggest contributor to working capital and one of the top costs on its P&L (up there with property and people). Think about the vast amount of product tied up in stores around the world. Retailers want to persuade shoppers to buy the product that is most profitable to them, but they also want to arrange the range and monitor the inventory level of each product or category to maximize stock turns. Putting these two together creates a measure known as "gross margin return on inventory investment"—a key measure for many retailers that we'll discuss in further detail in Chapter 13, "Motivating Retail Customers."

Finally, shopper marketers must consider the operational effectiveness of the availability plan. Products do not miraculously appear on shelves; they need to be put there. For most retailers, managing this is operationally challenging and costly (witness the high levels of out-of-stocks referred to earlier). Allocate too much space for a product, and you end up with too much stock. This impacts profits and contributes to the risk of aged stocks. Too little space and the product runs out too quickly, leaving gaps on the shelf and failing the shopper. In today's world of lean stores with minimal or no inventory in the storeroom, many retailers want to empty a complete case of product onto the shelf. Half a case of product is hard to store and is highly likely to be damaged (or stolen) in the stockroom.

Slow-selling products are hard to deal with, but bulky ones are the worst. Just a few units of diapers and toilet paper can take up expensive shelf space. Have too little space and you'll end up out of stock; too much and—well, how is the retailer going to fit all the other products in? The breadth of a range has a significant impact of the economics of shelf-space management. Having too many products in a range compresses the amount of space per product, making it harder to keep the product in stock. Having too many products also makes it harder for shoppers to find what they want. Too few products means the shopper definitely can't find what he wants!

To manage this challenge, a number of tools and principles should be applied, all of which require a clear understanding of how shoppers view products and categories. Without looking from a shopper point of view, it is highly unlikely that the decision you make is going to work very well.

The ranging question

Range and merchandise go hand in hand, but the process is actually iterative—beginning with the ideal range of products, then working out how to merchandise them, then reviewing and adjusting the range to fit the merchandising plan, and so on. The starting point, therefore, should be a decision about which products to make available in a store. Clearly, stocking *every* product is impractical for most physical stores, which are limited by the space they have. Most retailers are limited also by the sheer cost of stocking every possible product, most of which wouldn't sell. But even if this were possible, it has been proven to be counterproductive. Studies show that having too many products to choose from actually makes it hard for shoppers to find what they want; paradoxically, they feel they have less choice rather than more. So the challenge for most retailers (and the manufacturers who attempt to influence them) is finding the optimum range.

The starting point of this analysis is to understand how shoppers view the category, and in particular, how they segment it. To understand what products can be omitted from a range, we must know how shoppers substitute products in this category. Since we know that not all products can be placed on the shelf, the task is to eliminate the products that will be missed least by shoppers. Products that sell less or products that would readily be substituted for something else are naturally safer to eliminate than those that have large bands of fiercely loyal shoppers who may storm out of the store if they cannot find their preferred product.

Marketers need, therefore, to segment the products in the range into products that are more or less substitutional. Each segment can then be analyzed, and the marketer can choose the optimum range that balances operational, financial, and shopper needs. The analysis typically applies something close to a Pareto principle—a small number of products will cover a large amount of sales and of shoppers' needs. The term *market coverage* can be used to describe how much of the market is covered by a range. For example, 80 percent market coverage refers to a range of products that represents 80 percent of the total market's sales (or at least the sales in that channel). Retailers can set different levels of market coverage depending on how important a particular segment or category is to them and to their shoppers. In a category where the retailer wants to be seen as having a comprehensive range, the market coverage target may be high. A top-end retailer may choose to set higher market coverage thresholds for premium segments than for value ones, and so on. Strategy, too, may play its part. A desire to promote a healthy image may result in higher market coverage for health-oriented segments.

The type of store also has an impact. A convenience store may have very high market coverage for beverages (where a great selection is critical) but very low coverage for staple products bought in distress, where the shopper is likely to be less fussy about what she buys. In every case, the shopper perspective drives the selection.

However, as we said earlier, it isn't all about the shopper. There are also some practical considerations. The number of products required to achieve a certain level of market coverage varies dramatically. Adding one more product may increase market coverage by several percent (that would be very efficient); in other circumstances, it might take several products to move market coverage up by a fraction of a percent. This concept is called *fragmentation* and is illustrated in the following figure.

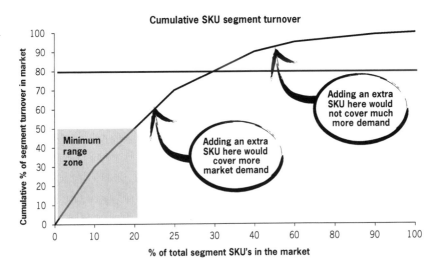

Graphing the number of products against product coverage results in a curve. Where the curve is steep, adding a single product increases coverage enormously. Where the curve is flat, each additional product makes little difference. As with all compromises, it is a fine balance.

Here, it is important to differentiate not just between products but also between shoppers. If we assume that some products must be absent, then some shoppers may be disappointed. Clearly, our most valuable shoppers should be prioritized. Target shoppers should be prioritized. Ranges must be adjusted not just to facilitate the average shopper's purchase but also to help the most valuable shoppers. When Tesco first launched the Clubcard in the UK, there was a myth (of unknown origin) that one of Clubcard's early triumphs was the rescue of a critical product: feta cheese. This relatively specialized segment of the cheese category, which sold very little in total, was on the verge of being delisted, but then analysis of Clubcard data showed that while the number of shoppers who bought it was small, they were all big spenders in Tesco. The segment survived.

Which products go where? The art and science of merchandising

With a first-cut range in hand, the next challenge is where to put the products. In most retail environments, there are two broad categories of location—the "home shelf," where a particular category of products is usually found, and a "secondary" or "off-shelf" location. Secondary locations are often (but not always) temporary. Products are placed on secondary locations primarily to interrupt shoppers—to intercept them and to put something in their path that they might not have noticed in the course of their usual shopping routine. This is the best way to trigger purchases among shoppers who were not planning to shop that category. But the home shelf is by far the most important area of the store—these are the places where similar products are grouped together in categories, regardless of the store type. This is where shoppers go week after week to browse, compare products, and buy. Our research has shown repeatedly that the bulk of sales regularly come from the home shelf, even if there is a secondary display. Shoppers' attention may be sparked by a display, but they often still go to the home shelf to check, browse, and complete their purchase.

The home shelf needs to be configured to help shoppers find what they want and to persuade them to change their behavior in a way that meets with the shopper objective that has been set. If the goal is to switch shoppers from one brand to another, then products should be arranged to encourage that. Further, if shoppers have a tendency to switch away from our brand (we obviously don't want that), then make it difficult for this to happen.

Case study: A milk shake-up

In a project studying kid's milk, we found a tendency for shoppers to switch to cheaper brands as children grew older. From a consumption point of view, some of this was natural (as kids are weaned, they rely less on formula for nutrition, so trading down is more acceptable). But by studying shoppers, we found that people were comparing products at the shelf, deciding what to buy. At this point, how the shelf was configured became important. Products were grouped together by the age for which the product was suitable (zero to six months, six to twelve months, etc.). Shoppers stood comparing many products and, unfortunately, found it difficult to differentiate. (Have you tried to read the back of a kid's formula pack? It's complicated!). They assumed the products, which were grouped together, had some sort of equivalence. They bought the cheaper product, but not because they were happy to buy a lesser product. Instead, they made this decision because, in their minds, the brands had the same ingredients and did the same thing, but one was cheaper. This merchandising, seemingly logical when considered from a consumer angle (grouping products by the age of the end consumer), actually made it hard for the shopper to make an informed decision. The solution to this trading-down problem, which was costing brands and retailers millions, wasn't expensive advertising; it was re-merchandising—shuffling the product around on the shelf. By grouping premium and economy products separately, the retailer allowed shoppers to compare comparable products. They made better choices (and many more of them stayed with the premium brand). Those who wanted a cheaper product could find it. Products were laid out in a way that helped shoppers find what they wanted and encouraged them to do what the manufacturer (and the retailer) wanted—stay with a premium brand.

Merchandising needs to make it easy for shoppers to find what they want, but it also needs to encourage them to do what we, as marketers, want. At the same time, the merchandising plan has to ensure enough space for all of the products in the range, has to ensure sufficient space per product so that nothing goes out of stock, and has to optimize the space allocated to each product to maximize the stock turn and the gross margin return on inventory investment (GMROII). Sounds complicated, doesn't it?

There are few hard-and-fast processes to help either. Tools that help manage the operational and financial efficiency of a shelf exist, but little of this helps in optimizing it for the shopper. Most shelf-management software merely calculates space allocation based on historic sales and profit. The best approaches involve researching different layouts with shoppers to see what happens. In the past, this would have been difficult (involving either changing stores around or mocking up shelves), but these days, virtual store technology has been proven to create statistically meaningful results and enable rapid and cost-efficient testing of shelf concepts.

Having said that, consider the following principles as a guide when laying out a shelf.

1. **Make it easy to see the products you want people to buy.** Most people's eyes naturally fall just below eye level when looking forward, which makes this area a hot spot. To help people notice a new product, put it in this "hot zone." Hot spots are unfortunately not universally in the same place: key brands create hot spots, too, as do signs, offers, etc. Pillars, posts, and other displays often create cold spots. In big stores, it is impossible, or at least impractical, for shoppers to scan every shelf and every product, so it is important to understand where their eyes go and what attracts them, and to ensure that your brand is in the firing line. Research technologies like virtual shelves and eye-tracking—where the shopper wears special glasses that follow the movement of his eyes— can be used to create a more refined view of where hot spots might be.

2. **Put impulse products where they are hard to avoid.** In every category, certain products drive traffic—they bring shoppers to the aisle. Other products don't, but they are nevertheless an important way to grow category sales. For example, in the oral care category, toothpaste is the traffic builder. But it's hard to get people to use more toothpaste, so manufacturers and retailers rely on other products to grow the category. Positioning toothpaste low down on the fixture (hard to find but not impossible) will mean that shoppers can still buy their desired product. But putting toothbrushes directly above toothpaste, in a hot spot, improves the chances of an incremental sale.

3. **Put premium products in hot spots.** Getting shoppers to trade up adds value immediately, so make it simpler to buy the more expensive product.

4. **Group products by your strategy, as long as it doesn't prevent shoppers finding what they want.** The challenge is to make it possible for shoppers to buy what they want to buy, but to encourage them—to make it eas- ier for them, if you will—to do what we want them to do. Sometimes research suggests that shoppers want to have certain products together. A research technology called "decision trees" is often used to create a

map of how shoppers decide what to buy, and that is used to build a merchandising plan. While decision trees do indeed provide useful insight into how a shopper thinks, simply applying this to the shelf is dangerous. For example, in one case, shoppers said that they viewed all stout (dark beers) as similar. The result was that all the stouts were merchandised together in the beer case. The problem was that Guinness, the premium brand, ceded sales to its cheaper competitors, reducing value for the retailer. Separating the two brands was found to give shoppers no trouble in finding what they want but reduced the trade-down situation immensely. If the merchandising approach doesn't make it so difficult to find the product that the shopper gives up, then it is a legitimate option.

5. **Get big packs off the bottom shelf.** As long as it is not too hard for the shopper to buy what he wants to buy, then we can encourage him to behave differently. If we want the shopper to buy more, then we should try to make it easy for them to buy big packs. Too often, big packs are placed on the bottom shelf in stores. This is often driven by operational efficiency: big packs take up more space, and the bottom shelf typically juts out more and can therefore hold more product. But operational ease should not automatically outrank shopper strategy. In another beer case study, we found that while shoppers were happy to buy big packs—and there was a huge opportunity to grow in-home consumption by encouraging bulk purchases—all the shopper could see at the shelf was single cans and bottles. Many shoppers dug out the multipacks from the bottom shelf, but many didn't. Moving the big cases up to waist-level grew sales enormously. In addition, it probably helped save many sore backs—no shopper needs to bend over to pick up a big, heavy case of beer.

6. **Horizontal blocks are easier to see at an angle.** In a supermarket aisle, the shopper approaches the fixture from an angle. Narrow, vertical blocks are much harder to see than long, horizontal ones. If you want to get noticed, block horizontally.

7. **Understand where people go and where they pay attention.** Shoppers walk around stores in many different ways, but they rarely go to all shelves, and they rarely pay equal attention to all the shelves they visit. By mapping how shoppers navigate a store and identifying which parts of the shelf they see and do not see, it is possible to optimize product location.

Once these shopper objectives are reflected in shelf layout, you can run the numbers. Space can be increased or decreased to maximize returns, but each change needs to be considered against its impact on the strategic goals, as well as the finances and operational issues. As the amount of space allocated to each segment is adjusted, the range may need to be reviewed, too; hence, the process becomes iterative. Finally, a decision can be made and the availability is set.

Availability in the digital world

The constraints that apply to the physical store disappear, to a certain extent, in a virtual one. The absolute physical limit on range either disappears or is extended enormously. Product does, of course, need to be stored somewhere but not necessarily in one place or in a logical, shoppable way. Online retailers like Amazon push this even further—many of their products have zero or virtually no stock or are stocked by a third-party vendor who is simply selling via Amazon's site. In the realm of online, the expense of holding massive ranges of product is also diminished. Downloadable music is a good example—the cost of stocking a huge range is arguably no more than stocking a small one.

The online environment also removes some of the problems of merchandising, though there is still a need to apply shopper insight to the process. In place of fixtures and locations, the online environment gives us categories, search, and page layouts. Knowing which products to group together in which tabs requires just as much insight and research as knowing how to group products on a shelf. And web pages must also apply the same concepts behind hot spots and which products should go next to others.

One exciting possibility is the idea of unique stores for shoppers. In the offline world, there is only one shelf, and it needs to work for every shopper who walks in the door. When you put certain products side by side, for every shopper being encouraged to trade up to a more expensive product, another shopper is tempted to trade down by the same layout. But in theory, each online shopper could see a different page and a different layout, modified according to the knowledge the retailer has about how that individual shops. Certainly, the ability to tailor different layouts to different segments is even more reason to really understand and segment shoppers.

Many grocery retailers are yet to grasp this, which presents both a challenge and an opportunity for vendors. The Tesco iPhone app, for instance, displays products alphabetically or by special offer. In this case, if a shopper is looking for Colgate, she is presented with Aquafresh first—great for Aquafresh but bad for Colgate, especially if Aquafresh is on offer. As shopping moves more online, there is a growing urgency for consumer goods marketing teams to build capability in developing and executing online merchandising strategies.

COMMUNICATION

Walk into any store, and you'll find it awash with messages. Even in so-called "clean stores," where manufacturers are not allowed to put up signs, there are typically hundreds—if not thousands—of messages from the retailer. Every piece of packaging is a potential communication media. A digital-age shopper has a smartphone, too, which she can access passively at any place in the path to purchase, and the retailer or manufacturer can also deliver messages to her via the phone. In the midst of all these messages, the shopper marketer must be able to answer four simple questions:

- Who is the target shopper?
- Which messages are required to guide this shopper along the path to purchase?
- Where and when in the path to purchase should this message be delivered?
- By which media should this message be delivered?

As with all marketing, understanding the target is critical to how we communicate messages to her. What is most valuable to know? Who is the shopper? What is her relationship with the consumer? What are her key motivations on this trip? And (perhaps most critically) what are the barriers that prevent her from buying? What is required to overcome those barriers and allow her to move along the path to purchase?

It is profoundly important to understand whether the shopper is also the consumer. It is, of course, impossible to create a clear divide between the two in how we market, and communication is no exception. Many marketers assume that the shopper is also the consumer, so they proceed to market to the shopper as both, which only works if this assumption is correct. Consider an attempt to encourage people to buy a new beverage. If the shopper is also the consumer, perhaps offering a sample of the product will be very effective. But if the shopper is not the consumer, there will be two limitations: first, the sample needs to be transportable, and second, it's less likely to yield a purchase today since the shopper needs the consumer's approval first. If the consumer isn't in the store, then all consumer-oriented messaging must be filtered through the shopper. The marketer can only hope that this messaging is transported home effectively.

Of course, this only applies to consumer messaging. If the messaging is targeted at the shopper, then the challenge is to understand what messages will move him along the path to purchase—what messages will unblock his journey, so to speak. Is the challenge to trigger an impulse in him? Or is it to make him consider a brand he's never had before? Is the challenge to persuade him to buy more than he normally does? If so, what typically limits his purchase?

With clarity on who the target shopper is, the appropriate messaging can be selected. This takes us to the second of our four key questions: What information is required to encourage the shopper to behave differently? What message is most likely to catch her eye and disrupt her shopping patterns? How complex is the message? What action do we wish the shopper to take as a result of this communication?

Even a perfect message delivered at the wrong time is wasted, so we must consider the third question—where and when should this message be delivered? Informing a shopper of a new product formulation at the check-out may or may not be too late. Informing the shopper of where to find a product in the store while they are still at home may be too early. Complex messages may be better absorbed when the shopper has time. Messages that create urgency may be best delivered at the point of purchase.

The final question is the choice of media. Shelf signage, displays, sampling, leaflets, product/brand ambassadors, in-store TVs, magazines—the range of media continues to grow. Increasingly, shoppers are using smartphones while they shop, opening up further possibilities to connect with them. The media choice questions in shopper marketing are similar to those asked in other marketing disciplines:

- Which media is appropriate for this audience?
- Which media is appropriate for this message?
- Which media is the most cost-effective way of achieving the shopper objective?

Different shoppers notice different things in a store. Some pick up leaflets and check out every sign. Others can walk past towering displays and signs but never notice them. All that matters is which media are engaging for this specific target market. It matters little if, as we found in a recent study, 93 percent of shoppers ignore a sign; all that mattered to this manufacturer was that *all* its *target* shoppers noticed it and took action.

Not all media are appropriate for all messages. It is difficult to put a complex message on a sign, for example. Complex messages may be best delivered in leaflets or brochures. Messages that require dialog or affirmation may require brand ambassadors or more sophisticated interactive displays. Messages that are more experiential may require sampling or video. Different messages require different media.

Determining the effectiveness—and, indeed, the cost-effectiveness—of communication efforts is a matter of trial and error. Research can tell how different shoppers respond to different messages and media, and measuring the impact of what happens is critical to success.

This is all very well, but we've so far ignored one small complexity in all communications that is particularly important in a store. Creating a structured communication plan is straightforward, but the challenge (and the opportunity) lies in the fact that *everything communicates*. Everything the shopper sees and hears (whether consciously or subconsciously) sends a message. A product's position on the shelf; a discount; an out-of-stock; aged product; being in a particular store; not being in a particular store; being in a specific section of the store—shoppers can't help drawing conclusions from all these things. Procter & Gamble placed Sunny Delight in the chiller because by being there, it sent a message of being "real juice"—even though it wasn't.

And lest we forget, the shopper journey begins long before the store. Whether deciding which store to visit, checking out websites, or comparing prices, the shopper is receiving messages. If he has rejected your brand by the time he reaches the shelf based on the messages already sent (or not sent), then it may simply be too late. While it is in many cases perfectly possible to encourage shoppers to switch brands at the shelf, sometimes it is not. It depends on the shopper, the category, the type of shop, and the message. A complicated message may be simply too much to digest in the 30 seconds the shopper spends in a convenience store, for example.

Communication in the digital age

The digital shopper is empowered but is also bombarded. Brands invade Facebook pages, browsers, and smartphone apps; they send us tweets and messages based on our location. Many stores now routinely provide wifi access, encouraging shoppers to surf in-store. While the full impact of digital remains to be seen, one thing is certain—cut-through will be critical. The world of the shopper is already complex and overrun with messages— and will only get worse. Retailers have already lost control of the media environment in their stores. Anyone can, in theory, communicate with a shopper in a particular store. A retailer may ban brand messages from the shelves, but that doesn't prevent a shopper from checking out a brand's Facebook page or website while he stands at the shelf. In this digital world, the principles of effective communication become even more important, and the discerning marketer will be successful. Surgical precision in making the right information available in the right format at exactly the right point on the path to purchase will pay dividends. Shoppers in this age have less patience. They want what they want, and they want it now. A shopper may be prepared to browse though pages and pages at home while nursing a coffee, but standing in a store is quite a different story. A shopper wants the information he needs—no more and no less. An introductory video laden with imagery may be beautiful, but if the shopper just wants to know which sizes are available, the video will fast become a turnoff.

The largest change, though, is likely to be in the area of targeting and personalization. The ability to send different messages to different shoppers is already with us: smarter use of analytics will surely lead to more targeted and efficient marketing. In many ways, this is a must: without targeting, shoppers will be flooded with messages and will simply switch off or filter out more and more.

The advent of digital marketing changes everything, yet in many ways it changes nothing. Communication is still communication, and it still follows the same simple principles. Understand your target. Understand what she needs to receive, when she needs to receive it, and the media most effective for conveying that message.

OFFER

For a purchase to be made, an offer must be made. A retailer (or a brand) offers a deal: we give you this in exchange for that. If the offer isn't made, the purchase cannot be completed. Offers can be simple ("You give me $6 and I'll give you this item") or complex ("You give me $46 in monthly installments and I'll give you this item, in a few weeks' time, and I'll fix it if it stops working in the next 30 days as long as you . . ."). But either way, an offer is always made. Offers encompass not just price but also an entire value equation; the shopper weighs this equation as she enters that final phase of shopping: purchase.

The offer part of the shopper marketing mix focuses on (1) the normal price of the product, and (2) the special promotional deals that are made periodically to sweeten the deal for the shopper—X amount off, buy-one-get-one, 50 percent extra free, free premiums, or gifts. These promotions are used extensively in the consumer goods industry. In many cases, they are the default activity a retailer places in front of a shopper. Unfortunately, it's unusual that much is done to understand the precise impact these promotions will have on the shopper.

When planned correctly, promotions can have value. They are often used tactically, and as pragmatic marketers, we don't exactly frown on this behavior. Short-term successes are sometimes needed. But as part of a Total Marketing mix, they can also have strategic value. Reducing the price of a product lowers the barrier to entry and may be the extra incentive required to encourage trial. A discount for a set of ingredients used to make a particular meal may prompt a shopper to try something new. Encouraging a shopper to buy a brand that's slightly more expensive may require reducing the barrier to purchase just enough to tip the balance—perhaps the consumption experience is so delightful that the shopper will deem the full price worth paying in the future.

As discussed previously, offer has a huge impact on profitability, so handle it carefully. Consider who the target shopper is and what impact the promotion will have on his behavior.

Given all we know about the potential dangers of promotion and the high stakes involved (see Chapter 6), a planned approach is critical. Researching and understanding the impact of promotional deals on different groups of shoppers is desirable. And whether or not this is possible, effective evaluation after the promotion is critical.

Promotional objectives should be set in three levels: the impact on the behavior of the target shopper, the impact on the manufacturer, and the impact on the retailer. Each possible promotion should be evaluated on its ability to positively impact the shopper's behavior and drive gains for the manufacturer and the retailer.

Offer in the digital age

One would hope that in this connected world, the myth of price as a differentiator would finally be put to rest. In a world where shoppers can compare prices in an instant, the zero-sum game of pricing would surely be used less, and more sophisticated tools would be used to win the hearts and minds of the twenty-first-century shopper. But alas, as we go to press, this is far from the truth. In fact, the UK's main retailers are using technology to up the pricing ante. Sainsbury's "Brand Watch" instantly tells the shopper whether they got a good deal today and issues a voucher for the difference if he could have bought his basket of goods cheaper elsewhere. Even upmarket Waitrose promises to match Tesco on a limited range of products. Walmart-owned Asda went one step further, promising a basket of goods from its stores would be 10 percent cheaper than the same basket from Tesco.

But the digital age's biggest impact on promotions and price will surely be the shift of power as online retailers reach scale. Digital retail has already hit hard in audio, video, and books, and Amazon now sells all of these and groceries in some markets. Online-only retailers will be formidable competitors to the established offline retailers. Online-only retailers turn the current retail model on its head: the very stores that have been big retail's biggest competitive advantage could become a millstone around their neck. The ability to compete on price may become less and less tenable, and then we might see a more balanced marketing mix applied to the world of shoppers.

Promotions are also likely to become much more personalized. Technologies

Here is a simple procedure to follow when planning a promotion:

1. Take your current gross margin and write it as a number.

   e.g., 25 percent margin = 25

2. Write your discount as a number.

   e.g., 10 percent discount = 10

3. Subtract your discount from your margin.

   e.g., 25 minus 10 = 15

4. Divide margin by this number.

   e.g., 25 / 15 = 1.66

This is the sales increase required if you want to break even. In this case, sales must increase by a factor of 1.66 (an uplift of 66 percent).

Of course, if the discount offered is greater than the margin, then no amount of uplift in sales will deliver a profit!

such as Catalina (a receipt-based coupon system that provides a coupon at the checkout depending on what has just been bought) tailor promotions to different shoppers depending on what they've bought in the past. Retailers who run loyalty card programs target deals based on purchase history and demographics. In the future, this trend is likely to grow. It may even help consumer goods marketers finally avoid deal shoppers altogether.

INTEGRATING THE MARKETING MIX

As discussed earlier in this chapter, once the consumer marketing mix and the shopper marketing mix have been defined, the two need to be integrated. Although the consumer and the shopper must be considered separately for all the reasons stated previously, there is no hard-and-fast line between the consumer arena and that of the shopper. The truth is that there never really was. In the past, the assumption that consumers and shoppers were the same was a poor approximation of the truth that was nevertheless once sufficiently accurate; similarly, the idea that shopping only occurs inside the store—once an adequate representation of reality, even though it wasn't always true—is no longer good enough. Seven years ago, in China, it took up to six months for the average shopper to buy a TV, and they didn't spend those six months in the store. They talked to friends, read brochures, and used the Internet. They shopped—outside the store.

Digital may not have created this reality, but it has brought it into stark relief. It is simply no longer tenable to believe that these two marketing mixes can be considered independently. Today, more than ever, they need to fit together.

The integration approach is, in theory at least, quite simple. Each element of each mix needs to be tested against the other target. Each element of the consumer marketing mix must be considered from the point of view of the target shopper; and vice versa. Each element then needs to be reevaluated based on whether it has a positive or negative impact on the other target. In the case of a negative impact, marketers must consider whether to change the element, add other activity to mitigate the downside, or adapt the element so that it works for both target markets.

Each element of the "4 Ps" consumer marketing mix can be challenged in this way. Products must be perfect for consumers, but they must also be easy to buy. For example, a product with a short shelf life might deliver perfect taste and freshness, but if the shopping cycle is too long, it won't work for shoppers. Packaging needs to deliver brand values when a consumer spots it in the home, and it needs to keep a product fresh; but it needs to be visible and trigger purchase in a store, too. When planning consumer communication, the marketer must also consider how these messages will affect the shopper—whether the shopper will see it, and if so, whether it will deliver for them. Consumer media designed for a consumer who is prepared to spend a few minutes watching a video may be a turnoff for a time-poor shopper who's stressed at the local store.

Likewise, shopper activity may have an impact on consumers. Price deals on a retailer's website may appear in Google searches and attract or repel the consumer. Run too many discounts in-store (be it virtual or offline), and the consumer may start to doubt the quality of the brand. Positioning a premium brand on a shelf with cheap products may affect its brand value in the eyes of consumers (even putting it in a specific retailer may do this). And, of course, the messages delivered in stores by signage, staff, retailer, or leaflet may make their way back to the consumer, even if the consumer wasn't in the store.

CHAPTER 12

OPTIMIZING RETAIL INVESTMENT

One of the hardest aspects of consumer goods marketing to explain to people from outside the industry is the idea of retail investment. To those not intimately connected to the industry, it seems strange, if not downright weird, that nearly twice as much money is spent in retail than is spent on traditional advertising. After all, advertising is by far the most conspicuous part of the consumer goods marketing mix, and no one would be surprised that huge amounts of money are spent annually on TV ads, sponsorship, billboards, celebrity endorsements, Facebook ads, and all the media regular consumers see every day. "How is it possible," the layperson asks, "that those companies could spend more money in retail?"

Yet it's true. One survey, conducted by Accenture CAS, showed that leading consumer goods companies more than tripled their expenditure in retail as a proportion of revenue (from approximately 8 percent to nearly 26 percent) between 1980 and 2005. This makes retail expenditure the largest single cost to the consumer goods industry after the cost of goods.

Similarly, Nielsen reported that today, expenditure in retail accounts forms 60 percent of total advertising and promotions funds (A&P). A more detailed analysis by Donnelly Marketing and Accenture showed in 2005 that expenditure on trade and consumer promotion had more than doubled as a proportion of total A&P since 1975, while traditional advertising and media had fallen by a third.

More recent research by MEI Trade Insight showed that 87 percent of CPG brand marketers intend to increase or maintain their spend on trade activities in the year ahead.[83] This is especially surprising because in all our interactions with leaders in the consumer goods industry, we find that escalating trade spend is one of the largest threats to future profitability.

So why is so much money spent in retail environments?

Well, the first part of the answer is historical; as we explored earlier in the book, as media became more fragmented and retail consolidated, marketing at the point of purchase became not only possible but also attractive. But the second, and perhaps more important, part of the answer has more to do with the economics of retail than with a solid marketing rationale. The mega retailers of today would lose money were it not for the cumulative funds that they extract from manufacturers in return for providing marketing services.

Our friends outside the consumer goods industry are often surprised when we tell them who pays for what in a retail store. Think about what you see when you go to the average grocery store. The posters on the windows and doors advertising deals—the manufacturers paid for those. The leaflets presenting offers—the manufacturers paid for those. The big displays in the first aisle—the manufacturers paid for those, too. The product displays at the end of every aisle, the banners hanging from the ceiling, the "shelf talkers" highlighting deals on every shelf—all paid for by manufacturers. The product-sampling booths and the people offering the samples—the manufacturers funded them. The lucky draws and inventive competitions—also paid for by manufacturers. The displays on checkouts and the fridges stocking soft drinks and the ice cream freezers—all paid for by manufacturers. The coupons used at the till, the loyalty card used to accrue discounts—also funded by manufacturers. Even some of the people who work filling the shelves are paid for by manufacturers. All of this adds up to a whole lot of money—and that's just what you see!

Now think about what you don't see. Almost every manufacturer pays a slotting fee or a listing fee to have its product placed on shelves. Manufacturers fund more than just the obvious promotional discounts; it's their cumulative investment that helps retailers be cheaper than their competitors. Manufacturers pay retailers to distribute products to their store, and they pay no-returns discounts to avoid taking stock back. Most retailers insist that promotion funds be guaranteed in a contract, securing a discount on every sale. Carrefour even asks manufacturers to pay an "anniversary fee"

---

83 Michael Bollinger, "Shopper Marketing & The Big Miss!" Smith Brothers newsletter, accessed March 7, 2013, http://www.smithbrosagency.com/newsletter/spring-12/shopper-marketing.aspx.

to pay for the stores' birthday promotions. In fact, the only limitation on what manufacturers pay for seems to be the imagination of the retailer. When we tell our friends that, they are often staggered.

It's ironic that retailers' biggest customers are actually their manufacturers and that the income they generate from manufacturers is one of the most important contributors to their total profitability. If retailers tried to sustain themselves on the difference between how much they buy products for (the invoice price) and how much they sell them for (the retail price), it's very unlikely that many would be around for long. This was illustrated to me by a friend and former colleague at Tesco. He explained that in the market in which he ran Tesco's commercial operations, the "front margin" (a retail term for the percentage difference between retail price and invoice price) was approximately 8 percent. He went on to explain that in order to break even on operating costs, the chain needed to make at least a 13 percent margin. How then does a company like this make money?

Simple—through the funds its manufacturers contribute in marketing, promotions, and other fees. These are often referred to as "back margin." We recently modeled the front and back margins that Carrefour made in one of its biggest categories in one major operation in Asia. Our analysis showed that Carrefour lost 0.39 percent in the front margin equation—in effect, they sold the product for less than they paid for it. The back margin, however, totaled 10.1 percent, returning the retailer to profit. It is a fact of retail economics that in order to remain profitable, retailers depend, to a degree, on manufacturers' investments, and by extension, the easiest way for them to continue to grow profits is by securing greater levels of investment from their suppliers.

Anyone with experience working with a major multinational retailer will attest to the importance of this agenda and the continued pressure that these retailers place not only on their suppliers but also on buyers to secure an ongoing improvement in front and back margins. Retailers offer a clear and compelling logic to drive this: numerous outlets attract a great deal of shoppers, making stores both efficient to supply and an effective marketing channel; this efficiency justifies both lower prices and direct investment from manufacturers. By securing lower prices from manufacturers, retailers can offer lower prices to shoppers; the lower prices offered across numerous outlets attract yet more shoppers (and so the cycle continues). This cycle has become known as the "cost price reduction" (CPR) cycle, and it is the economics of CPR that drive spiraling expenditure in retail.

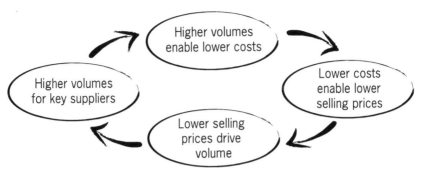

Source: Retail Outsourcing Ltd.

RETAIL COST OR RETAIL INVESTMENT?

The big question, though, is this: Do these funds represent an investment (as retailers would have their suppliers believe) or a cost of doing business (as one senior manager witheringly described to us recently)? In truth, this is such a big question that when we pose it to teams around the world in workshops, it often prompts furious debate. To help us answer it, let's first be clear on what we mean by "investment" and "cost."

The act of investing is well described by Princeton University's wordnetweb.com website as "laying out money or capital in an enterprise with the expectation of profit." That is to say that when a sum of money is spent with the direct expectation that more money will be returned, it is an investment. By contrast, Dictionary.com offers the following definition for *cost*: "the price paid to acquire, produce, accomplish, or maintain anything."[84] So, one might say that when one spends money *without* the expectation of profit, it is a cost.

We have already discussed the levels of return that manufacturers accrue in promotions (they lose money on up to 70 percent of the promotions they "invest" in), and recent data from POPAI suggests that there is a one in 150 chance of a target shopper even seeing a promotional message in a store.[85] As you can see, today's expenditure in retail has many of the characteristics of a cost rather than an investment.

---

84 "cost," Dictionary.com, accessed March 7, 2013, http://dictionary.reference.com/browse/cost.
85 Larry McManis, "Newsflash: The Shopper Doesn't Even See The Display You Spent Millions On," *Shopper 360*, August 8, 2012, http://www.myshopper360.com/newsflash-the-shopper-doesnt-even-see-the-display-you-spent-millions-on.html.

Indeed it's entirely possible that most managers in the consumer goods business have no idea what the potential returns on retail expenditure are. Our interactions with sales and trade marketing teams have taught us that the industry rarely evaluates its expenditure in retail. Most businesses evaluate only the very largest activities, and this analysis is often relatively simplistic. The technology consultant Gartner reported that the leading tool used by consumer goods teams to evaluate promotions expenditure is Microsoft Excel[86]—hardly a sophisticated way of managing funds that run into the billions.

Even where trade spend is evaluated, the calculation of return on investment is often flawed. In a recent interview with a former manager at Dunnhumby—Tesco's loyalty, data, and consulting division—we were told that participation in Tesco's targeted couponing campaigns delivered an average ROI of 400 percent. "Really?" we said, "How can you calculate ROI without knowing the margins of each manufacturer?"

"Ah," said the manager, "in fairness, when we say ROI what we really mean is that if you spend, say, $1,000 on a program, you can expect at least $4,000 in sales."

What this illustrates is the most common way the industry evaluates ROI—by dividing incremental sales value by the cost incurred. Of course, this gives a beguilingly positive picture. The truth is that ROI should be calculated based on the incremental profit accrued from the activity. Given that consumer goods companies make 8.5 percent margin on average,[87] in the previous example, the manufacturer loses $680 (incremental profit = $4,000 × 8 percent = 320; incremental cost = -1,000 +320 = -680), delivering a true ROI of 0.32.

So it seems that the truth behind retail expenditure is that it is a cost and not an investment. But what if it was an investment? What if the consumer goods industry did make a profit on its expenditure in retail?

Well, then things would be dramatically different because the profitability of the entire industry would leap forward. We estimate that today, 10 percent of total sales are spent on promotions, and we assume that this delivers a return of 30 cents on the dollar. We said earlier that this represents a net

86 Alarice Padilla, "7 Considerations for Choosing a TPM Solution," Consumer Goods Technology, November 21, 2011, http://consumergoods.edgl.com/trends/7-Considerations-for-Choosing-a-TPM-Solution76876.

87 Deloitte, *Global Powers of Consumer Products 2012: Connecting the Dots*, accessed February 28, 2013, http://www.deloitte.com/assets/Dcom-Guam/Local Assets/Documents/Global Powers of CP 2012_Deloitte_Web.pdf.

loss of 7 percent per annum. Just breaking even, therefore, in an industry that makes just less than 8 percent on average would almost double profitability. Integrating shopper marketing into the Total Marketing equation makes this possible.

WHY INVEST IN RETAILERS?

Why do we invest in retailers, then? This simple question is often asked by naïve consumer marketers as they see their advertising budgets whittled away by the "profligate guys" on the sales team. And retailers have a clear, simple answer to this—retailers own the shopper. After all, the retailer invested in the real estate and marketing to draw shoppers to its stores. Retailers have invested in the infrastructure to supply the stores, putting the products to be bought by shoppers on their shelves. It's the retailers' real estate assets that are used to market products in the stores, so why shouldn't manufacturers invest in them in order to get shoppers to buy? So the argument goes.

One can go on to assert that without the retailer's support, little can be done to conclude the sale. All of the essential decisions that lead to a purchase are made by retailers: they decide which products to stock, how and where products will be merchandised, what promotions to run, what advertising will be run in-store, and the final price a shopper will pay. Given that retailers control these decisions, if a manufacturer wishes to influence these decisions, part of the equation must be the level of investment the company is willing to make.

This is a simple, strong argument for investing in retailers, right? Wrong!

This simple rationale, while factually accurate in all of its key points, misses the major point entirely. This argument makes a case for treating the funds offered to retailers as a cost. It simply says that in order to get things done in a retail environment, the manufacturer has to pay. This is as close to the definition of a cost that one can get.

If this is all a manufacturer's funds achieve, then money spent on retail is merely cost. But with so much being spent, surely brand owners should aspire to more: aspire to make some return on all this expenditure. The financial laws that govern return on investment dictate that one must make more profit than was spent to deliver a positive financial return. Most vendors have an ongoing relationship with a retailer—they have a relatively stable base of sales that will continue. This relationship includes a built-in assumption that, all other things being equal, costs should remain static too. So, in order to justify an investment in retail, the investment must create incremental profit. This can only come from changing the sales base or reducing costs overall. Logically, one would only invest in a retailer if either of these outcomes were possible.

The five-step approach enables marketers to navigate this logic. Let's take, for instance, the kids' milk case discussed in the previous chapter. The company involved stood to gain significant sales and profits by ensuring that *consumers* continued to use its more expensive brand in favor of the cheaper one. In order to do this, the company sought to prevent *shoppers* from switching to a cheaper brand. The outcome of this change in behavior is a quantifiable increase in profits. Since shoppers in hypermarkets regularly compared brands, reducing the level of comparison in this *channel* was important. So in these large format stores, changing the merchandising of the shelf was a great *marketing* strategy to prevent switching. Since the costs associated with re-merchandising were relatively low and the potential to create incremental profit was high, it made sense to *invest in retailers* who owned hypermarket stores.

So, why invest in retail? To implement activities in priority channels where influencing shoppers' behavior is likely to increase consumption. This rationale turns the simple answer companies often offer on its head. It forces teams to make a clear distinction between cost and investment, but it can also have a dramatic impact on a company's P&L. However, this can only happen if retail investment is the last decision marketers make in the five-step process.

INVESTMENT IN RETAIL—THE LAST DECISION YOU MAKE

In many companies around the world today, there is a constant internal negotiation between the sales functions and the marketing teams as to how much money should be spent and where. Budgets are often cut in very traditional ways. First, a sales value target is agreed upon, often based on last year's performance and an acceptable growth rate for the coming year. Then an A&P budget is defined by multiplying the sales target by a constant percentage developed by the finance team; this budget is then subdivided between the sales and marketing functions. What then follows is a debate about whether this budget is adequate for either party (often it's not), and a new number is eventually agreed upon. The budget that stays with marketing is split by brand, and the sales budget is prorated across the customer base, normally based on the size of the company's sales to each customer. As customers' demands escalate, the sales team soon finds it doesn't have enough money to meet these demands, and the negotiation begins again. It's quite easy to see that this approach puts the company at the mercy of its biggest customers and drives the constant increase in total retail cost.

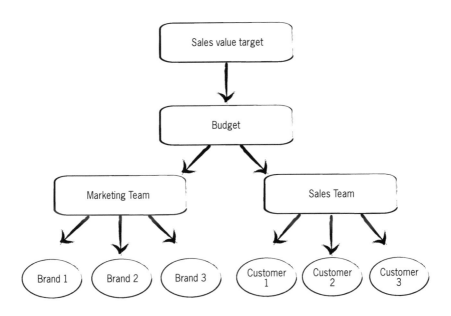

What's at fault, therefore, is the way that consumer goods companies often plan their growth and investment. We believe that to get better results, a better approach is needed—one that places customer investment at the end of the process, not in the middle as it is now. By now, you'll know how we believe these decisions should be managed—namely, using the five-step process:

Step 1: The team defines which opportunities for consumption growth it will prioritize.

Step 2: The team identifies the shopper behavior that's needed to deliver this consumption.

Step 3: The team defines which channels are to be prioritized to deliver this behavioral change and set sales targets for brands in each channel.

Step 4: The team defines the marketing mix needed to deliver the sales targets.

Step 5: The team determines which retailers can implement this marketing mix in each channel and develops a trade investment framework to secure this implementation.

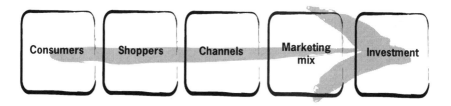

This process breaks the traditional model in three very significant ways. First, it focuses the team on driving incremental consumption. As a result, the basis of growth targets is no longer last year's sales plus an estimate of acceptable growth. Instead, it is a quantified view of the achievable sales number that can be gained from the existing consumer base as well as from new consumers. These growth targets are more tangible and realistic and thus have much more meaning for the individuals who will ultimately deliver them.

Second, this approach focuses the marketing mix on prioritized segments of the consumer, shopper, and retail base. This makes the task of marketing in a complex environment more manageable and much more specific. It enables manufacturers to market a given brand in a much more integrated and coherent way.

And finally, this approach puts the importance of a channel ahead of individual retailers. This prevents a small number of customers from driving the escalation of retail expenditure and offers the company a more expansive picture of where retail investment should be targeted.

However, this five-step approach to retail investment requires significant change, and in most cases, manufacturers faced with such a significant change find that inertia steps in and prevents action. So why would a company embrace such a wholesale change in common business practice?

Having worked with a number of companies through this process, here's what we've observed. First, this way of working reduces conflict. By working through the process, managers who once positioned themselves as having dramatically different roles in the organization come to see a common purpose. With this common purpose in view, each person's role in the achieving an objective becomes clearer, and ownership increases. This breaks up the divisive silos that apportion blame for poor performance more often than praising great performance.

Further, we've found that investment decisions become both easier and more focused with this approach. This will become increasingly important as digital blurs the lines between traditional "above the line" and "below the line" investments. By looking at the total investment requirement to drive consumption, the company no longer needs to consider what "consumer investment" is and what "trade investment" is in the same way—it simply becomes "necessary investment."

More interestingly, we've seen that companies that embrace this approach have gained competitive advantage with retailers. This might seem counter-intuitive, as inevitably the transition from an approach that credits the size of the retailer to one that favors the value a retail channel can deliver is likely to see some retail customers losing out. But this doesn't seem to happen.

We alluded to an interview with a former Dunnhumby director earlier in this chapter. He was particularly impressed with one manufacturer that explained why investment in Tesco's Clubcard data was not an important priority despite the retailer holding high market shares. He talked about how the team had demonstrated that Tesco was of lower importance to the company for a key brand, so they would not be investing in his data. What struck him was that far from being marginalized in discussions with Tesco, this manufacturer was actively sought out for its insight and opinion, and it received greater support proportionally on the brands for which Tesco was a priority. This manufacturer is the only company applying the five-step approach in Malaysia, where the interview took place.

Finally, we have seen this approach deliver results. In most cases, it is rare to find examples where companies have been able to reduce their expenditure with major retail players; yet over the last two years, one of our clients has reduced overall expenditure in 20 key accounts by more than $5 million.

We think that there are some compelling reasons for taking a customer-last approach to trade investment, but we anticipate that, by now, most readers will be asking how this is practically done. So, for the rest of this chapter, we'll examine how, with a marketing mix in hand, a management team might go about structuring investment and then defining the principles that should be applied when making investments. (And in the next chapter, "Motivating Retail Customers," we'll deal with the thorny question of how to persuade a retailer that this new approach is a great idea!)

STRUCTURING TRADE INVESTMENT—BEGIN WITH THE END IN MIND!

One of Stephen Covey's "seven habits of highly effective people" is putting the end goal at the beginning of every activity. Let's follow Mr. Covey's advice and look at the ultimate goal of trade investment. What is it? To make more profit.

Without incremental profit, there is no payback on any investment.

It certainly doesn't require an MBA to know that there are only two ways to increase profit—you can either reduce costs or you can increase sales. So, logically, the outcome of an investment in retail must be one or both of these.

Investments that drive sales growth are those that focus on changing shopper behavior. The investments spend money on activities that encourage existing shoppers to buy more often or to spend more, or they spend money on activities that encourage new shoppers to buy the brand. Naturally, these investments are configured to support availability, communication, and compelling offers.

Reducing costs between retailers and their suppliers generally requires that the two businesses become more efficient in dealing with each other rather than simply taking items out of a cost line. Investment funds can be targeted to promoting reductions in working capital—by reducing inventory, for example, or improving cash flow or reducing overhead. Generally, these investments either reward efficient working relationships or fund changes in operational processes.

The investment strategies one has to choose from are numerous, so it's important to construct a clear framework that identifies what money should go where. This requires some rigorous thinking, but it has to start with a fundamental notion that one invests only in channels that have a high potential to deliver a significant change in shopper behavior. At this point, channel prioritization becomes an essential input.

In Chapter 10, we introduced a model defining which channels are most important. We concluded that we prefer channels that are both highly relevant to target shoppers and are more easily managed:

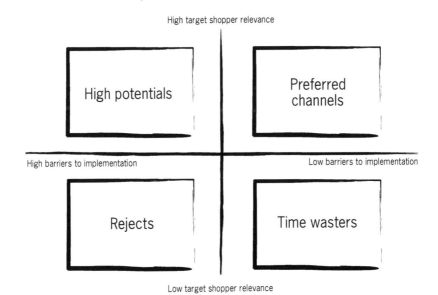

High target shopper relevance

| High potentials | Preferred channels |

High barriers to implementation ——— Low barriers to implementation

| Rejects | Time wasters |

Low target shopper relevance

This model is tremendously valuable because it guides the business in making investment decisions at the channel level. In a "preferred channel," a company should be able to expect exuberant growth and relatively high returns on investment. It makes sense for the management team to focus heavily on investments that will deliver this growth and less so on enhancing efficiency. In "high potentials," the inverse might be true—since it is harder to realize higher levels of growth, one might be more circumspect on the amount of funds earmarked for growth, while seeking to make initial gains in efficiency.

"Time wasters" have the potential to suck up growth funds for little or no reward, so seeking efficiency is perhaps the only viable option here. And while the company might not wish to sacrifice the volume created in "rejects," any funds deployed in this space would be better allocated to "preferred channels" or "high potentials."

For one of our clients in Korea, this approach has driven real value. The particular company sells vitamins and mineral supplements and owns major brands in the space. Korea, a vibrant and growing market for supplements, has a new generation that is seeking to blend traditional ginseng with more

Western alternatives. Yet in Korea, only 4 out of 10 consumers use such products, while penetration in Australia is close to 7 in 10. Driving growth in this market depends on acquiring new consumers while they're young since, as the aging process sets in, those who already use supplements have a tendency to consume a wider range of products. Korea's hardworking and relatively youthful population has rapidly adopted Internet shopping sites, and our analysis of this market demonstrated that Internet-based outlets are absolutely the preferred environment for investment:

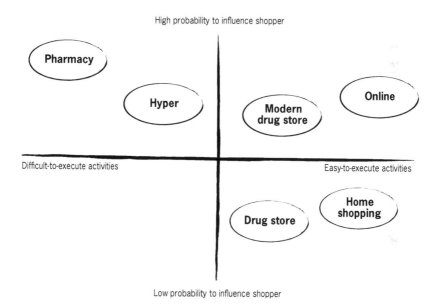

Before its ultimate breakup, Sara Lee was a client of ours, particularly in Southeast Asia. While planning investments for the company's coffee business in Thailand, we were able to apply the same methodology. This business was particularly strong in urban areas and in hypermarkets, supermarkets, and convenience stores. Its performance was much poorer in more rural environments and especially in traditional mom-and-pop retailers. To rebalance its business, Sara Lee considered increasing its investment in the rural mom-and-pop trade. The company planned to invest heavily in distribution to these outlying areas and asked us to help. Having commissioned some research, a number of striking facts came to light. Perhaps the most important was that Sara Lee's weakness in rural areas had less to do with distribution and more to do with its brand. But of equal relevance in configuring retail investment was the fact that some 30 percent of the purchases shoppers from rural homes made were actually in urban supermarkets, hypermarkets, and convenience stores. Given the company's existing strength in these channels, we advised the team not to invest further in its planned strategy but to gain greater leverage in the "modern stores." By following our advice, Sara Lee grew its market share by 15 percent.

This simple step first step creates significant focus, but it doesn't automatically break the cycle of escalating trade costs. What happens, for example, if hypermarkets are a preferred channel, but they are dominated by major global retailers, as might be the case in China? There, the hypermarket channel is full of major players, including Walmart, Auchan (who trade as RT-Mart), Carrefour, Tesco, and a number of nationally important retailers.

The next logical step, therefore, is to conduct a further prioritization of retailers in each channel. Using the same model, one might look at each retailer to refine the framework. So, Walmart's extensive network of stores in China and its ability to execute nationwide might make it a preferred option over Carrefour, whose local trading practices make it difficult to secure execution without going directly to the store manager. RT-Mart has an equally good store network and is known to be easier to deal with than Carrefour. Tesco has a less developed store network, despite its operational expertise. Taking all this into account, a company wishing to drive growth in hypermarkets might prioritize investment in Walmart and RT-Mart, as shown here:

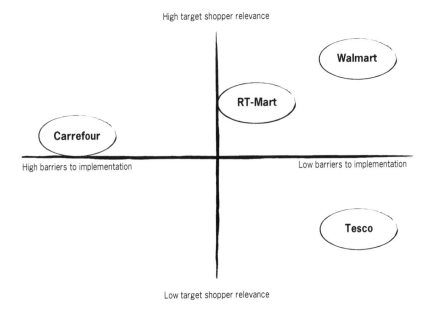

In this case, and in markets where this does not contravene legislation, as would be the case in the US, the funds allotted to the channel for growth might be disproportionately allocated to Walmart and RT-Mart, while maintaining an even allocation of funds to drive efficiency to each.

With a general framework in hand, the company is then able to consider the principles it will apply in actually investing funds.

RETAIL INVESTMENT PRINCIPLES—THE GOLDEN RULES OF INVESTING FOR GROWTH

For the marketer, by far the most important component of an investment strategy is that which drives growth. So, rather than providing lengthy technical instruction on how to engineer more efficient working practices, we feel that offering guidance on how to structure investments in this area is more valuable.

In the last chapter, we talked about the three components of the marketing mix and how they can be combined to deliver behavioral change. Converting this integrated mix into a structured investment approach is somewhat like creating a recipe. As in baking, where different combinations of flour, water, raising agents, fats, salt, and sugar can deliver dramatically different outcomes, different combinations of availability, communication, and offer can have equally diverse outcomes. In every category and for every brand, investment is in all three—but in varying degrees. Yet in our experience, one component will almost always take the lead in terms of its potential to change the shopper's behavior, and this is where most investment needs to be focused.

Take, for example, a category where shoppers' behavior is highly planned and where they consistently buy to that plan. It's unlikely that investing more in offer will drive a change, so the focus of investment might tilt towards availability, where the potential to disrupt shoppers' behavior is higher (one thing guaranteed to interrupt a planned shopper is a lack of availability), or communication, which might help drive additional purchases over that which was planned. One such client found that 80 percent of its retail investment was focused on offer, with approximately 10 percent each on the other two components. By changing the mix from this to 50 percent on availability, 30 percent on communication and 20 percent on offer, the client was able to execute merchandising strategies that encouraged complementary purchase and enticed new shoppers into the category. The reduction in spend on offer meant that the manufacturer and the retailer alike enjoyed higher value sales and ROI.

To define which element should take the lead for investment, we established three golden rules that govern growth investment on almost every occasion.

The First Golden Rule

"Invest in availability when changing shoppers' behavior undermines planned or habitual consumption."

In Chapter 11, we talked about the potential cost of lack of availability, and we discussed a situation where a shopper, faced with not being able to buy the product he planned to purchase, had three options:

Defer purchase   **Buy a substitute**   **Buy nothing**

What if any one of these actions were to materially change the consumption of a brand or category? Let's take a habitual coffee drinker, for example. Many coffee consumers have a preferred brand, and many consume that brand on a regular basis. Some Nescafé consumers drink two cups before work in the morning and one cup on their return home. This is what we might call habitual consumption, and you can find it in all sorts of categories—milk, laundry detergent, toothpaste, diapers, pay-as-you-go phone cards, razor blades, and many others.

In categories where consumption is habitual, leading brands seek to cement loyalty by reinforcing habitual behavior while their competitors constantly seek to switch shoppers to their own brand and create new shopping habits. Since the easiest way to change a shopper's habits is to make a product unavailable, anyone with the potential to gain from such behavior would be wise to prioritize investment in availability.

The Second Golden Rule

"Invest in communication when changing a shopper's behavior will have a profound impact on long-term consumption."

Have you ever noticed the lengths cosmetics brands go to in order to secure sales in department stores? In high-end stores, you'll find elaborate booths not offering ranges of products per se but the opportunity to try those products. Many companies provide full-time makeup artists whose sole job it to evangelize for the product. Potential shoppers are invited to have a complete makeover at great cost to the company. Why is this?

Think about what happens when someone has such a makeover. She learns how to blend foundation, blusher, lip gloss, mascara, eyeliner and so on. She also sees the actual impact of doing so right on her own face. The result? The shopper now has a compelling reason to buy not just one product but a whole range of products. An average user might take six months or more to consume the entire suite of products, but when the time comes to repurchase, the chances that she'll buy from the same range are much increased. Not only does this lock out a competitor, but in some cases, this one makeover can also convert the shopper into a brand advocate who shares her experience with friends and peers.

Not all categories are like cosmetics, but some are. Think about sportswear, premium wines and spirits, skin care, health foods and supplements, TVs, and mobile phones. Marketers in all of these categories have the potential to create committed users by communicating effectively at the point of purchase.

Let's take a real case: one of our clients has a specialist high-calcium milk product that reduces the risk of osteoporosis. Many women consume too little calcium and are at risk of the condition, but few women are aware of this risk until it's too late. The company ran a campaign in large stores, giving women free bone scans to identify their risk of developing osteoporosis. At the end of the process, they were offered the company's product. On average, 33 percent of shoppers who had never bought the product made a purchase on the day of the bone scan, and two-thirds of these shoppers remained committed users three months on.

If your brand has the potential to dramatically change consumption behavior in the long term, a heavier focus on communication investment would be justified.

The Third Golden Rule

"Invest in offer when changing shoppers' behavior
expands consumption."

Ice cream is an awesome product. Nothing quite delivers the combination of indulgence and satisfaction at such a keen price point. Beyond personal preference, though, it's also a really interesting category—the thing about ice cream is that it almost doesn't matter how much is bought; it all seems to get eaten. Confectionery is the same: put a bag of candies in a jar and see how long it lasts. Now buy a bigger bag and see what happens—it disappears at almost the same rate. Do the same with chocolate and, as if by magic, it disappears, too. Beer's like that, as are whiskey and sodas, because the number of potential consumption occasions and the amount that can be consumed at a given occasion almost exceeds the purchase volume in most cases. For all these categories, consumption is expandable. That is to say, if it's in the home, it will probably be consumed.

Good mothers know this, which is why they limit the volume of candy, soda, and ice cream they buy. The same dynamic is probably also true for couples in which the female buys beer—buy too much and the male will end up comatose on the sofa every night! We have spoken much about the costs of investing in offer. Unless consumption is expandable, overinvestment in offer will yield low or negative returns. But in expandable categories, judicious investment in offer can educate shoppers and encourage them to buy more over an extended period of time. When mom sees that a larger pack has been consumed, there is a good chance that she may buy a larger pack next time. This is the positive impact of shopper conditioning from a commercial perspective, and it largely accounts for the migration of snack foods and carbonated soft drinks from single-serve packs to larger packs over time.

This third golden rule of in-store investment is worth bearing in mind for all consumer goods manufacturers; it contemplates a change in the rationale that drives promotional spend. Our earlier analysis, we hope, proves that overinvestment in offer has grossly negative consequences, yet nearly 80 percent of management time in consumer goods marketing and sales teams is spent on configuring promotions.[88]

It's unrealistic to expect that consumer goods companies will stop investing in offer, and particularly in promotions, but in applying this rule, perhaps marketers will become more circumspect in the volume of money they spend in this space and more conscious of what might be gained from an offer.

---

88 **engage** research.

PAYING FOR PERFORMANCE—THE DIFFERENCE BETWEEN CONDITIONAL AND UNCONDITIONAL EXPENDITURE

By working through this process, a theoretical framework will be created for how money should be spent in the trade. However, this is often a long, long way from the actual situation faced by most manufacturers.

This is mainly because there are two broad ways of making retail investments. The first is generally in the control of the consumer goods company—these are investments made on behalf of retailers. This sort of investment includes the development and deployment of advertising materials like display stands or shelf talkers; the training, management, and deployment of merchandising teams and in-store promoters; and the creation of bespoke promotions such as in-store giveaways and bundled products and gift packs. This discretionary expenditure is relatively flexible and can be transferred between channels and into specific activities by choice.

The second way of investing is significantly less flexible and consists of either payments made directly to retailers in the form of contracted commitments or ad hoc payments in support of specific activities. Since these payments contribute directly to a retailer's "back margin," they are subject to high levels of scrutiny and are a constant source of pressure. They also, unfortunately, are often a significantly larger part of total trade investment than the former.

The fact is that most of these deals with retailers are stacked in the retailer's favor. In some markets, manufacturers sign standard terms documents, most of which consist of photocopied contracts that are made up of a series of checkboxes and blanks that the retailer's buying team fill in and pass to key account reps to sign off on.

These contracts make little provision for creativity and even less for delivering the kind of focus we have described. But there is hope. While the terms retailers demand are often fixed, the conditions they need to achieve these terms often remain open, and the investor can play in this space.

In many cases, consumer goods manufacturers fall into a trap. For instance, they may pay Carrefour a "common assortment fee" that is a set percentage of total turnover. The common assortment fee is Carrefour's way of managing listing or slotting fees with larger vendors. Implicit in the fee is the presumption that Carrefour will continue to stock a range of the supplier's products and, by mutual agreement, will add or remove products to this range as new products are introduced. However, this agreement does not make explicit the responsibilities of either party in ensuring that these products are available.

In effect, this fee is exacted simply for maintaining a list of the manufacturers' products on a computer. As long as this most basic term is met, Carrefour is legally entitled to the agreed percentage, regardless of what product is actually present in-store. This sort of fee is rapidly becoming "unconditional"—that is to say that in order to secure this funding, the retailer has no legal requirement to meet substantial conditions.

There are numerous other terms and conditions like this. It's common practice, for example, to negotiate a percentage of manufacturers' sales as a promotional fund. In return for this fund, the retailer might commit to a number of gondola end displays and a number of insertions in its mail campaigns. However, very rarely do these negotiations detail which products will be featured and where, or what space will be given, and there is almost never a condition that a proportion of funds will be paid upon proof of execution. Again, these funds are potentially lacking any substantial conditionality. So manufacturers that wish to employ these funds more effectively must convert these broadly unconditional funds into conditional investments.

This is perhaps best explained with an example. A.S. Watson is one of the world's largest drug store chains; it is headquartered in Hong Kong, with store operations across Asia and Europe. Like many global retailers, Watsons seeks to create a global contract with major multinational consumer goods firms. These contracts seek to secure a small percentage of sales from each market in which the two parties do business in order to fund mutually beneficial global initiatives. Typically, global manufacturers might pay between 1.5 and 2 percent of total global sales into this fund, but what they secure in return is massively negotiable.

Many manufacturers complain that, in return for this global funding, they get little or no support in return from Watsons. Yet Watsons places the onus on the vendor to determine which projects might be of value. As a result, some contracts have little or no conditions attached to them, while others—such as the deals done by Procter & Gamble and Unilever—have literally pages of conditions attached, all of which must be met for part or all of the payments to be made.

The same is true of almost any deal made by a manufacturer. It appears that there is no limit to the volume of conditions that one can negotiate with a retailer as long there is a clear rationale for the condition. Creating conditionality can be as simple as asserting the right to pay on execution, or it can be much more involved, specifying exactly under what conditions a payment or proportion of a payment can be made.

By defining the conditions that must be met in terms of availability, communication, and offer, a manufacturer can convert expenditure that might be considered a cost into an investment.

Let's think again about a common assortment fee. Conditions that might be attached legitimately to this would be a specific range made available in different sizes of store. It might specify minimum merchandising standards, minimum stock depths, monitoring and compliance methodologies, and so on. By insisting on greater conditions, this entire fund can be directed at creating much better availability. Interestingly, this greater level of conditionality doesn't necessarily require an increase in the scale of the payment, meaning that companies might be able to secure better execution without increasing expenditure—*and* might be able to convert what is today a cost into a meaningful investment.

In the next chapter, we'll discuss practical steps that can be taken to secure agreement in these sorts of negotiations. However, getting an agreement to this type of change is impossible if a manufacturer has no clear view of how funds might be used to drive changes in shopper behavior, hence the importance of placing decisions about customer investment at the end of the planning process.

CHAPTER 13

MOTIVATING RETAIL CUSTOMERS

At the heart of the concept of Total Marketing is the need for today's consumer goods companies to satisfy three customers: the consumer, the shopper, and the retail customer. We have written extensively so far about the first two customers and the importance of investing effectively in the retail environment to stimulate the behavioral change to drive growth. As of yet, we've largely ignored the third customer: the retailer. In this chapter, we'll address this more fully. At the end of the day, without retailers' support through execution in-store, the needs of the other two customers can't be served. Motivating retailers to support a manufacturer's brands is therefore an essential component of the Total Marketing mix.

WHY EXECUTION IS SO IMPORTANT

An Anecdote from Toby

Early in my career, I was lucky enough to work for Columbia Pictures. My role was with the home video division, and I looked after our business with major UK grocers like Tesco, Asda, and Sainsbury's. I was in my mid-twenties, and it was a really exciting time and a great job. And though VHS tapes have since been consigned to the museum, I learned some valuable lessons during my time in that industry. In those days, a major video release might sell 90 percent of its total volume in the first two weeks of launch, so perfect availability was an absolute must, and getting your product on display in volume was a major success factor.

During the early 1990s, Disney had been incredibly successfully in getting its classic titles out to the mass market via grocery stores. They'd created a marketing machine that powerfully combined heavy TV advertising with great in-store displays to convince grocery shoppers to add the latest digitally remastered copy of *The Jungle Book* or *Snow White and the Seven Dwarfs* to their shopping baskets. They were the envy of all the other studios. So when Columbia's *Matilda* was a huge summer box office success, we knew we had a chance of emulating the Disney model for the VHS release later in the year.

Working with Tesco's buying team in Cheshunt, UK, we built a plan. *Matilda* was to be displayed in a freestanding display unit in every store. As a special offer to Tesco's shoppers, we added an exclusive Tamagotchi (a small handheld gaming device that simulated a pet—the player had to look after this "pet" by "feeding" it, "cleaning" it, and so on), which at the time was the must-have toy for preteens. The launch was set to be huge.

On the day of release, I began visiting stores to bask in what I believed was going to be the glory of a top-notch release. By 9:30 a.m. I'd been to three stores, but not one had the video, let alone the Tamagotchi, on display. The VHS tapes and toys all languished in the stockroom, with no one to merchandise them on the shop floor. By 11:00 a.m., my phone began to ring; and by lunchtime, I was in emergency meetings with the team at Cheshunt.

It became clear that in-store teams had decided not to put up the display. Some felt it was too big; others felt it was too difficult to erect; some claimed that the display didn't stand up when it was built; many said they hadn't been informed; and I suspect many others just felt that the video wasn't important enough to warrant the extra effort it would take to put the product on display.

At the end of the day, just over 20 percent of Tesco's stores had actually executed the plan. By the end of the week, we got this number up to just under 40 percent, but by then the key selling window was closing. As a result, both Columbia and Tesco lost out. Despite months of planning and negotiating, and thousands of pounds in mutual investment, piles of videos and toys went unsold that week and in the weeks after that. It took three more months and large amounts of additional negotiation and investment to finally clear the stock we'd accumulated.

For a young key account manager, this was a deeply humiliating experience, but it is far from an uncommon one. A recent survey conducted by TradeIn-sight suggested that 31 percent of consumer packaged goods manufacturers cite trade compliance as a major issue in their business.[89] It's an issue that has far-reaching implications.

Take, for instance, a typical new product introduction. The process of developing a new product requires many thousands of hours and huge volumes of research dollars to bring to fruition. It takes entire teams months of effort to build marketing plans, packaging and creative designs, and media budgets. Production and logistics investments are required, and sales teams are deployed. After configuring, executing, and evaluating promotions, it is new product development and introduction that absorbs the greatest amount of marketing and sales management time. Yet the success or failure of a new product is dependent on one thing—a shopper being able to buy the product in a store. This means that without outstanding execution at retail, new product introductions are destined to fail.

WHO MAKES EXECUTION HAPPEN?

So who makes retail execution happen? Well, the retailer does! Even if you want your product on display in the smallest stores on the planet, the store owner has to decide that it's worth diverting some of his disposable cash to buy a case of your product. He has to take time to find space on his shelves to merchandise the product. Then he needs to make sure that his investment of time, money, and effort has delivered enough return to keep buying and merchandising the product.

In sophisticated chain stores, the same principle is true. All the key decisions are made within the retailer's business, except these decisions are much more complicated and involve a whole bunch of people working in different departments across the business.

The buying team must ensure that investing in a company's product is financially sensible and must establish a base retail price. The merchandising team must then reconfigure shelf layouts to accommodate the product. The marketing team needs to ensure that the product is included in communications to shoppers. The finance team must ensure that purchase orders can be raised, sales can be accounted for, and invoices can be paid. An operations team plans when changes are going to be made in the stores, and a logistics team will be charged with making sure that stock gets from a

---

89 "2010 Trade Promotion Management Trends" TradeInsight (Powered by MEI) http://www2. tradeinsight.com/rs/meicpg/images/2010 Trade Promotion Trends Whitepaper.pdf.

distribution center to the stores. In the stores themselves, section managers and store managers figure out whether stock levels are right and amend or place orders for the product. It may also be at their discretion to decide whether, where, and when they will display a product in the store. In some cases, in-store teams are entitled to change the price of a product based on local competition. Finally, someone has to find the product in the warehouse, get it onto the shop floor, and put it on the shelf.

To give some context to the complexity of all these decisions, it's worth thinking about the organizations with which you might be dealing. For instance, according to the retail consulting firm Hypertrade Consulting, the average Carrefour hypermarket might sell 100,000 items every day and might carry over 25,000 separate items in one store. These might be displayed on 12,000 linear meters of shelf space in a store that could be up to 15,000 square meters in size. Each store employs nearly 300 staff members, including a team of 50 managers, 60 security guards, and over 40 cleaners. There may be between 39 and 50 checkout lanes that will be fully staffed at peak periods, and the teams working in-store will put in over 1.3 million hours a year.[90] And this is just in one store; in March 2013, Carrefour had over 1,450 stores like this around the world.[91]

Clearly, then, securing in-store execution with a giant like Carrefour takes some doing, yet many organizations unwittingly leave much of this to chance. Around the globe, it's quite normal to assign one individual to manage all the business a company does with a big retailer. Sometimes, that person might also be responsible for working with other key retailers. Often, these salespeople only have time to interface with the buying and merchandising teams in a head office, and while they maintain steady and regular contact with these teams, each interaction rarely lasts longer than 30 minutes, in which time the agenda will be full of issues ranging from minor to major. Yet, in these meetings, salespeople must convince their contacts not only to make a decision but also to take sufficient action to ensure that all the other departments involved execute as they should. This is a big thing to ask!

Let's go back to a typical new product launch. On average, a key account salesperson will get 5–10 minutes to pitch a new product to a major retailer.

90 **engage** research; direct reports from Hypertrade Consulting.

91 "Hypermarkets: The Retail Business of Today," Carrefour Group, accessed March 14, 2013, http://www.carrefour.com/content/hypermarkets.

Why so little time? Well, the first 5 minutes of the meeting are taken up with pleasantries; the next 15 minutes will be absorbed in discussing and resolving what's on the buyer's agenda, so all that's left is 10 minutes to make the sale and agree on action points. In effect, all the preceding months of effort come down to one five-minute presentation, which has to secure a buyer's agreement to act—and encourage him to persuade scores of other managers across the organization to act, too. So you might say that these are the most important five minutes in the life of this new product.

MOTIVATING ACTION

Regardless of how well structured a retail organization is, the decision made by a retail buyer in those five minutes is a deeply personal one. When the buyer decides to invest in a new product or initiative, she must spend considerable amounts of incremental time to persuade and communicate with many other people. Since buyers work extremely hard, this extra effort requires a lot of motivation.

In our experience, people only act when two things are true: the individual understands that action is important *and* the individual believes that he will benefit personally from that action. When I think back to my *Matilda* debacle, I have to conclude that I didn't do enough to ensure that in-store teams knew that putting the displays up was important, and I certainly did nothing to ensure that these teams felt they would benefit from doing so. In fact, quite the opposite is probably true. We were asking teams to erect a complicated stand, to take time to merchandise it with products they knew nothing about, and to distract attention from their core job, which was to make sure shoppers could buy groceries. With the benefit of hindsight, I did nothing to motivate the in-store teams to act.

My struggle in securing operational execution is a common one. Most sales managers would struggle to secure the resources required to speak individually to everyone involved in getting things done in-store. So the onus is placed on the retailers' buying teams to act generically to secure the support of their counterparts across the business.

Successful salespeople know how to motivate, and they make sure that when they pitch, they communicate clearly why it's important for a buyer take action—but they also give the buyer personally compelling reasons to act. They do this by understanding one simple truth in business: employees work hard every day so they can take home more money, which enables them to do the things they want to do.

Now, no salesperson can deliver this money directly—it's neither ethical nor legal to hand over a check or a pile of cash. What a salesperson can do, though, is help a buyer get better results. When buyers achieve better results, they get paid bonuses. Bonuses fund school fees, holidays, hobbies, and new homes and cars, or inflate a pension plan, so they are personally important to a buyer. In order to trigger a bonus as a buyer, you have to meet or exceed your key performance indicators (KPIs). Great salespeople make sure they understand these KPIs—and that the propositions they bring to the table help buyers achieve them.

GETTING IT WRONG AND GETTING IT RIGHT

Organizations set KPIs for managers to ensure that they work toward achieving the company's objectives. Almost all corporations have two very broad groups of objectives: *strategic objectives*, which relate to the long-term direction of the business as a whole, and *commercial objectives*, which relate to the short-term outcomes the business needs to achieve to meet financial expectations. But when consumer goods organizations work with retailers, they find that the objectives of the two parties are rarely aligned—and often they downright conflict.

For instance, manufacturers will focus effort on growing the market share of a brand or group of brands that requires them to beat the competition in the marketplace. To see this in action, just look at decades of cutthroat competition between Coca-Cola and Pepsi. By contrast, retailers will focus on driving *their* market share in a category—it doesn't matter in this case whether they sell more Coke or Pepsi, just as long as they sell more carbonated soft drinks. This automatically puts Coke's strategic objectives at odds with Walmart's.

At the same time, retailers' and manufacturers' commercial objectives are often at odds, too. Both might seek to increase profits, but the fastest way for a retailer to increase its profits is to secure greater investment from a manufacturer. As we've already seen, this is a great way for manufacturers to lose money. In many situations, then, the drivers of a manufacturer's success might be diametrically opposite to those of a retailer, as can be seen in this figure:

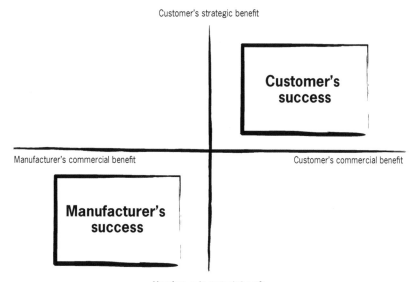

This has some interesting implications for salespeople who want to motivate buyers to act. Since there is always a possibility that their actions could make retail buyers less successful, salespeople often get it totally wrong.

Armed with a presentation from the marketing team, a sales manager will often talk about how well the company brand is doing against its competitors. She might demonstrate how to get more shoppers to buy the brand, though shoppers are rarely referenced, especially when the presentation is prepped by a consumer marketing team that is still operating under the delusion that the consumer and the shopper are one and the same. She'll demonstrate to the retailer how an activity will grow sales of this brand. But here's what the buyer hears: "We are interested in making our brand more successful, and we want you to help us do this by adopting our strategy. As a result, you will end up spending more money on our products."

As the sales manager is talking, the buyer is thinking, *How does this help me? If I make you more successful—does that mean I'm more successful? Why should I change my strategy just for your brand? Do I want to spend more money with you?* As a result, many buyers complain that their suppliers simply don't understand their needs, which means the supplier can't help with the buyer's KPIs. When KPIs aren't achieved, bonuses don't get paid. So, naturally, at an emotional level, the buyer rejects these sorts of propositions.

However, many buyers are pragmatists. Believing that manufacturers have deep pockets, they look for the easiest way to meet at least one of their KPIs—which is to seek more funds from the manufacturer. "Very interesting," a buyer says. "Since this is clearly important to you, what levels of cooperative investment can we expect from you to support this?" At this point, the checkbook comes out and the cost of doing business with the retailer immediately increases.

Sometimes salespeople get the proposition part right, but they'll explain how their ideas support a commercial KPI without thinking about the strategic impact on the retailer. And again, the buyer, knowing that this undermines at least one objective, seeks additional funding. Alternatively, a salesperson will demonstrate how he is supporting the buyer's strategy but fails to give a compelling commercial result in the short term. Faced with the compromise of winning in the long term but making no short-term gain, the buyer seeks additional funds once more.

The only way to get it right and avoid increasing costs is for the manufacturer to enter the retailer's mind space and meet both the commercial and the strategic objectives that have been set for the buyer:

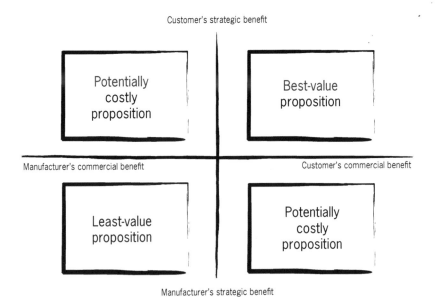

Here's the unavoidable conclusion: to be successful in the long run, the sales team must have an intimate understanding of a buyer's KPIs.

UNDERSTANDING RETAIL KPIS

Though every retailer is different, there is a surprising consistency in the commercial KPIs set for buyers. Having worked in numerous markets on projects that ultimately involve hundreds of different retail operations, we see that most buyers typically have three KPIs in common.

The first and always primary KPI of almost every retail buyer is **margin**. It doesn't matter whether this is expressed as a total gross profit number or as a percentage difference between invoice cost and retail selling price—buyers will be required to deliver an increase. Some organizations expect the buyer to drive front margin (see Chapter 12) or back margin, or a combination of both, so KPIs are often set in these terms. Margin KPIs are commonly set at a category level, so a buyer might have to deliver a higher total margin across sales of all sodas, leading him to make choices about how the company treats vendors who deliver low margins compared to those who contribute more to the total pool.

The second retail KPI we see is **business growth**. A buyer may have a value sales growth and a volume target set against a category. These KPIs may be more sophisticated in some cases. Especially at senior levels, targets might be set for underlying growth, same-store growth (which measures the health of retail sales in existing outlets and is sometimes known as "like-for-like growth"), as well as for total sales, which might account for new stores. Increasingly, improvements in shopper measures such as category penetration (which measures the percentage of total shoppers buying a specific category) and basket size (which defines the average transaction size) are also used to measure growth. Of course, buyers act according to the weight each KPI is given; for example, buyers charged with increasing penetration might favor price-down promotions or lower-cost brands.

The third common retail KPI will be in the area of **inventory**. These KPIs might be expressed in "stock days" (also known as "inventory days") or in "stock turns." "Stock days" refers to how many days it will take to sell all the stock held at a given time based on an average rate of sale; holding 21 days of stock means that if the rate of sale remains steady, all of those products will be sold in three weeks. "Stock turn" refers to the same data but in terms that describe how many times the company could sell, or "turn," their current inventory in a year. Three weeks of inventory, for example, will be turned just over 17 times in a year. Invariably, buyers are expected to reduce inventory, so they seek to buy and hold less product on their shelves, or they favor lines that are deemed to move quickly.

It's important to stress that these are not the only KPIs a buying team will have, but these KPIs consistently appear across buying operations. Some retailers (e.g., Tesco) subscribe to the idea of a balanced scorecard of KPIs that looks to counterbalance financial measures with measures of improvement in the quality of personnel, and to balance measures of customer satisfaction with operational efficiency. Tesco also includes social responsibility in its scorecard, but even within this model, buyers must still deliver higher margins, better growth, and lower inventories.

There is an exceptionally good reason for the ubiquity of these KPIs, but it requires an understanding of how retailers really make money.

Retailers are businesses just like any other—they exist to provide their shareholders with a return on their capital investment. Traditional manufacturers do this by seeking to increase the profits of the business by driving top-line sales and by reducing costs. While this is true for retailers, too, you only have to look at the relative profitability of the world's leading retailers and compare it to the world's leading manufacturers to see that there must be more to the retail equation than profits. The top 250 manufacturers make an average profit margin of 8.5 percent, but the world's leading retailers make much less than this on average:

Retail revenue rank	Name of company	2011 group revenue (US$m)	2011 group net income (US$m)	% of group revenue
1	Walmart Stores, Inc.	446,950	16,387	3.67%
2	Carrefour S.A.	115,277	563	0.49%
3	Tesco PLC	103,244	4,502	4.36%
4	Metro AG	92,905	1,032	1.11%
5	The Kroger Co.	90,374	596	0.66%

Source: Deloitte, Global Powers of Retailing 2013: Retail Beyond, accessed March 7, 2013, http://www.deloitte.com/assets/Dcom-Australia/Local Assets/Documents/ Industries/Consumer business/Deloitte_Global_Powers_of_Retail_2013.pdf.

Yet, these retail businesses deliver comparatively similar returns on capital to those created by consumer goods, so clearly retailers have something else "under the hood."

The secret of retailing lies not in how much profit a company makes but in what the company does with the cash it takes. Big retailers take a huge volume of money through their tills every day. Walmart, the biggest of the lot, is taking in over $1.22 billion every day, and this cash is used every day to pay for stock, salaries, electricity, and so on. But in the hands of a competent treasury team, such huge volumes of cash can also be invested on overnight and short-term markets for gain. The longer a retailer can hold on to cash, the more can be invested. For large retailers, there is a real imperative to make this happen.

Since inventory is the largest cost a retailer has, creating as much cash as possible from the sale of this inventory is key. Retailers do this by leveraging what is commonly called the "golden period."

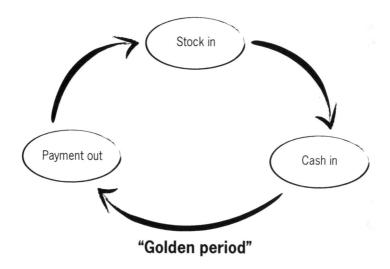

"Golden period"

The golden period enables retailers to make money on the credit they receive from their suppliers. Here's how it works. Let's say I buy a case of goods, and it takes me three days to sell those products through my store. If I don't have to pay for those goods for another 11 days, that gives me 11 days in which I can use or invest the cash I've made.

Logically, if I can reduce the amount of money I ultimately have to pay back to the supplier as a proportion of the money I take in, I stand to make even more money. Equally, if I can sell the case of products I've bought in less than three days, or if I can put off paying my supplier for a little longer, I will have more time to use my cash, and I can make more money. So the game of retail can be won in four ways—make more money from the goods I sell (by increasing margins); sell goods faster (by getting more shoppers into my store, more often, which increases my growth); hold less stock (by buying less inventory); or pay slower (by increasing credit days). The successful retailers win by combining all four.

It's these fundamental principles of retail that drive a buyer's KPIs, and while a buyer can't personally contribute to increasing returns on capital, he can be responsible for the return on the investment the retailer makes on inventory. Within retail, this idea is expressed in a little known but highly influential calculation called the gross margin return on inventory investment (GMROII for short). GMROII tells retailers how much money they can expect to make in a year from a dollar invested in inventory. The easiest way to calculate this is to divide the annual gross profit of a retailer by the cost of the inventory that it currently owns. So, to make a higher GMROII, you have to either increase profits or reduce inventory costs. This is why the three KPIs of margin, growth, and inventory are so consistently used:

- Increases in margin lead to higher annual profits, which leads to higher GMROII.
- Increased growth rates leads to faster stock turns, which reduces inventory costs in relation to sales and leads to higher GMROII.
- Reduced inventory holdings leads to faster stock turns, which reduce inventory costs and lead to higher GMROII.

If manufacturers want to improve retail execution and reduce the cost of working with retailers, they must use this knowledge to sell better. And the five-step process we have described throughout this book actually makes motivating retailers to support the brand much, much easier.

USING THE TOTAL MARKETING APPROACH TO MOTIVATE RETAILERS

Great marketing works because the right messages get to the right people at the right time to change behavior. So applying a great marketing approach in interactions with retailers makes implicit sense. The five-step process makes this possible. Think about it—the best retailers on the planet are successful not just because they are great at logistics or managing their suppliers. No, the main reason for their success is that they are great with shoppers.

Shoppers are a retailer's lifeblood. Without a constantly increasingly flow of shoppers into stores, without those shoppers returning to the stores regularly, and without those shoppers spending more in the stores, a retailer's business will wither and die. Why did Borders and Blockbuster ultimately fail? Simply because shoppers moved to more convenient, more effective retail environments online.

The five-step process enables consumer goods companies to help retailers grow by harnessing the latent power of untapped consumption by changing shoppers' behavior in the store. The five-step process equips sales teams to work with retailers to achieve strategic and commercial goals, and it enables sales teams to motivate buyers—because the buyers see that the manufacturer can help them deliver on their KPIs.

The Total Marketing approach delivers a compelling rationale for action: it demonstrates where the opportunity to grow consumption lies; it shows which shoppers to target; it establishes the retail environments where purchase can be activated; and it identifies what is needed in-store to make this happen. And, of course, it speaks to retailers.

Retail buyers meet with up to 40 companies a week, each one claiming that its initiatives add value. But few can articulate what the retailers really need to hear, which is this:

1. There is an opportunity to grow consumption in the long term.
2. The shoppers who can make this happen are in your stores, and there is a plan to grow sales to these people.
3. Executing this plan will improve your business performance overall.

These three points—we call them the consumer proposition, the shopper proposition, and the customer proposition—become the structure for a highly motivating sales pitch.

THE CONSUMER PROPOSITION

Just like manufacturers, retailers must understand the consumer. Retailers know that while a single sale can deliver value today, a repeated sale delivers value far into the future. Repeat sales ensure that the GMROII equation works in the long term, and retailers know that if there's no real demand for a product, that equation will fail. So the first component of any proposal should focus on the consumer.

The consumer proposition should demonstrate the manufacturer's understanding of which consumers the manufacturer is targeting. It should explain the consumption opportunity in concrete terms. If the target consumer group has needs that aren't yet satisfied, it should explain who these people are and how many of them there are, as well as the incremental growth in total consumption if they did use the product. If there is an untapped consumption occasion, define it and show how often it arises; then quantify the opportunity that filling that occasion represents. If there is a gap between actual consumption on each occasion and potential consumption on each occasion, show that in the proposition, too. If people could be using a different product that might meet their needs better on that occasion, show that instead, and demonstrate the potential value of this.

Let's take a simple case. In discussion with an Indonesian marketing director some years ago, we were told that the way to drive yogurt consumption was to get people to eat it more often. At the time, consumers enjoyed the product once a week, so getting these consumers to eat twice a week would double consumption. Looking at it this way, the opportunity to grow was clear.

But only three percent of Indonesians ate yogurt at the time, so we looked consumers that weren't. About 16 percent of Indonesians were affluent enough to afford yogurt and weren't lactose intolerant—so they were potential consumers. That represented an opportunity to grow consumption by over five times, which doubled if these people ate it twice a week! This sort information is powerful and gives retailers a reason to support a company.

Wherever the opportunity lies, the consumer proposition should be specific and quantify the opportunity, then show that the company has a plan to reach out actively to consumers in the target groups. This plan should detail the range of consumer-focused marketing activities and make it clear that the company is serious about the opportunity.

THE SHOPPER PROPOSITION

The shopper proposition sets out to demonstrate that a retailer could really take advantage of a consumption opportunity. It should demonstrate who the target shopper for this opportunity is and that the target shopper segments are actually in this retailer's stores (or could be if the appropriate actions were undertaken). It should also show how these shoppers currently behave and, more importantly, that it's possible to influence their behavior. The shopper proposition should then explain exactly how the retailer could apply improvements in availability, communication, and offer to capitalize on this potential.

A practical case of where this worked particularly well is Procter & Gamble's launch of Sunny Delight in the UK, which we talked about in Chapter 4. While this took place a long time ago, it's worth reflecting on how clearly P&G created a shopper proposition. Sunny Delight was targeted at kids, and P&G hoped to encourage those children who drank alternatives like Coke to switch. However, P&G understood that the best way to drive consumption of the product was to persuade moms to buy it.

To persuade moms to buy Sunny D for their kids, P&G had to communicate not that Sunny D was better than Coke since Coke was significantly cheaper, but to demonstrate that Sunny D was a more affordable alternative to juice. Here P&G took a particularly clever line. They showed retailers that in order to capitalize on this untapped opportunity, they need to make Sunny D available in a way that would persuade moms to buy. They recommended that major grocery stores display the product next to juice in the chiller, since displaying this (long-life) product in that environment gave the appearance of it being as fresh as juice.

THE CUSTOMER PROPOSITION

The final section of the proposal is the customer proposition. At this point, the business benefits of supporting the brand are made clear to the retailer. This is the tipping point between explaining that action is important and demonstrating that the buyer can achieve his KPIs by acting.

The customer proposition illustrates the business value of changing shopper behavior in terms that meet key KPIs. Let's start with growth: changing shopper behavior has a direct impact on retail sales, and it's important to illustrate how this happens. Earlier we wrote about the three dimensions in which behavior can change: you can attract more shoppers to buy, which increases penetration of a category; you can get shoppers to buy more often, which increases frequency of purchase; or you can get shoppers to spend more, which enhances weight of purchase or transaction size. Enhancing each one will lead to a commensurate increase in sales. For instance, if penetration increases by 10 percent, the sales will improve by 10 percent. What's interesting is what happens when multiple changes happen.

Let's consider the sales implication of increased penetration, frequency of purchase, and weight of purchase at the same time. In the following table, one million shoppers buy products in the category, twice a month (24 times), and spend on average 100 units of currency every time they buy.

	Today	Add 10%
Penetration	1,000,000	1,100,000
Purchase frequency	Twice Month (24 times)	26.4
Weight of purchase	100	110
Total sales	2.4bn	3.2bn
Sales growth	-	133%

Adding 10 percent in penetration increases the shopper base by one hundred thousand. Increasing frequency by 10 percent adds an extra 2.4 trips each year, and a 10 percent increase in purchase weight adds 10 more units of currency. Individually, each change only adds 10 percent to the sales line, but together total sales increase by 33 percent. This is because the total sales number is not the cumulative outcome of each change but the product of each change. Since Total Marketing enables companies to define the value of these changes effectively, these calculations become easy, and the demonstration of potential growth to a retailer is more compelling as a result.

Unfortunately, however, this analysis tends to look at the brand in isolation, and the buyer is not paid a bonus for growing a brand—her job is to grow the category. So, it's not enough to leave the story there. Unless it's clear that the initiative is guaranteed to only attract shoppers who have never used the category before, it's logical to assume that changing shopper behaviors in favor of one product is likely to lead to some negative impact on another.

Say that there is an opportunity for shoppers to trade up to a higher value brand—for example, getting shoppers to choose a premium ice cream product instead of a mid-price one. The penetration in premium ice cream will go up, but the penetration in mid-price ice cream will go down:

	The category today				The category tomorrow			
	Number of shoppers (Penetration)	Frequency (per year)	Average Price	Total Sales	Penetration	Frequency (per year)	Average Price	Total Sales
Premium Ice Cream	100	12	$5.20	$6,240	200	12	$5.20	$12,480
Mid-price Ice Cream	900	12	$3.60	$38,880	800	12	$3.60	$34,560
Total				$45,120				$47,040

As a result, sales of premium ice cream boom, but the loss in mid-price ice cream sales tempers the gains across the category. While the hardcore sales guys might not like this approach, it demonstrates an understanding of the total growth picture from the buyer's perspective.

The same analysis becomes significantly more important when we consider margin. Let's look at the same figures, but now bring the profitability of each segment into play.

	The category today				The category tomorrow			
	Total Sales	Average Margin	Gross Profit	Category average margin	Total Sales	Average Margin	Gross Profit	Category average margin
Premium Ice Cream	$6,240	12 percent	$749	-	$12,480	12 percent	$1,498	-
Mid-price Ice Cream	$38,880	8 percent	$3110	-	$34,560	8 percent	$2,765	-
Total	$45,120	-	$3859	8.6 percent	$47,040	-	$4,263	9.1 percent

Since the premium product carries a higher margin than the mid-price one, this proposition not only grows sales by four percent; it also increases the total category's profit by nearly six percent.

Now let's look at the impact of the same activity on inventory. Let's assume that in order to attract new shoppers to premium, we've increased the display by a factor of two and reduced space on mid-price ice cream to make space. We are now holding twice as much stock on the premium product, but the products are selling twice as fast, so the inventory measures remain the same. But the rates of sale on mid-price ice cream have slowed, and despite holding lower stocks, the inventory measures have worsened. What's interesting is that when you consider the category view overall, inventory levels have dropped.

	The category today					The category tomorrow				
	On-shelf inventory (units)	Inventory Value	Total Sales	Stock Turns	Days inventory	On-shelf inventory (units)	Inventory Value	Total Sales	Stock Turns	Days inventory
Premium Ice Cream	30.00	$137	$6,240	45.45	8.03	60.00	$275	$12,480	45.45	8.03
Mid-price Ice Cream	300.00	$994	$38,880	39.13	9.33	270.00	$894	$34,560	38.65	9.44
Total	330	$1,131	$45,120	39.90	9.15	330	$1,169	$47,040	40.25	9.07

So this whole idea, which starts with getting shoppers to buy one product instead of another, has had a major impact across the whole category and has been positive overall for the retailer—its business has grown, margins have increased, and inventory has come down. As a result, the overall returns on the category have increased. The GMROII, initially 3.41, has increased by just under 7 percent, to 3.65. Assuming that the consumer proposition and the shopper proposition are equally strong, this should be a very motivating proposition for the retailer.

This really works in the real world. Some years ago, we were working with GlaxoSmithKline (GSK), and among its splendid brands was Sensodyne, a toothpaste that reduces the pain caused by sensitive teeth. According to data they shared at the time, 81 percent of the adult population experienced this condition. However, it's not an acute condition, so many consumers do little or nothing to treat it. For the brand to grow, they needed to persuade more shoppers to buy it. The problem GSK faced was that the brand is niche, and therefore small in oral care as a category. As result, Sensodyne rarely enjoyed prominence on the shelf and, in most cases, was tucked away close to the floor, where it was simply not visible (read: not available!) for many shoppers.

But Sensodyne also had some of the features that premium ice cream had in the case described—it was both more expensive than its competitors and it delivered much higher margins. As a result, despite its tiny market share, it delivered significant profit to the total category. To get more shoppers to buy the brand, we all agreed that Sensodyne needed an availability boost, both to increase its space on shelf and to increase the brand's overall visibility. So GSK coupled a great consumer and shopper proposition with a simple customer one. It illustrated that every time a shopper switched to Sensodyne from a competing brand, not only did sales value increase (remember, the product was more expensive) but also profit—the retailer made 7.5 times more cash profit from selling Sensodyne than from selling its closest rival.

This simple proposition led to a complete change in execution, and Sensodyne acquired significantly stronger displays in every market where this approach was used.

GETTING AGREEMENT—NAVIGATING NEGOTIATIONS

The Sensodyne case is special in many ways. It was a great combination of consumer, shopper, and customer propositions, and it was so motivating that retailers rarely disagreed with it. What was most unusual about it was that few retailers even tried to negotiate incremental investment. But some did, and for those seasoned in dealing with major retail players, this should come as no surprise.

Indeed, we often tell sales teams to be shocked if a buyer asks for nothing—"nothing" should be a surprise, we say. This is just the retailer's way of winning the retail game. Remember, there are four paths to success in retail: increase margins, drive growth, hold less stock, or increase credit days. For buyers, the game of retail is one of chance. Choosing one strategy today does not guarantee success, so buyers are schooled in finding multiple ways to deliver their objectives.

This is not a negative thing; it's just a commercial reality, and this means that to expect a buyer to ask for nothing is naïve. The idea that "nothing" should be a surprise is a way to encourage salespeople to plan for a negotiation, even when they believe they have the strongest proposal. And let's be clear, negotiation is far from a negative thing; we only negotiate when we want something. Negotiation—the process of giving an item of value to one party in exchange for an item of equal or greater value in return—can sometimes increase the value of the deal and leaves both parties in a better position than they were in before. For this reason, smart salespeople always prepare for negotiations no matter what the situation; they know that a good negotiation only leads to better results in the end.

This being the case, if you are serious about motivating your customer, not only will you use the five-step process to create a great proposition, but you'll also use your investment framework to prepare for the negotiation that will almost certainly follow. This book is not designed to be a treatise on negotiation, as many writers have created texts on how to prepare for and conduct negotiations (as a follow-up to this book, we might even write one!). An equally great number of courses that teach practical steps to get better at negotiation are available. Indeed, before we founded **engage**, we worked for a business that used to teach a seven-step process to prepare for a negotiation.

Whichever school you choose, however, two fundamental principles drive the preparation and delivery of a negotiation: (1) know what you want, and know what your counterpart wants; and (2) trade what is valuable to you for what is valuable to them.

These simple principles are applied more easily when there is a clear investment framework in place. The investment framework describes what you are prepared to invest in and, against a known return, how much the company might be prepared to invest. This makes preparation easy. If availability is the priority, then any action by the retailer that improves availability has value—likewise with communication and offer. This foresight gives salespeople a long shopping list from which to work.

Similarly, if you know the rules of the retail game, then it's relatively easy to identify what a retail buyer might ask for. Retailers in the past, especially aggressive ones like Carrefour, have gone to great lengths to invent long lists of demands. Placed in their proper context, these are simply schoolboy tactics to drive margin, reduce inventory, or extend payment terms (since growth is not an outcome that is easily negotiated in an uncertain world). In an increasingly difficult world, tactics that take advantage of manufacturers are neither tenable nor valuable, so it's more useful to think about the retailers' imperative to increase returns as simple commercial reality.

Armed with this knowledge, the parameters of a negotiation are likely to be clear: there will be things that are of mutually high value, where no negotiation is necessary. Some retail requirements will be of high value to the retailer but low value to a manufacturer. In the same way, manufacturers will want some things that have little or no value to the retailer. Negotiations happen between these two points.

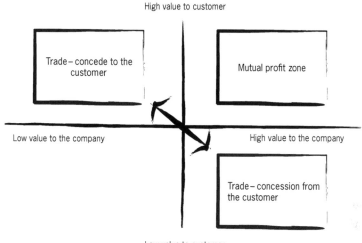

For instance, say the retailer demands a listing fee to take a product. This is of high value to the retailer, as it increases (back) margin, but of low value to the supplier, as it reduces profits. But exchanged for a guarantee of execution of a specific mix of availability, communication, and offer activities, all of which might have high value to the manufacturer, this listing fee might actually represent a reasonable exchange.

What's important is that any investment made by the manufacturer is clearly tied to an action by the retailer, regardless of how either party wishes to label it. As long as it is contractually clear that a fee has been paid on the condition of execution of a specific component of the marketing mix, then that fee is conditional and the funds can be apportioned to their proper place in the investment framework.

With these relatively simple realizations, we've seen salespeople achieve what they once believed was impossible.

RYAN'S STORY

In our careers as trainers and consultants to the consumer goods industry, we've worked with thousands of salespeople to help them motivate their customers. But a guy named Ryan always comes to mind when I'm asked whether our approach can really make a difference. Ryan has an awesome story. He began life in a poor neighborhood in Manila, and he worked consistently throughout his career to build a better life for himself and his family. By the time we met Ryan, he'd held almost every job in sales. Having started as a merchandising supervisor, he eventually landed a job with a major fast-moving consumer goods company, where he was in charge of business with the Philippines' largest retailer, SM.

It's fair to say, though, that things weren't going so well when we met Ryan. Sales were down; worse yet, the company had spent so much money unconditionally that it was probably losing money on every case it sold. Ryan was determined to turn this around. With a little bit of help and a lot of great research behind him, he did just that. Ryan was lucky in that he handled a brand that was just like Sensodyne.

What was great about what Ryan did, though, was that he prepared to sell and to negotiate. He felt there was huge latent demand for his product and that he could lead shoppers to trade up incrementally by making some relatively simple in-store changes . Knowing SM's past form, though, Ryan also figured out what they would probably ask for and had a list of requests in return. The results were spectacular—not only did the retailer buy in, but Ryan was also able to secure hugely valuable conditions against the extremely small number of concessions he made. As a result, he was able to save over 30 percent of his trade spend budget and grow sales for both his company and SM to boot.

Ryan now leads the team he was once part of, and he's taught his way of working to numerous young salespeople.

This isn't just good sales practice, though—it's great marketing. Ryan proved that in motivating the customer to act, the whole marketing process is brought to life. Without a great consumer proposition and a clear understanding of how to motivate shoppers to behave differently, Ryan's negotiation would have been impotent. By viewing this entire approach as continuum, companies place equal value on the consumer, the shopper, and the retail customer.

By applying this simple philosophy, we have helped numerous companies around the world get better retail execution at lower cost. They are seeing their sales improve because they are actually motivating shoppers to buy for consumers who want to use their products, and these results are both measurable and tangible. In the next chapter, we'll look at how these results can be measured in the long term.

CHAPTER 14

MANAGING THE METRICS

etrics are essential for any business, project, function, or activity. "You can't manage what you can't measure" may be an age-old management mantra, but it still holds true. Great measurement enables better, more informed decision making, and that, in turn, should create more effective and more efficient programs. In a modern consumer goods world of slim growth and pressured profits, this is all the more true. And in the world of shopper marketing, where most activities lose money for the manufacturers who fund them, surely metrics would be almost mandatory, right? Apparently not. Many activities are not evaluated at all, and many organizations track little more than their sales. According to a 2008 Deloitte/ GMA report, "Organizations report that they are not able to calculate the impact of their shopper marketing efforts . . . or identify which programs, partners, or tactics are the most successful." Further, "barely half currently use performance data to measure program performance, evaluate partners, or determine marketing mix." And to put these statistics in context, this data was based on surveys of 100 companies in North America with an average annual turnover of around $10 billion. These companies are arguably the leaders in the consumer goods world. It would be fair to say that the many companies and operations that fall outside this group are almost certainly far less sophisticated in their approach to measuring the performance of their shopper marketing activities.

The lack of effective metrics and measurement against them must be a significant contributing factor to the poor financial performance of many shopper marketing activities. In an Interscope study in 2009 covering 150 companies, 82 percent of respondents suggested that the inability to calculate ROI was a roadblock to the development of shopper marketing in their organization. Even among retailers, the frustration exists: a 2011 GMA report stated that not having an effective way to measure effectiveness of shopper marketing was the top scoring "pain point" for retailers, with over 70 percent scoring it as "significant."

Metrics are critical in all marketing activity. Metrics allow for the assessment of marketing performance; without them, it is almost impossible for an activity, a strategy, or even a department to be objectively evaluated. It is impossible to refine activities or improve the mix without understanding the impact of an activity. It is impossible to understand whether a strategy is working without some form of measurement towards a goal. And as margins come under greater pressure, the swathes of money spent on marketing could (and should) come under greater scrutiny from the C-Suite (and shareholders). In a study by Fournaise, 77 percent of CEOs say that their marketing teams (note that we are not just talking about shopper marketers here!) fail to connect their actions to the business measures that matter (ROI, revenue, profit). Additionally, 74 percent believe that their marketers focus too much on new trends but fail to explain how they will create new sales, and 72 percent say their marketers are always asking for more money but rarely demonstrate what return the investment will generate. In a fabulous sound bite, Tim Cook, CEO of Apple (arguably a very "marketing" company), allegedly told his marketing team, when they presented a new initiative to him, "Tell me how it helps me sell more phones."

Effective measurement to prove, and improve, the performance of marketing activities will become increasingly important for marketers as they are asked to justify their budgets and their existence. And what is true of marketing in general is even truer for the fledgling discipline of shopper marketing. As we have seen elsewhere in this book, expenditure in the area of shopper marketing is growing fast—both in absolute terms and as a share of total marketing spend. There appears to be a grave danger that without an effective measurement approach, the rapid acceleration of expenditure in this area will erode profitability further, putting even more pressure on consumer goods companies. As Neil Weitzman, vice president of shopper marketing and strategy at Nielsen Canada, puts it, "No one really knows if they're getting their money's worth." Arguably, if shopper marketing cannot rapidly add demonstrable value, it's likely that plugs will be pulled across the globe. Whether marketers like it or not, senior management increasingly holds marketing accountable for its contribution to the financial performance of the company. Without robust, objective metrics, CEOs can hardly be blamed for questioning the efficacy of marketing activity. The converse may also be true: for organizations beginning their shopper marketing journey, instilling a metrics culture from the beginning may lead to more attention, resources, and funding in the future.

In this chapter, we will explore the reasons why metrics in marketing, particularly in shopper marketing, are not universally applied; we'll look at what metrics should be measured; and we'll make suggestions as to how they can be measured. We'll also take a pragmatic look at the data that might be typically available and how proxies can be used to at least indicate performance, before making some suggestions as to how to get started with shopper marketing metrics, regardless of budget. Finally, we will look at the exciting future of shopper metrics in a world where technology is increasingly used to understand exactly what is going on in stores, often in real time.

METRIC AVERSION

As marketing has evolved over the last few decades, the application of metrics has, too—and thank goodness it has. The days when marketers could cheerfully shrug their shoulders and quote John Wanamaker regarding the half of their budget that was probably wasted are a dim and distant memory. While they may not be universally applied, there are now a slew of metrics available to marketers, and these metrics cover all sorts of activity. Advertising can be measured in terms of reach (the percentage of the target market that will see the message), frequency (the number of times that audience will see the message), and GRPs (gross rating points, the product of reach and frequency, such that if 40 percent of a market will be exposed to the advertising six times during a campaign, then the GRPs delivered would be 240). Public relations metrics may include media impressions (how many people will see the piece) or advertising value equivalency (a measure of the value of the PR expressed in terms of how much it would have cost to achieve the same results using paid advertising). Marketers can measure how people think or feel about a brand (awareness, understanding, belief, favor) and people's behavior (when, how, and where they consume; where, when, and what they purchased)—to mention just a few. And with each new marketing element, a new language and a new set of metrics is born. David Berkowitz of digital marketing agency 360i blogged a list of over 100 metrics for social media alone.

Many marketers are using metrics, yet many are not. Many are measuring some of what they do but ignoring huge amounts of activity (and therefore expenditure). It is often surprising how many managers we encounter who insist on setting objectives as part of any planning process, but when it comes to measurement against that objective, they repeatedly let their people off the hook. But if the application of metrics is so clearly important, and if there are plenty of metrics to use, why aren't metrics universally appreciated and more rigorously applied?

Shopper marketing faces some unique barriers to the development of a meaningful metrics culture. This discipline has evolved in a space that is organizationally and conceptually between marketing and sales. If the traditional marketing metrics focus on brand awareness, market share, and brand equity, and if the traditional sales metrics revolve around revenue, volume, and (in some cases) trade spend efficacy, then what metrics are wholly owned by shopper marketing? For shopper marketing, lack of a clear role is clearly a critical contributor to this problem—if there is no clarity on what shopper marketing is, then understanding what it is supposed to achieve and then measuring its efficacy are rather difficult. Hopefully, we have argued enough by now for a clear and distinct role for shopper marketing; with time, this specific issue should decline.

THE PERFECTION BARRIER

The most common reason cited for not measuring something is that it's "difficult." Another excuse might be "There's no way I can accurately measure that." This pervasive argument is used frequently in the world of shopper marketing. Practitioners argue that it is impossible to effectively isolate one action in any evaluation—there are many other factors that may or may not have influenced the result that is being measured. This is true. The firm's other activity at the time will also have had an impact; in this world of integrated activity, it is rare that one activity is conducted in isolation. How much of the impact is due to advertising out of store (targeted to consumers) and how much to the shopper implementation? How does a shopper marketer isolate the impact of the consumer advertising campaign? Beyond this, other factors have a potential impact on shoppers' behavior, and all could cloud the results of any evaluation. The weather, competitive activity, other activity in other categories or stores, what was on TV last night—all these can and do impact shoppers, their behavior, and therefore any metrics that might be measured.

One of the root causes of this belief among marketers is the desire for an immediate response to a question: a yes-or-no answer to a simple question. Unfortunately, that is difficult (or expensive) to achieve. But tracking over time and measuring (and learning) repeatedly delivers a bank of data on performance. With enough data, most other variables can be removed by regression techniques to give a more accurate response. The alternative, running blind with no metrics and no measurement, should be clearly less appealing. Any measurement, as long as it can be proven directionally indicative, must surely be better than working on gut feelings, assumptions, and received wisdom. If metrics are putting some science into the art of marketing, then metrics form part of scientific method: an attitude and approach of continual exploration, building and proving or disproving hypotheses by developing relevant data over time.

These arguments could be made for any other discipline, yet accountability is largely in place elsewhere in the corporate world. Sales teams are graded on their revenue or volume, both of which largely depend on the successful implementation of great marketing activities. This dependence does not prevent the use of revenue as a sales metric, nor should it be used to prevent the use of effective metrics in shopper marketing. Every effort should be made to strive toward high-quality, accurate measurement, but strong indicators should always be preferred over the rather unpalatable alternative of running blind.

Despite the difficulties and potential inaccuracies of applying metrics, the alternatives currently employed by many consumer goods organizations are clearly far less acceptable. The alternative is to make decisions based on gut feelings, traditions, or rules of thumb and to allocate funds based on history ("this is what we did last year"), myths ("that doesn't work here"), and percentages ("we spend 20 percent of our total budget on promotions"). Decision making by percentage is perhaps the most insidious, as it is often justified or defended by the belief that it is the industry norm, and therefore "right." Again and again, managers plan spending based on allocation: "Tesco is 20 percent of my business, so they will get around

20 percent of the spend." Or, "Most companies spend approximately 30 percent of sales on in-store promotions." But following the market rarely leads to competitive advantage.

Marketing is, at its heart, about getting away from these "absolute approximations" and moving toward making better judgments. Better judgments require science, and that requires data. Data and science are not, however, about absolutes, and it is easy to get lost in the drive for a perfect solution and to be frustrated when that is elusive. Great management, in marketing and elsewhere, is about judgment. If there was a "right" answer, judgment would not be required, and there would be little competitive advantage in marketing decision making. Measurements and metrics enable the assessment of the effectiveness of previous decisions, and that, in turn, facilitates better decisions in the future.

Metrics also support the "art" of marketing—lending credence and support, as well as making the reasons for judgment transparent and explicit. But to acknowledge that perfect knowledge is currently unattainable is no excuse for a full-blown retreat into art alone. That would do a grand injustice to shopper marketing. Shopper marketing, with its natural opportunities in terms of data availability, should be leading the way into a future of more accountable marketing in total, not just in the shopper realm.

The difficulty of measuring accurately should not be a barrier to the application of metrics. So, which metrics should we focus on to create accountable, effective shopper marketing?

WHAT TO MEASURE

The ability to "crunch the numbers" is (or should be!) almost mandatory for marketing professionals. It would be disingenuous to suggest that marketers the world over are making decisions without any data or analysis, though many are. (A recent survey by the Corporate Executive Board, a consultancy and research company with thousands of members from the marketing community in the United States, suggested that marketers used data in only 11 percent of customer-related decisions.) The roots of marketing lie in ideas and innovation, and this part of the role will never—and should never—fade away. But with so much data now available, the opportunity to back up inspiration with data should be irresistible. However the sheer amount of possible measurements, metrics, and methodologies means that what will divide the most successful marketers of the future from the pack isn't their ability to manipulate and analyze data but their ability to make a precursive decision—they will know which numbers they should crunch and therefore what metrics they should track.

When selecting metrics, there are a number of criteria to consider (see sidebar): whether the metrics are relevant and measurable, whether the activities of the company can impact them, and whether they are cost-effective to measure.

Organizations that apply metrics frequently limit their measurement to the data that is currently available. Worse, many individuals limit their analysis to the data that they personally have at hand—ignoring valuable resources elsewhere in the business. Starting with what you have is a quick fix, but it does introduce a bias and is likely to reinforce the current way of looking at the world and current perception or norms (assuming, of course, they were based on any data at all). The most obvious and frequent of these is the use of ex-factory sales data (a measure of sales out of the factory, and therefore into retail) to evaluate the impact of a shopper promotion. The continual measurement of this may reinforce a belief that a particular promotion drives sales. If what the organization wants to measure is sales to a customer, then ex-factory sales data is a pretty good metric. But if it is being used to demonstrate whether or not a particular activity changed shopping behavior, it is limited. The data measures sales to a retailer, not out of the stores. Inventory may have been

KEY METRIC CRITERIA

Relevance: The metric must be connected to, or reflect, the desired business results. Further, the metric should be something that actually drives business results.

Impact: It must be possible for the activities of the organization to affect the metric; otherwise, there is little value in understanding the performance, as the company has no power to affect it.

Measurement: The metric should be something that can be measured consistently and with a reasonable level of accuracy.

Cost-efficacy: In theory, anything can be measured. But the value of measuring must outweigh the cost of measurement. The balance often lies between cost and accuracy.

273

stockpiled at the customer's warehouse or stores, creating a peak in sales at the factory door: it does not necessarily mean that shoppers bought more.

We encourage marketers, to a certain extent, to make the best of what they have, but we do not propose starting with what is at hand. The best way to start setting metrics for marketing is to understand what the desired business results are and then identify the best metrics to measure this. From that point, each metric can be analyzed in terms of its cost and value. If, at that stage, the only cost-effective way is to use existing data, then so be it. But by stepping through this process, the marketer has a much clearer idea of what the company is trying to measure and of the compromises a particular methodology may introduce. Armed with this knowledge, the compromise might be mitigated by measuring other factors that will help get closer to the desired measure (see the following figure). In the earlier example, perhaps measuring inventory levels at retail as well as ex-factory sales would at least give a clearer idea of real uplift in a store.

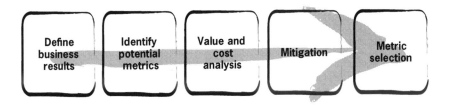

The five-step Total Marketing model supports the definition of specific, desired results. As has been discussed in previous chapters, working through the five-step process creates absolute clarity on the desired end result.

First, there is a clear definition of the **Consumer Opportunity**. This is described in terms of understanding the desired change in consumption behavior: which consumers are being targeted, and what behavior is desired? Ideally, this is quantified (for example, a 20 percent increase in penetration among a particular market segment). Clarity in terms of the consumer opportunity fuels clarity in terms of **Shopper Behavior**: which shoppers need to behave in a particular way to fuel that consumption opportunity? Again, if the consumer opportunity is quantified, then shopper behavior change can be quantified, too. **Prioritizing Channels** involves focusing on the environments that this shopping behavior will take place in, and enables a quantification of the behavior that should be observed in any group of stores. The **Marketing Mix** describes the stimuli we have chosen to create this behavioral change, and the last step, **Investment**, describes the investments required to make this happen.

By utilizing this model, we can describe business results of an activity with a high level of accuracy. Let's say the desired business result is to create 55,000 new long-term users of a brand who use it at least once a week. If that is the business result, it is therefore possible to set a shopper objective, or several shopper objectives. A shopper result might be to persuade 150,000 new shoppers to try the brand (assuming there is not perfect conversion from trial to long-term usage). From here, a result in a specific channel can be defined easily. In terms of in-store marketing, results can be broken down by thinking about the three elements of the in-store mix. Was the product available and visible? Did the communication affect the way the target shoppers felt toward the brand? And did the offer create purchase? Finally, the investment completes the data set to calculate arguably the most important measure in marketing—the return on investment.

By defining activities using this five-step approach, it is clearer and simpler to connect specific activities to business results and therefore be confident that the appropriate metrics are being used.

From here, you can brainstorm metrics that will support those business results. Rather than looking at what is available, consider potential metrics. In the example earlier, trial rates (ideally along with a measure of retention) would be a great metric to study. If you want detail about the effectiveness of specific elements of the marketing mix, then perhaps test stores that feature only certain elements of the mix could be established (some stores with a promoter in-store, some without). Or perhaps shoppers could be observed or interviewed to better understand what they interacted with and what potentially influenced them. All of these mechanisms have some potential error or bias, but as long as you understand that, then progress is being made.

At this point, you can select specific measures based on an analysis of the value and cost of each. From a shopper marketing perspective, the most frequently desired result is a specific change in the behavior of a certain group of shoppers (the target shoppers). All activity should support that goal, so the most valuable metrics are likely to be those most closely associated with it.

At a strategic level, metrics should be set around whether the desired behavior is successfully created. If the target market could be isolated, specific measures of penetration and purchase frequency would create clear indicators as to whether the group of target shoppers was buying the product in the desired fashion over time. Tracking studies, if configured effectively to isolate the target shoppers, can track performance over time against these metrics very clearly. Shopper panels may also be useful in this area, depending on how the target shopper is defined and whether that data is collected as part of the panel definition.

It is when shopper metrics move from strategic to tactical that things begin to get complicated. Strategic metrics, by definition, take a long-term view of things, and time smoothes out many of the peaks and troughs caused by other factors. Setting metrics at a tactical level has additional complications, as we shall see.

For example, say an organization wishes to drive penetration of its brand. Existing data suggests that a large group of target consumers are not aware of the product, that many of these consumers shop for themselves, and that they shop in supermarkets. A big campaign is devised, with TV advertising, press ads, and an in-store marketing campaign with sampling, posters, wobblers on the shelf, and gondola displays in major stores. What are the most important metrics around this? And how should those metrics be used to evaluate the performance of each element of the marketing mix? The advertising might have created awareness, but surely the display or the sampling may also have done this, right? How can you isolate the different elements? Would shoppers have bought the product without the offer? Would they have bought without the advertising?

Realistically, it is almost impossible to isolate one element from another unless stricter test conditions are created. Employing different elements of the mix in different combinations can help isolate the impact of each activity, but this can easily become time consuming—just four elements creates 15 different permutations (without counting different levels of deals, or media weights). You may need to save this for only the most significant (highly important or expensive) initiatives.

If you want to measure the impact of a particular activity or element, the measurement mechanism must endeavor to isolate that interaction. And the further the interaction from the point of measurement, the harder it is to get an accurate take on its impact. Measuring the sales impact of TV advertising has been traditionally difficult because between the TV viewing and the actual purchase, a million other things happen, including loads of in-store action.

In most environments, for most marketers, the answer lies in statistics and regression. By continually measuring the impact of all or most activities, it is possible to spot the impact of individual elements over time. While the results are far from "real time," they are statistically accurate and are a long way ahead of the alternatives.

It is fair to say that getting accurate data to complete the entirety of a shopper marketer's wish list is likely to be an expensive endeavor (and one that would probably reduce the return on investment rather than increase it), but this approach also enables better use of existing data. By focusing on what is important, the marketer can identify new ways of using existing data.

And for many organizations, there is a surprising amount of data about shoppers around. Although the available (or easily available) data may not be perfect, in many cases, it is reasonably accurate. Ex-factory sales data lacks a degree of accuracy in terms of understanding how much was bought, but it is better than nothing. Listed here are a number of common data sources that may add value to a shopper metrics approach.

- **Ex-factory sales data:** Data on sales out of the factory and into the retailer does not measure what a shopper buys and gives no understanding of specific shopper behavior (other than the chain or store where purchases may have taken place). Low-cost, low accuracy.

- **Retail scan sales data:** Measures what was bought where, and when. Doesn't detail who bought. Scan sales deliver highly accurate data that can be tracked to the hour and the day. The cost depends on the relationship with a retailer.

- **Loyalty card data:** Adds in the "who" question. Gives a highly accurate, high-level view of who bought what, when and where. Limited only to the purchases that a shopper made at that retailer and only to the shoppers who have and use a loyalty card; therefore, the data is inevitably skewed. The cost depends on the relationship with a retailer.

- **Retail audit:** Retail audit data details what was sold where, when; in some geographies, gives details of availability, too. Accuracy varies depending on data collection method and geography (for large chains, the data usually comes from the retailer's scan systems, but for small stores and independents, this may be gathered by visiting a sample of stores, which inevitably introduces inaccuracy). High cost.

- **Household panel data:** Individual shoppers scan the product they buy when they get home (or as they shop, in some cases) or scan in their receipts. Typically, the panels are large and continuous, so longer-term trends can be analyzed. Due to the large sample, results are often very accurate; but errors can be introduced when product is consumed before it is scanned or for smaller shopping trips, where the scan may not happen due to panelist error. While there are some dangers in more impulsive categories, this data creates a very rich library of which shoppers bought what, where, and when, and covers all of a shopper's trips, not just those in one retailer (as a loyalty card does). High cost.

- **Brand tracking:** Many marketing teams habitually track key brand metrics, and many of these can be used to evaluate shopping behavior. Brand teams are usually tracking consumers instead of shoppers, so the data may be skewed, particularly if a significant number of shoppers are not consumers. Many studies track "brand bought" and perception. While this data is based on recollection and is therefore less accurate than data collected in a store, it is "free" if the marketing team is already gathering it.

- **Usage and attitude:** A staple study in the armory of most consumer goods marketers, this study asks consumers about their usage and attitude towards categories and brands within it. As with brand tracking, the studies often target consumers, but changes in consumption can be a proxy for changes in purchase. If a consumer is using more of a brand, then someone must have bought more. In addition, there are frequently shopper-related questions ("Where do you buy?") that may be of some use. They are limited because of a lack of proximity to the shopping occasion ("Have you bought this product in the last three months?" is a difficult question to answer accurately), and shoppers who are not consumers are not usually surveyed. While there are accuracy issues, if the consumer marketers have already invested in this, then it may be a useful place to start.

WHERE TO BEGIN

The process outlined previously is designed to help any business at any stage of development select appropriate measures. But getting started can be daunting. Measuring and evaluating potentially hundreds of shopper marketing activities can be expensive and incredibly time consuming. The challenge for most organizations is to decide what to measure and to prioritize these specific metrics.

Shopper marketers should focus on the really big questions—the ones connected to their biggest strategies and objectives. If the single biggest objective of a particular brand is to drive new usage out of home, then shopper marketers should use the five-step process (outlined earlier in the chapter) to identify the most appropriate shopper metrics, and work on how to monitor and measure those. In addition, marketers should review the activities that are either costly or happen very frequently (such that their annualized cost is high), and consider how those could be monitored and measured to determine their effectiveness.

Finally, and in particular where incremental expenditure may be required to effectively measure a situation, marketers should form a hypothesis around the activity ("Gondola ends do not drive higher trial than the home shelf," for example) and then build evidence from existing data that might indicate whether the hypothesis may be correct. Armed with this evidence (assuming, of course, it is supportive of your hypothesis), you can understand the cost and value of additional measurement to prove the hypothesis, enabling you to build a business case for additional investment. This is the process by which existing data can be brought into use. Most organizations we work with have significantly more data available than they actually use. Framing a question in the form of a hypothesis enables the marketer to review existing data and purposefully quiz other departments to gather data. In our experience, this approach frequently leads to new discoveries in existing data that can often shortcut the metrics process or help build a case for additional investment.

A WORD ON COMPLIANCE

One area we would argue is a "must" in terms of measurement is compliance (rather, the measurement of the stimuli that a shopper actually faced). Too often, activities are evaluated merely based on the results that were achieved, with little or no consideration as to what stimulated the shopper. Without an accurate view of this, it is very difficult to measure the efficacy of an activity. The issue of compliance is certainly more apparent in the shopper marketing arena. Media companies have long tracked the actual delivery of advertising versus a media plan, but in the world of shopper marketing, this issue seems to get less attention.

Compliance is important. Without a compliance measure, it is possible to judge whether an activity was effective, but it is not necessarily possible to understand why the result was achieved. Products go out of stock. Displays do not get set up (remember the Tamagotchi?), they are positioned incorrectly, or they don't stay in position for the requisite time period. Activity doesn't get implemented in all the stores. Staff doesn't show up, or shows up but doesn't follow the script. It happens all the time. Not only does compliance cost a vast amount of money (research in 2008 by POPAI in the United Kingdom suggested that poor compliance was costing manufacturers over $600 million per year), it also skews the interpretation of any results. Damning an activity because it didn't achieve the desired results creates a certain amount of value. Understanding why the activity worked or didn't work creates the potential to improve the activity in the future and perhaps helps save an otherwise effective mechanic from the scrap heap.

Compliance-testing methodologies fall into two camps: one is in-store observation, and the other is mystery shopper. While observation can show you what's in the store at a particular time, mystery shoppers can reveal whether more complex elements of the in-store mix (namely, the people) played their part correctly. A word of warning on compliance—the measure only signals what was in-store at a particular time. It does not mean that the situation was the same the following day or the following week. The decision of whether to take a "spot observation" as a positive indicator of compliance versus continuous observation is in the hands of the marketer—it's often a trade-off between value and cost.

THE FUTURE OF SHOPPER METRICS

Technology is rapidly changing the availability, affordability, and efficiency of creating and tracking shopper marketing metrics. There is a continuous stream of activity as organizations strive to create better ways of understanding *exactly* what happens in a store.

The advent of scanning at the checkout created (or at least supported) the first wave of interest in shopper analytics. For the first time, data on exactly what was bought, and when and where it was bought, was available in a fabulously efficient and low-cost way. Retail loyalty cards stepped this forward, with the ability to understand who was buying, as well as what and where.

As more transactions take place in a digital environment, it will become even easier to track behavior. All digital interaction has tracking built into it—the tracking is automatic. It is possible to track the paths shoppers make through a digital environment and to identify exactly which stimuli created which results. The ability to test many combinations rapidly, to measure the results, and even better, to make changes to the campaigns in real time is incredibly empowering. Compared to this, setting up test stores feels positively archaic. No longer does the marketer need to wait until days or weeks after an activity is completed to understand whether it worked. She can now see activity in real time and can therefore make immediate adjustments to the campaign, thus remedying shortcomings or amplifying elements that are particularly effective.

And marketers are looking to use technology to better understand what happens in brick-and-mortar stores, too. Radio-frequency identification (RFID) tags can be attached to shelves to monitor where a product was purchased (and also to monitor the inventory level). One company in the United Kingdom uses the tracking signal from mobile phones to understand store traffic flows—where shoppers actually go in a store. Scanning trolleys, where shoppers scan the product as it goes into the basket, could be used to measure how long people spend in a particular part of a store. Cameras can be positioned in-store for lower costs than ever before, and they can help marketers observe shoppers (and monitor compliance!). As smartphone usage becomes more ubiquitous, and as smartphones become a more integrated part of more shopping processes, the ability to track where people are and the types of decisions they make at that physical point grows even stronger.

There is an abundance of data already available to marketers, and enhancing this with additional pertinent information is not a difficult task. In the near future, marketers, particularly in more developed markets, will be bombarded with new data options, and the ability to use these effectively will be an enormous competitive advantage. Shopper analytics—identifying, monitoring, and evaluating the effectiveness of shopper marketing against its objectives—will be mandatory for the shopper marketer of the future.

CHAPTER 15

ORGANIZING FOR SHOPPER MARKETING

A s we have argued, shopper marketing represents a fundamental shift in the way consumer goods companies think and operate. It makes sense that this could have dramatic consequences for the way teams are organized, as organizational structures should follow the core strategic thrusts of the organization. Organization and business strategy have a strange intertwined relationship. On the one hand, strategy should drive organizational structure; businesses decide what their priorities are, and organizational structures, with a dose of pragmatism, are designed to deliver on them. On the other hand, and in part because of this, organization drives the way a company operates and thinks, and (consciously or subconsciously) the organization therefore affects strategy. Whether this is an insidious trait or not depends on your view of the strategy (assuming that the organization serves it). If the priorities, and therefore the strategies, are no longer valid, then organizational structures tend to act like quicksand—holding people and practices in place and sucking in any deviation. In a typical consumer goods company (and there are many notable exceptions), we think this is the case. The fundamental structure of the commercial part of this business has remained largely unchanged for decades, and this structural inertia has (in part, at least) contributed to the current and future difficulties that face consumer goods companies.

The introduction of shopper marketing, then, represents challenge and opportunity. The core challenge is that shopper marketing demands different priorities for the business, and that, by definition, demands a fundamental review of the structure of the organization. There are always barriers to changes of that magnitude: inertia, politics, and fiefdoms have often prevented the optimization of business structures. However shopper marketing also offers an opportunity to organizations that truly see its potential. Shopper marketing offers the opportunity, *the rationale*, for a radical rethink about the way marketing and sales teams are structured and operate; an opportunity to dissolve the paradigms that no longer serve companies in the industry and to create a very new way of looking at this part of the business. Further, the arguments put forward thus far in this book would suggest that this review is long overdue and potentially mandatory for companies that wish to thrive in the future.

In many ways, this offers further evidence that shopper marketing is indeed a *revolution* in the way consumer goods companies market and sell their products. As with any revolution, not everything in shopper marketing is new. Many of the ideas and practices have been around almost as long as marketing itself. Revolutions come at a time of need, where the overthrow of the status quo is essential. The reach and impact must go and will go far beyond the individuals involved. And so is the case with shopper marketing, which is why any new approach must be a Total Marketing solution rather than one merely focused on the shopper arena. There is a dire need for change in consumer goods, and we will see in this chapter that the overthrow of the status quo is essential before the power of shopper marketing is truly felt.

A lack of consensus on the definition of shopper marketing is reflected in the variety of organizational approaches to the area. And while there is no blueprint for organizational perfection (organizations, as discussed earlier, should be driven by strategy) and there may be variations for different companies in different situations, there is strong evidence that there are "better" ways of doing it, if not a specific "right way." In this chapter, we will explore the different ways companies have chosen to organize for shopper marketing, and we'll examine the pros and cons of each. We will consider the challenges of creating an effective shopper marketing organization and suggest key approaches that have proven successful for others. Finally, we will offer some thoughts on the critical success factors involved in bringing shopper marketing into the organization. But first, let's consider what doesn't work with existing organizations (or at least pre-shopper marketing ones).

THE LAND OF SILOS

Our discussion will be limited to the parts of a consumer goods company's organization which are responsible for the task of serving the three customers: the challenge of creating desire and need for the company's brands in the eyes of **consumers**, enabling and encouraging purchase of those brands by **shoppers**, and the motivation of **retail partners** to support the company's brands. In many definitions, all this is "marketing" (Peter Drucker suggests that businesses only do two things: "innovation and marketing"). Yet while all of these elements could be known as marketing in a typical consumer goods company, the term "marketing" is used typically to describe the team responsible for and focused on the first customer: the consumer. Throughout this chapter, we must be careful to differentiate between (1) the act and discipline of marketing, and (2) the business function, department, or team that is called marketing.

Across these three core tasks of reaching out to consumers, shoppers, and retail customers, there are myriad structures in play around the world, but most have one thing in common, with a few notable exceptions. These tasks are broadly split between two core functional teams: sales and marketing.

Sales teams have existed for as long as there have been customers; and in many businesses, marketing grew as an adjunct of sales, as a support function designed to make the selling of product to the customer easier. Marketing broke free as a separate department as the power of media and branding was discovered, and the value of longer-term brand equity was realized. CEOs recognized that there was a need to focus on the longer-term value of the brand, as well as this quarter's numbers, and created departments that could be held accountable for that. Over time, marketing departments developed their own place at the boardroom table, with distinct metrics and responsibilities. While sales departments remain responsible for hitting the sales numbers week in and week out, marketing teams took on the responsibility of managing the longer-term equity of a business's brands. This relationship functioned well for some time, with both sets of metrics balancing each other—long-term equity versus short-term sales—albeit with an element of constructive tension thrown in.

Over time, these structures—once devised out of strategic focus—became hardwired into organizations. New priorities have been force-fitted into existing structures and departments as the strategic agenda moved in the last few decades. As customers grew in scale and importance, elements of the sales team were converted to "key customer management." Key customer managers, and then key customer management teams, were created after manufacturers recognized that larger customers required more effort and focus. Companies soon realized that their relationships with these mega customers could deliver strategic long-term value, or equity, in the same way that consumer relationships could.

The need for better, stronger propositions to these customers became apparent, and trade marketing was created *as part of the sales team.* As new thinking entered businesses in the form of Category Management, it was either merged into the trade marketing team, or separate Category Management teams were created as a sub-function of sales. And in some cases, category managers were embedded into key customer teams. Whatever the route, Category Management was part of the sales team in virtually all cases. Why? Because it was related to retail, and that pointed to sales. No matter that Category Management actually started with an understanding of a category from the consumer point of view (which is surely a consumer marketing task). No matter that these changes were the early indications of an enormous shift in business priorities. Very few CEOs saw either of these shifts as a big strategic change—it was, after all, a "sales issue." Over the decades, marketing departments cemented their reputation (and self-belief): they were the drivers and owners of company strategy, so anything to do with stores, customers, or sales teams was clearly not a strategic issue. Whether or not this view of marketing was true, it created the lasting impression (still pervasive today) that sales was clearly *not* strategic; it was merely tactical, there to execute the plans of strategic marketing overlords. Marketing directors and vice presidents were the guardians of strategy, and long-term equity; value lay in understanding consumers, not retail customers.

Most marketing gurus accept that serving the customer is a key priority—"the customer is king" is a well-used marketing mantra. Drucker describes marketing as "the whole business seen from the point of view of its final result; that is, from the customer's point of view." Over the decades, consumer goods companies managed to pervert this truth with the simple substitution of the word *consumer* for the word *customer.* Therefore, in the majority of cases, key customer management, trade marketing, and Category Management were sales (and therefore tactical) issues. Whether this was ever valid is largely moot; as we have argued elsewhere in this book, it is certainly not true anymore. Consumer goods organizations must recognize three customers (consumer, shopper, and retailer). An organization designed to focus on only one of these is likely to be suboptimal.

The results of these changes to sales functions have been well documented elsewhere and referred to earlier in this book. Rather than creating bridges and connections between marketing and sales teams, departments such as trade marketing created bigger barriers between these two functions and reinforced the belief that "sales equals retail equals tactical." Brands were where long-term value and equity lay, and brands were about consumers.

Of course, this generalizes enormously. There are sales and marketing teams that function well together, with high levels of alignment. There are many more that function well with less alignment, with both parties content in their exclusive roles of strategist and tactician. There are cases where trade marketing departments have been set up alongside sales and where there are separate Category Management teams. And there are many cases where true alignment is elusive.

In most cases, however, it is into this environment that the concept of shopper marketing arrives.

THE PRECURSIVE ORGANIZATIONAL QUESTION

One might think that the biggest question facing any company wishing to take its first steps on the shopper marketing path might be "Where does it sit?" The obvious choices appear to be to have shopper marketing as part of the sales department, part of marketing, or as a standalone structure reporting to a general manager. Interscope, in a survey in the United States, found that of the 150 companies who responded, 25 percent had shopper marketing functions reporting to marketing, 23 percent reported to sales, and 24 percent to some executive level. The rest existed as part of Category Management, trade marketing, or shopper insights groups. However, we would argue that there is a better, precursive question.

Shopper marketing is not a goal, not an end in itself. Rather, shopper marketing is part of a bigger Total Marketing solution and, as argued in this book, is a culture, an attitude, a way of working. Shopper marketing is one element of a fully integrated business process. Any organizational structure that achieves a fully integrated solution that profitably addresses the needs of consumer, shoppers, and retail customers is probably perfectly fine. With this in mind, remember that organizational structure is the last decision made; first, you must answer a number of questions.

- What does the business want to achieve?
- What is the role of shopper marketing in achieving this?
- What is the role of other functions in achieving this?

engage, our consultancy business, has helped many companies with organizational design. Whether as part of a strategic review or as part of a people-development program, getting the right organization structure is a critical part of deriving value from brands and people. We use an approach we call People First™. The first step of People First is an understanding of the priorities of the business.

Business priorities drive organization design. Business priorities are driven by strategy, and these priorities tell us which brands, channels, and customers are important for the business's success. They help identify all the tasks the business will need to do to deliver those priorities and how these tasks need to be completed. Further, they make it possible to prioritize some activities over others. This is critical, because it helps define the type of resources required to complete these tasks to the desired standard and tells us how long that might take. They drives definition of role (which "jobs" the business might need to create), as well as headcount (the number of people in any given role required to deliver all the tasks required to deliver the priorities). Add to this the development requirements of the organization (which can be identified by knowing who exactly needs to be able to do what, to what standard, and what competency is required to deliver it), and you'll be able to map out an organization that can deliver its priorities.

Therefore, a better (dare we say mandatory) precursive question is "How does the concept of shopper marketing affect the business priorities and goals?" A business should answer that question before attempting to answer structural questions. For some organizations, the sales/marketing model is so hardwired that the first question is unfortunately about organizational orientation. For many more companies, however, the shopper journey began by stealth, with almost no questions being asked, let alone answered.

For many organizations, the concept of shoppers and shopper marketing crept in the back door, often at the behest of large retailers or in hopes of deriving greater value from Category Management. The concept of shopper research and shopper insights became en vogue as part of the Category Management movement but very much within the paradigm of understanding the consumer in the store, rather than considering marketing to shoppers in and of itself. Research projects were tentative and one-off, often linked to a specific category project. From there, trade marketing (or Category Management) slowly began to morph into shopper marketing.

This chain of events perhaps led to many shopper marketing departments reporting to sales, although it appears that the number is declining. According to the Interscope survey, over half of those surveyed in 2006 had shopper marketing functions, or at least shopper marketing resources, residing within the sales camp. By 2009, that had declined to 23 percent. It is not clear whether this was caused by companies moving shopper marketing or by later entries taking a different approach, but it is clear that there was once an organizational tendency for shopper marketing to default into the sales department.

THE ORGANIZATIONAL QUESTION

Assuming that business priorities have been established, there are two broad organizational questions to be answered. First, where should the shopper marketing team be housed—within marketing, within sales, or as a standalone function? Second, how should the team be structured? Should there be a discrete shopper marketing unit within the sales or marketing team, or should resources be somehow integrated?

Beginning organization design with a company's unique strategic business priorities should lead to solutions that are different from what other companies do. There is still no dominant model for how shopper marketing should fit into the organization structure, and looking at leading companies offers little reinforcement of one route over another. Campbell's has shopper marketing linked into marketing, as does ConAgra. The shopper marketing team at Hewlett-Packard, however, reports into sales. Unilever has pulled Category Management out of sales and combined it with its headquarter-based shopper marketing teams. All of these companies are highly successful in the shopper marketing arena—evidence that there's not one "right" way. So, if there is no definitive model for success, what are the pros and cons of each approach? And which approach will drive into the ascendancy?

SHOPPER MARKETING AS PART OF SALES

As discussed previously in this chapter, the sales department is often the default home for a fledgling shopper marketing team. There are many organizations, such as Hewlett-Packard, who also seem to be remarkably successful with a sales-based approach to shopper marketing structures. Yet we have observed many common shortfalls in this approach, especially when the shopper team has grown organically from a trade marketing or Category Management base.

The largest benefit of this type of structure is the strength it can potentially deliver in the area of retailer understanding and collaboration. Shopper marketing initiatives, in most cases, require retail permission for execution, and retailers are increasingly looking to their suppliers to collaborate on shopper initiatives in much the same way that Category Management projects were conceived. Retailers have vast reams of data on shoppers in many cases (particularly in more developed markets)—the retail proximity that this structure creates certainly enables closer relationships with key customers.

Unfortunately, this often comes at the expense of closer working relationships with marketing teams and sometimes limits how effective that collaboration can be, especially to the manufacturer. As with many Category Management projects, the manufacturer sometimes makes significant monetary and time investments, yet the vast majority of the spoils fall to the retailer. This, too, can limit the strategic impact shopper marketing can have on the business. True, this depends on the strategic clout of the head of the sales department—if sales is seen as a strategic "big hitter," then the limitations are smaller. However, the danger that shopper marketing is led more by the strategic direction of key customers is a very real one in any company where shopper marketing is embedded in sales. Retailers do not have the strategic well-being of a manufacturer's brand at heart. Therefore, any agenda led by them, or even driven in collaboration with them, will run the risk of putting the growth and well-being of the manufacturer's brands second to their own. This can manifest itself in a poor return on shopper marketing efforts—manufacturers do a lot of work, and retailers glean the benefits—but worse, it means that initiatives with much higher potential may be left on the shelf. Opportunities to grow do not always come in the stores where a brand currently sells. Nor do they always come in the stores with the most data or resources, or those owned by retailers who are willing to engage in shopper marketing initiatives. Much as with Category Management, shopper marketing that is led by retail or driven by retail collaboration runs the risk of missing the real opportunities to drive brand growth with less sophisticated retailers. In 2011, a senior manager at Saatchi & Saatchi X suggested that the development of shopper marketing in India was slow because the modern trade was tiny—did this person think that Indian kirana stores don't have shoppers? Wherever there is a shopper, there is an opportunity to market to him.

The biggest areas of limitations for this model can often be related to the targets, metrics, and KPIs of the head of sales. Typically, her agenda is one of revenue, volume, and debtor days. The KPIs of a shopper marketing function should be very different, and while the rest of the sales team will have KPIs that are aligned to the head of sales' KPIs, the shopper teams' KPIs will not. Too often, the shopper KPIs will be sacrificed for the "greater good" (i.e., this month's sales numbers). It is a brave sales director indeed who is prepared to take poor sales results into the boardroom and offer brand equity with shoppers in return.

Beyond this, shopper marketing is, after all, a marketing discipline. As we have demonstrated throughout this book, shopper marketing is about applying marketing techniques and approaches to a different target market in a different environment. It is not sales, and therefore, it is unrealistic to expect the typical sales director to have a marketing skill set honed to the requisite levels. The majority of sales directors are not trained marketers, and while the better ones have a strong appreciation of the value of marketing, few would suggest that they are the best person in their organization to lead a team dedicated to marketing to consumers: why, then, would they be any better placed to lead a team that markets to shoppers?

Under these circumstances, ineffectively allocated or insufficiently protected budgets are common. Shopper marketing is seen as initiative- or project-based rather than as part of ongoing business. As a result, shopper marketing is often underfunded and underdeveloped when housed in the sales realm. Sales leaders may be reluctant to commit funds to activities that cannot be directly connected to short-term sales, and marketing teams are not likely to cede their budgets to activities that are not of their realm where the budgets may quietly slip into the trade promotions pot (heaven forbid!). When funding does come from marketing, it is often project-based and does not create a lasting way of working.

Finally, positioning a shopper marketing team within sales can affect the perception of the concept itself within the business. Marketing teams are more likely to see it as a tactical activity—one to be engaged with at the end of an activity stream, as a task moves into execution; they will not see the shopper marketing team as strategic partners who should be involved much earlier in decision-making processes. This perception can also have a negative impact on external or internal recruitment. To marketing talent, the sales team can sometimes have a stigma attached to it, and a move to shopper marketing may not be seen as the great career move it could be.

Should the decision be made to house shopper marketing within the sales team, the organizational options fall into two broad camps. Shopper teams can sit as a unified team to the side of the customer teams, or shopper resources can be integrated into customer teams. The decision depends on the company's priorities, the scale of the shopper resource, and the scale and requirement of the company's major customers. Big businesses with big customers often embed shopper resources within their customer teams, particularly where those customers are strategically important. Smaller companies may find this completely impractical, and there is an important word of warning. Putting extra resources into the team that services a major customer is relatively easy—but taking it out can be rather tricky!

SHOPPER MARKETING AS PART OF MARKETING

Many of these shortcomings can be overcome by positioning shopper marketing within the marketing department. In many of the largest consumer goods organizations, marketing already has a number of sub-functions reporting to a chief marketing officer, and it is thus quite possible to add an additional team into this structure.

Under these circumstances, shopper marketing is seen in a different light, as something new, something less likely to be labeled as an interesting adjunct to the sales team. Involving the shopper marketing team in strategy development is simpler, and the opportunity to manage brands in an aligned way is increased. Typically, shopper marketing teams embedded in marketing departments automatically behave like marketers, sharing a common DNA and language with their consumer counterparts. Recruitment, both within and outside the organization, can be simpler, too. Most importantly, the team is better configured to integrate consumer and shopper activity effectively, a capability that is already key to managing today's complex paths to purchase and fragmented media options. As mobile and online trends grow, the (external) line between shopper and consumer will become ever more blurred. As argued before, the idea that shopping only occurs within the four walls of a store is patently false, and this will be become more apparent.

While this structure enables far closer collaboration and integration between consumer and shopper teams, it does have the potential to underperform in the area of retail collaboration. Shopper marketers can become distanced from the reality of retail, and indeed suffer from an inability to integrate retailers' strategies into their own shopper work.

Again, once a decision is made to house shopper marketing in the marketing team, there are options as to how the team is structured. We believe that integrating consumer and shopper resources to create brand teams creates the best chances for the development of a truly integrated marketing plan. Many organizations (particularly large ones with a chief marketing officer and a number of sub-functions already within marketing) prefer to keep shopper resources together and create a sub-function under a head of shopper marketing. In the same way, those with a relatively small team will find it impossible to spread their people across the various brand teams.

STANDALONE SHOPPER MARKETING

The final potential reporting relationship is one where shopper marketing reports directly to the executive level. This structure clearly supports the focus on shopper marketing and ensures that shopper marketing is seen as a "big hitter" around the boardroom table. With the right management, this structure can also create effective integration with consumer marketing plans and reduces the chances of a gap opening up between shopper and customer teams. It does not, however, guarantee integration, particularly with a marketing team that is accustomed to being insular.

The primary drawback of this structure is that there is a danger of shopper marketing becoming a wedge between the consumer and customer teams, making that relationship even more distant. Consumer marketers confer with shopper marketers, who in turn confer with customer teams. The dangers of duplication, of Chinese whispers, and of shopper marketing becoming a middleman are high. The last thing a consumer goods company needs to do is create a third silo!

The other limitations of this structure are of a more practical nature. This type of structure may suit large organizations, but an additional head at a vice president level may not be palatable (or necessary) for smaller businesses, whose shopper marketing team may be quite small.

AND THE WINNER IS ... MARKETING!

It is true that none of these options is inherently good or bad, as that would have to depend on the organization's priorities, scale, and available resources. There is no right or wrong; in addition to the archetypes described here, hybrid options may work well, depending on what the company is trying to achieve.

Plenty of case studies of success from each model exist, but integration of shopper marketing into the existing marketing team is the preferred option. The appeal of fully integrated insights and strategies across consumers and shoppers is far too strong, as is the appeal of knowing that all marketing efforts are aligned and that campaigns work in harmony. Chris Hoyt of Hoyt & Co. suggests that economics support this, too. He states that housing shopper marketing in the marketing department delivers, on average, a better ROI. While a sales-based shopper marketing team can lift ROIs to around 1.1–1.0; teams housed in marketing can deliver a significantly better performance of 2.5–3.1.[92]

Large organizations can overcome the retail collaboration/alignment issue by having shopper experts embedded in customer teams, having dedicated resources for key retailers within the shopper team, or creating matrix organizations. Some maintain Category Management approaches within sales and separate only shopper insights and marketing. We strongly support the creation of a "commercial head" role in some cases, sitting above sales and marketing heads, ensuring that the two functions are aligned. Either way, it appears that there are routes to mitigate this situation, and the returns can be significant.

Even once the decision of where to house shopper marketing is made, there are many permutations. We think the integration card trumps all. It is critical to bring together consumer and shopper insights to create a clear understanding of what opportunities exist to drive consumption and which shopper segments are important to enabling consumption. The manufacturer must be clear on which channels are important to it before a retailer's strategy is considered. While the five-step process is not supposed to be truly linear in that it is an integrated model—nothing is complete until the customer-investment piece is complete—it does run from consumer to customer. Manufacturers should own their own brand strategy. This structure creates the possibility of marketing teams that truly manage brands rather than just managing the relationship between a brand and its consumers.

---

92 Shopper Structure, Chris Hoyt.

THE INTERNAL STRUCTURE OF A SHOPPER MARKETING FUNCTION

From this point, there are a plethora of options. Shopper marketing can sit alongside its consumer counterparts, or shopper-insights professionals may be positioned in the same team as consumer insights (if such a team exists). It is possible to create mini brand teams with a consumer, shopper, and potentially insight resource.

Decisions of this nature depend more on the scale of the organization, on the portfolio, and on those business priorities. Larger organizations have more of an opportunity to focus and specialize; if a consumer insight team already exists, this is an area of potential synergy. Organizations with few categories, or categories that are very differentiated, may find that creating consumer/shopper brand or category teams produces focus; other organizations may find that one of the core benefits of shopper marketing is to break away from the brand or category paradigms and consider the world from the shopper's point of view. In some categories, shoppers often look for solutions (e.g., a meal) rather than a brand. Too much brand focus from the shopper marketer might cause him to miss opportunities that a channel- or customer-oriented shopper team could exploit. For smaller businesses, where business units and teams are not appropriate, we believe the shopper team is best positioned as a separate group reporting to the head of marketing.

In consumer marketing teams, brand managers typically manage a brand or a portfolio of brands. The team structure is aligned, therefore, to the consumers the brand is targeting. Sales teams are typically aligned to their customers; so how, then, should shopper marketing be aligned?

Putting aside questions of scale and quantity of resources, which always need to be considered, it seems that shopper marketing teams should be oriented along shopper lines. If meal solutions across categories are what shoppers want, then that is how the team should be structured. It may be that integrating consumer and shopper managers into brand teams may not be desirable under those circumstances. If the company understands that there are fundamental differences in target shoppers in different channels, then a channel-based orientation may well be beneficial. What is important is that the jurisdiction of each shopper marketer is aligned with his target market and the behavior that he wishes to create in that target. An organization that attempts to mirror this as closely as is practically and commercially viable is more likely to succeed.

The most effective organization is the one that most effectively delivers the company's goals—there is not a right or a wrong. However, shopper marketing is a marketing function, and it will perform better when structured as part of the marketing organization under most circumstances. The case for placement in marketing will be made stronger as the emergence of mobile increases the need for integrated shopper and consumer strategies and plans. Within the marketing function, orienting resources as close as possible to shopper groups will deliver better results.

We hope that whatever structure you adopt is not allowed to stand unchallenged for decades; revisit it regularly to ensure that it still reflects the focus and strategies of the business. Let's not wait another 50 years—until we need another revolution!

CHAPTER 16

SHOPPER MARKETING— THE POST-REVOLUTIONARY AGE

This is an exciting time to be in the consumer goods industry—quite possibly the most exciting in the past 50 years. A perfect storm of pressures has brought an outdated marketing model almost to its knees, and a new form of marketing is emerging as a response to the conditions of this century, rather than those prevalent halfway through the last. Shopper marketing has been talked about for a long time, but in the last few years, some marketers have begun to see it as more than just a "bolt on" to existing marketing practices. Today, more and more see it as an integral part of the new marketing that is necessary if manufacturers hope to thrive in coming years. Even so, shopper marketing is still in its infancy—nothing but a concept for all but a few leading companies. Various definitions exist, and part of the growth in the shopper marketing "noise" is undoubtedly the sound of agencies and marketers jumping on the bandwagon.

The world of consumer goods is at a tipping point. What will happen next? In this final chapter, we will argue that change is both necessary and desirable, and that the current environment will encourage or possibly force companies to take stock and make the change. Further, while predicting the future is fraught with risk, we will paint a picture that suggests its conditions will support and embed that change, as well as reward those who take the plunge and join the revolution.

JUMP OR BE PUSHED

Those who see an industry beset by problems and challenges—riddled with outdated beliefs, structures, and working practices—are right. The consumer goods industry has, in many ways, gotten itself into a rut—perhaps even sleepwalked into this mess—and getting out of it is going to require a lot of work and effort.

The good news is that some of the sleepwalking giants are beginning to wake up and look around, and many of them don't like what they see. Investors and corporations are belatedly noticing the signs that things are not well and need to change. The cost and effectiveness of marketing, however, shows no sign of moving in the right direction. With the exception of a few notable successes, it feels as though the consumer goods industry is, rather than driving growth, merely "grinding it out." Even stalwart companies that saw great success in the past few decades, such as Procter & Gamble, are stumbling.

Retail continues to consolidate, and there is little suggestion that this trend will end. Nor are there any indicators to suggest that large retailers are likely to stop wielding their influence at the negotiating table. Retailers are likely to find themselves under even greater pressure at home and abroad. Digital retailers, not hampered by the large costs of real estate, threaten to eat away at share in home markets. That increased pressure will inevitably lead to pressure on suppliers.

All this bad news is, surprisingly, good news. The status quo is finally becoming untenable, or at least incredibly painful, for many companies. Forward-thinking organizations are already beginning to see the need for change and are attempting to comply. In the near term, others will feel compelled to do so as well. Significant changes only come about when there is so much pain associated with a system that a *revolution* becomes almost mandatory. If that point has not been reached, it is not far away for many companies operating in the consumer goods industry.

THE AGE OF THE SHOPPER IS HERE

As at any time of crisis, opportunity arises. Just when the pressures appear likely to break many consumer goods companies, things are beginning to change.

The source of retailers' power has been their control over the point of purchase, the "first moment of truth." Retailers' control over what goes on in stores is a fundamental part of the leverage gained by scale. In any industry, big customers have some power over suppliers, but the retailers' ability to "cut off" the shopper from the manufacturer made that power more tangible, more real. If the retailer didn't stock your product, you were in big trouble. Shoppers couldn't buy your brand, so all brand investment was at risk. All the advertising, product development, and design—potentially wasted. Not doing a deal with the retailer was impossible to contemplate. Any negotiator will tell you it's pretty darn difficult to negotiate effectively when you have to make a deal and the other party doesn't. It's very unlikely that even the best negotiator would strike a great deal under those circumstances.

This entire premise, however, was built around a simple conceit: first, that shoppers have no choice when it comes to where to buy, and second, that the primary point of influencing shoppers was indeed in-store, at the point of purchase. As you now know, neither of these is necessarily true. Shoppers now have more choice than ever before. Some independent retailers have continued to thrive and have developed offers based on convenience, service, and—in some cases—credit to serve their local communities. Convenience stores have grown at unprecedented rates. Warehouse clubs, discount stores, dollar shops, and specialists now offer more choice than ever before. And the online world merely affirms that which was already becoming true: shoppers now have more choice than ever when choosing what to buy—and more critically, *where* to buy. No longer is it sufficient to gather a selection of products in one place (a store) at a reasonable price. The "big retail" model of convenience, curation, and price is under threat. The walls that retailers (quite literally!) built around shoppers are crumbling. And the very tools that were their greatest strength—the stores—threaten to become their Achilles' heel. When all competitors had the same store legacy, this wasn't much of a problem. New digital upstarts have no such handicap. Digital can deliver greater selection, greater convenience, and potentially better prices. The retailers have blinked.

Beyond that, the myth that shopping only happens in stores has imploded. Voices such as Jim Lecinski at Google, with his work *Zero Moment of Truth* (ZMOT), have joined us in challenging the nonsensical argument that shopping only happens within the four walls of a store. Jim argues that other decisions are made prior to the store (in fact prior to any point of actual purchase). One might argue that Google has a vested interest in this, given its business interests, but it might also be fair to say that POPAI, the organization that pushes the "76 percent of decisions made in-store" rhetoric, likewise has a vested interest, given its mission and focus on "marketing at retail." The suggestion that all shopping decisions happen in a store never really stood up to scrutiny—any credence this notion has must surely evaporate in the *Zero Moment of Truth* era.

The implications of this shift are profound. This book is called "The Shopper Marketing *Revolution*" for good reason. The idea that a consumer and a shopper could be considered one discrete marketing target has been proven to be simply not good enough. All models are approximations, and while this model may have been sufficient in the early days of marketing, this is no longer true. Marketers must recognize that the shopper may actually be a different person than the consumer, and these two mindsets are different from a marketing perspective even if they are corporeally the same individual. A shopper has different motivations, different needs, and different behaviors than a consumer. Likewise, the marketing goals are different. We wish for a consumer to love our brand and consume it; we wish a shopper to buy it. Different target, different behaviors, different goals. It's a different kind of marketing!

And yet these two marketing mixes need to work together. Paths to purchase extend way beyond the store, so shoppers and shopping exist outside the store. Consumer-targeted activity will be visible to a shopper as well as a consumer. Likewise, in the age of mobile media, consumer media can now enter the hallowed, once-exclusive grounds of the retail store. In some markets, retailers still ban manufacturer signage and branding (the so-called "clean-store environment"), but they cannot (we hope!) ban the use of a mobile phone or the branding and messages that can be pumped into one of these devices.

Further, when the shopper and the consumer are indeed the same person (as is true in many cases), there is no longer a clear distinction between the shopper and consumer phases of the journey. Historic models looked at a more linear path to purchase—but this idea of linearity is patently false. Complex, nonlinear paths to purchase are nothing new, but the information age has brought their reality into stark focus. As media and messages become muddled, an individual can flit from being a shopper to a consumer and back again in a fraction of a second. And because one of the greatest influences on a shopper are her needs as a consumer, the idea that these two marketing challenges could be considered as completely isolated from each other is clearly nonsense. Consumer marketing and shopper marketing are separate challenges, but they need to be well integrated to be effective.

THE FUTURE OF THE CONSUMER GOODS ORGANIZATION

Shopper marketing as we envisage it will transform consumer goods companies. The current external environment creates both the pain and the opportunity required to encourage (or force) organizations to change the way they operate and how they organize their activities and resources. Shopper marketing, introduced to companies as both a new way of thinking and of acting, will force change onto other parts of the organization. For shopper marketing to fulfill its promise, it needs to be integrated fully into the way both marketing and sales functions work, rather than just the functioning of one of these entities—even though the latter was too often the case with trade marketing. This will require changes in the business practices of marketing and sales, and may well result in completely new organizational structures, as outlined in Chapter 15.

But what a future we might behold! Consumer, shopper, and customer teams with clear, aligned objectives, integrated strategies, and effectively designed key performance indicators that ensure that the efforts toward both long-term and short-term goals are encouraged; strategies and activities that are not implemented until the total investment requirement is understood; a clearer focus on what actually drives profitable growth and an organization that is aligned for and committed to excelling in the activities that deliver this growth. A nirvana? Not at all. We're already seeing it happen. And the starting point is a simple, five-step approach to marketing:

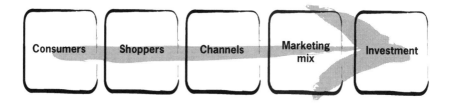

WILL IT LAST?

The world is changing fast. None of this is easy. Given the scale of the operational changes required, how can companies be sure that they will bring lasting change and improvements to their business fortunes? How can they be sure that the Shopper Marketing Revolution is ushering in a new *era*; that it isn't just the latest fad? Predicting the future is notoriously dangerous, but let's briefly take a look at what ours may hold.

DATA WILL BE KING

New technology will make data-acquisition mandatory. Marketers will no longer be able to hide behind the difficulty of measurement, and accountability will rule. Shopper marketing will lead this area, and the focus on understanding behavior and the results of that behavior will become the language of the boardroom. But data ubiquity will no longer necessarily be a source of competitive advantage. Retailers have long used their ownership of shopper data to their advantage, as have large manufacturers. But in the future, any brand owner could gather data from the source, one on one, with shoppers and consumers. This will affect not just the consumer goods industry and the retailers but also those that support them. Research agencies may find that the collection and analysis of data yields diminishing returns as the cost of both processes drops dramatically. In this world, data and analysis become the norms of business, so where can a company gain competitive advantage? Power will come in the ability to understand the implications of the data. In a word—*insight*. The discovery of insight, the burning heart of all great marketing, will set apart the winners from the rest of the pack. Already, shopper marketing organizations are filling their desks with analysts; the words *insight* and *analytics* are being used interchangeably. Organizations that encourage and nurture insight and discovery will do well. Organizations that expand this skill beyond their consumer teams and learn how to integrate data and insights across consumer, shopper, and customer teams will do even better.

TECHNOLOGY WILL CHANGE EVERYONE—ESPECIALLY SHOPPERS

Technology will touch every part of the world (and of course every part of the consumer goods world), but we will limit our discourse to the world of marketing. We talk of the Age of the Shopper because the shopper now has power. Power comes from two sources: information and the ability to make choices. Combined, these two sources allow shoppers to make informed decisions. Technology will support shoppers in both ways, and that power will force those who service shoppers to completely change the way they interface with these customers.

We've already seen transformations in the places shoppers can shop. Technology enables pop-up shops—temporary retail outlets that require little or no fixed investment to get going. Shopping on the go or at home is now rapidly becoming just as commonplace as shopping in a store. As virtual technology improves, the ability to sample things virtually will become a viable alternative to the heavy cost of shipping and returns associated with trial of the real product. Already, clothes and shoes can be fitted virtually, and furniture can be positioned in a room to see how it looks. It is possible to buy, in theory, from anywhere. It is easier to find independents or specialists—to be aware of their existence (search), to interact with them (personal media), and to find them physically (GPS). The costs of business drop, and the ability to reach a geographically disparate market increases. The chances of more retail competition both online and offline will continue to increase.

Shoppers will have more choice of where to shop and whom to buy from, and they will also have more choice of what to buy. The trends mentioned will make specialization and niche retailing far more viable than ever before. Closer relationships with individual shoppers will create the opportunities for more customization—targeting specific products or ranges of products at ever-smaller groups. Customization will become far more commonplace as technology enables individuals to design their own products, or at least to collaborate in the design process. All these niches require sharp targeting—another great marketing skill. As more and more shoppers come within reach (and as more and more competitors emerge) the need to be really targeted increases. Thus, understanding that target market will become more and more important. With more segments to choose from, prioritization of shoppers will become paramount. The successful companies of the future will be experts at targeting shoppers and experts at understanding shoppers—their behavior and their motivations—and they will focus on the shoppers who will yield greatest future returns. We call that *shopper marketing strategy.*

Engaging with consumers and shoppers will yield competitive advantage. As proposed before, convenience, curation, and price will rapidly become givens in the relationship with a shopper. Anyone can offer anything, anytime, and at a similar price to competitors. The winners in this world will be those who can create significant value. Adding value requires understanding what is important to the target; those who build meaningful relationships with their target market are likely to be those who can meet their needs better than others. All of this means more interactions. The quantum of messages and media will continue to increase, and again, choice will kick in for shoppers. Today, some commentators and marketers envisage a world where everyone is interacting with every brand—that message after message will be lapped up by a grateful shopper on every aisle as they are induced to spend a few moments with the brand. But in the future, the novelty will have worn off, and the sheer volume of messages will lead shoppers to choose. They will choose those brands (including retailers' brands) that add the most value. No value add? You're out!

However many brands or businesses the average shopper can be bothered to communicate with, the net result is likely to be a net increase in communication and interaction between brand owners and their target markets. All brands will have a different relationship with at least some of their shoppers and consumers. Customer service, or customer satisfaction, will become a significant part of *every* brand's mix. Apple has blazed the trail, demonstrating the brilliance of having a great product but simultaneously demonstrating that it's not all about the product. The Apple store may well go down in history as the single biggest innovation from that organization and potentially the one with the biggest marketing legacy. The Apple store stands testimony to the need for tomorrow's brands to understand the entire experience they offer to a shopper and to create it relentlessly in everything they do. "Total experience" marketing requires an understanding of all the potential touch points and the seamless integration of the brand across all of those (recognizing the need to appeal to different states of "consumer" and "shopper").

MORE COMPETITION

Consumerism marches onward. Distribution costs drop. Production costs in many markets continue to fall. Barriers to entry are significantly lower; there will be more competition within the consumer goods market. The definition of a "consumer good" will be challenged and will expand. When Toby started selling chocolate bars in small stores in the UK for Mars, the primary competitors were Nestlé and Cadbury. Five years ago, it was probably mobile phone top-up cards. Today, it might be apps for a smart phone.

Technology and innovation create more things for people to spend their money on, as well as more places and ways to spend it. More competition creates more losers than winners. Whatever is good enough today will almost certainly not be good enough tomorrow. Sharper, better offers delivered in the right way, at the right time—these will become the necessary deliverables of the consumer goods company of the future.

EVERYTHING STAYS THE SAME—EVERYTHING MUST BE DIFFERENT

A brave new world for consumer goods is on the horizon—but while the pieces on the board may change, the same basic rules apply. Companies will still thrive by driving the consumption of their brands in the most efficient way possible. In the past, this was desirable. In the future, it will be mandatory. The ability to drive growth will still require understanding, anticipating, and profitably meeting the needs of the target market (remember the definition of marketing?). What will change is the definition of that target market, its diversity and complexity, and the pace at which the environment changes. But it's still marketing. Consider the previous points. Insight will win. Segmentation will win. Targeting will win.

It's all marketing. That is, marketing to shoppers in an integrated way and, therefore, marketing in a radically different way. A *revolutionary* way. Yes—everything stays the same, but everything must be different.

WHERE FROM HERE?

So where to start? We hope we have articulated in this book what needs to happen, but what can you do to begin revolutionizing your business and readying it for the Age of the Shopper?

Clearly, what happens next depends on you. That's right—you. This is a revolution. It doesn't happen unless a lot of people play their part. Exactly how you contribute depends on two things: your level of passion for creating the change and your ability to effect that change. We quit our jobs, set up a company, employed a whole lot of people, and wrote a book—dedicating a huge amount of our time to jumpstarting this revolution. We know that not everyone will share *quite* that level of passion, nor will every reader be able to take those actions, but we implore you to do your part.

Different people in different situations (be they different types of roles or different types of companies) can take different actions. A CEO, for example, is empowered to make far more significant changes than an intern can. This book is designed to help everyone, so we've focused on things that anyone can do, no matter what your position is or what company you work for. Students can apply this to their thesis or to their job search and interview process. (Having read this book, would you want to go and work for an organization that doesn't buy into shopper marketing?) CEOs can directly influence change by incorporating these strategies into their company culture. Agencies can challenge their clients; clients can challenge their agencies. Whatever you are doing and wherever you are based, the following points will have a profound impact on you and probably many other people. We promise.

QUESTIONS

When developing anything—a strategy, a plan, a promotion, a new product, a TV commercial, or a Facebook page—or when presented with anything, use the five-step approach to frame a set of killer questions:

- What specific consumer opportunity are we targeting? Who will consume differently, and how much is that worth?

- Who is the target shopper? What do they do now, and what do they need to do in the future to enable the consumption defined? Why do we believe the change could happen?

- In which channels could this change in shopping behavior take place? Which channels are most important?

- What marketing activities are required to create the change in shopping behavior?

- What investment in which customers is required? Does the total growth opportunity justify the total investment across consumer, shopper, and customer?

By consistently asking these questions of your team, you will condition the team members to answer them and then to pose the questions to their own units. Questions change behavior, and behavior drives culture.

GOALS

Review your goals. They might be great, but they were written in the past; and hopefully, you have a new view of the future now. Even if you don't change a single goal, reaffirming that you are going in the right direction is not only sensible, but it's also invigorating! Challenge yourself to understand where the growth you're aiming for will come from, and ask yourself whether you've considered the implications across the consumer, shopper, and customer.

SET KEY PERFORMANCE INDICATORS

Create the standards against which you will measure the success of your activities. Key performance indicators (KPIs) should measure (1) desired change in consumption; (2) desired change in shopper behavior; (3) impact on brand performance; and (4) impact on customer performance. Set all four KPIs as your goal; if you achieve at least two, you are already light-years ahead of your current situation.

START MEASURING

Measure your progress to understand whether you are on track to achieve your goals and your KPIs. And don't forget to measure what *actually* happens, in-store or elsewhere.

START UNDERSTANDING SHOPPERS

Understanding is the starting point of all marketing, and marketing to shoppers is no different. We're not necessarily advocating a rush to divert budgets toward expensive shopper research projects; instead, we recommend a review of what the organization already knows, followed by an effort to use that information to glean shopper-related knowledge. Spend time in stores—get to know your shopper in whatever ways you can. And, yes, if you can justify the investment, invest in appropriate research.

CHALLENGE WORKING PRACTICES

Ask questions of yourself, your team, and your peers. Ask about the shopper in every decision. Challenge every process that impacts shoppers but does not include a shopper point of view. Even if the process works well today, ask how it would stand up in a more complex, connected world. How would this work with more channels, more segments, more complexity? Is it fit for yesterday, or will it hold up to tomorrow's changes?

START WITH THE FIVE-STEP TOTAL MARKETING MODEL

Print it out from the **engage** website (www.engageconsultants.com). Share it with everyone. Use it to frame everything you do. Go on. You know you want to!

BE READY FOR TOMORROW

Whatever happens today, tomorrow will be different. Ensure you and your team are up to speed. Buy them a copy of this book, and stay on top of the initiative with ongoing training and reading. Things move fast!

Shopper marketing can, and we hope *will*, transform the industry to which we have dedicated our working lives. We love the consumer goods industry. It has served us well for a long time. The consumer goods industry was once the vanguard of the marketing world, a place people wanted to work. We believe that our approach can make that true again. The idea of marketing to multiple customers along a value chain in an integrated fashion changes business results, but it changes much more. Organizations are more efficient and more collaborative. Decisions happen quicker. There is less confrontation, less frustration, and less blame. People get more satisfaction from what they're doing.

Isn't that a place you'd like to work?

Come on. Join the Shopper Marketing Revolution.

BIOGRAPHIES

MIKE ANTHONY   FOUNDER AND CEO OF ENGAGE

A pioneer in shopper marketing, Mike Anthony is a passionate practitioner, speaker, and trainer who has helped countless businesses discover new opportunities and achieve better brand returns. After a consumer goods career spanning 17 years and three continents, Mike redirected his energy and enthusiasm toward founding **engage**, a global management consultancy that leverages the power of a unique vision of shopper marketing and customer management to deliver phenomenal growth and transform business performance. As the firm's CEO, Mike has worked with the world's leading consumer goods companies, such as Nestlé, GlaxoSmithKline, Kimberly-Clark, Electrolux, Johnson & Johnson, Sara Lee, and Unilever.

TOBY DESFORGES   FOUNDER AND HEAD OF CONSULTING OF ENGAGE

Toby Desforges is a recognized expert in shopper marketing and customer management. He has worked with over 50 of the top 250 consumer goods companies globally, across three continents, in both line management and consultancy. A speaker, author, and blogger, Toby is passionate about shopper marketing but just as pragmatic in implementing change.

Toby Desforges began working in consumer goods in the 1980s. His career since then has taken him all over the world, and he has worked with leading manufacturers in more than 20 countries. As a line manager he has worked with Britvic (Pepsi's bottler) in the UK and Mars and Columbia Pictures across western Europe. When his wife went to work with the United Nations in Asia, Toby followed her and began a second career consulting.

In 2005, Toby cofounded **engage** with Mike Anthony. Toby now leads **engage**'s consulting business unit internationally.

INDEX

311

Horstman, Mark, 55
hot zone, merchandising, 211
household panel data, 278
Hoyt, Chris, 18, 29, 38, 64, 112, 125, 133, 294
hypermarket channel, 168, 186, 236
Hypertrade Consulting, 248
hypotheses, development and use of, 140–145
hypothesis-based differentiators, 160

I

ice cream marketing, 260–261
impulse purchases, 69, 80–81, 211
impulse sector, 168
incremental consumption, 231
incremental investment, 263
incremental sales, 211
India, 22, 167
"individual show-offs," 48–49
Indonesia, 258
insight, 122, 133–134, 302
insight story, 150–151
in-stock management, 91, 109, 110
in-store mix, 123
in-store promotions
    annual expenditures, 12
    and category management, 15
    in China, 49–50, 51–52
    hidden costs of, 110
    out-of-stock conditions, 109
    path to purchase and, 93
intangible asset, brands as, 116
integrated brand model, 121–122
Internet marketing, 14, 49
inventory (KPI), 253
inventory costs, 206
inventory days, 253
investment, in total marketing model, 46–47, 53, 275
investment decisions, 55
investment defined, 226
investment strategies, 233
iTunes, 14

J

Japan, 33

K

Kellogg on Branding, 117
key customer management, 286
key performance indicators (KPIs), 250–252, 253–256, 291, 307
kirana stores, 167

Klauser, Lisa, 133
Korea, 234–235
Kotler, Philip, 153, 195, 196

L

Lafley, Alan, 77
Lauterborn, Robert, 195
least-value proposition, 251, 252
Lecinski, Jim, 181, 299
Lewis, Elias St. Elmo, 83–84
"life enjoys," 48–49
like-for-like growth, 253
limited offers, 180–181
listing fees, 265
location, product, 180
long-term brand equity, 285
loyalty card data, 144, 180–181, 220, 277
loyalty programs, 14, 71–72

M

Malaysia, 171, 172–174, 177, 232
manufacturer profit margins, 254
manufacturer-retail relationship, 37–38, 224–225, 228–229, 250–251
manufacturer's strategic benefit, 251, 252
margin (KPI), 253
market coverage, 207–208
marketing. See also shopper marketing
    defined, 82
    purpose of, 30–31
    two definitions of, 285
Marketing Drive, 84
marketing message impressions, 78–79
marketing mix
    availability, 200–214
    changing components of, 97–98
    communication, 214–217
    consumption objectives, 199
    first acknowledged, 195
    in five-step model, 46
    4 Cs, 195–196, 199–200
    4 Ps, 5, 36, 195–196, 220–221
    limited offers, 180–181
    and metrics use, 274–275
    offer, 217–220
    price as a factor in, 108–109
marketing role, 27–28
marketing spend statistics, 79
marketing tools, 66
market research, 129–130
Marshall, Darren, 24, 29, 65, 88
Martin, Neale, 79

mass retailing model, 5–6, 7
Matilda promotion, 245–246
McCarthy, Jerome, 195, 196
McDonald's brand, 116, 120–121
media, in-store, 215–216
media expenditure, 9
media fragmentation, 5–6, 8, 11, 22, 154, 224
media personalization, 11–12
medical halls, 172–174
MEI Trade Insight, 223–224
men's fashion brands, 121–122
merchandising. *See also* product placement
    art and science of, 209–213
    defined, 205
    differentiated, 179–180
metrics
    aversion to, 269–270
    compliance measure, 280
    digital tracking, 280–281
    essential nature of, 268
    key criteria, 273
    low use of, 267
    perfection barrier, 270–272
    sales-marketing relationship, 285
    strategic use of, 275–276
    tactical use of, 276
    technology, 281
    what to measure, 272–278
    where to begin, 278–279
milk marketing, 53–54, 93, 185–186, 191, 209–210, 229, 239
mission-based differentiators, 160
mobile technology, 97
modern trade, 168, 169
Mohr-Value chain, 6
moments of truth concept, 77
Morrisons, 45
multi-channel retailing, 191–192
music, downloadable, 213

N

navigation, store, 212–213
needs and desires, 72
negotiation, 263–265
net margins, 101
network television, decay of, 8
Newcomer, Tia, 43, 55, 61, 68
new product introductions, 32, 33, 247, 248–249
niche marketing, 154, 302
Nielsen data
    channel definitions, 170–171

Chinese medical halls, 172–174
misleading nature of, 108
origins of, 129, 130
retail investment, 223
Nigeria, 167
Nike shoe store experience, 183
no-name brands, 6–7
null hypothesis, 140

O

offer, 123, 200, 218–220
off-shelf location, 209. *See also* product placement
Ogilvy, David, 117
Ogilvy & Mather, 84
online retail
    annual sales statistics, 167
    channel influences, 181–182
    Cyber Monday, 192
    digital change advantages, 179–181
    ease of entry, 177
    future potential, 192
    growth of, 14
    merchandising considerations, 213
    purchase-consumption continuum, 197
    and traditional retail decline, 191–192
online shopping, 68
operational effectiveness, 206, 212
oral care category, 262
order taking, sales *vs.*, 29–30
organizational change, barriers to, 284
organizational structure, 283
outlets, 137–138
outlet selection, 88–89, 92, 94
out-of-stock conditions, 91, 109, 110, 202–203, 204
out-of-store marketing, 78
out-of-store shopping decisions, 83, 88–89
own-label sales, 14

P

Pampers brand, 91–92
path to purchase
    barriers, 93
    complexity of, 97
    defined, 83, 85–86
    early intervention, 95, 112
    Ogilvy & Mather model, 84
    seven steps, 85–91
    technology changes and, 96
    traditional models, 83–85
Pathtopurchase.com, 84

317

8760R00192

Made in the USA
Middletown, DE
25 February 2015